The Arnold and Caroline Rose Monograph Series
of the American Sociological Association

Understanding events

Affect and the construction of social action

Other books in the series

J. Milton Yinger, Kiyoshi Ikeda, Frank Laycock, and Stephen J. Cutler: *Middle Start: An Experiment in the Educational Enrichment of Young Adolescents*
James A. Geschwender: *Class, Race, and Worker Insurgency: The League of Revolutionary Black Workers*
Paul Ritterband: *Education, Employment, and Migration: Israel in Comparative Perspective*
John Low-Beer: *Protest and Participation: The New Working Class in Italy*
Orrin E. Klapp: *Opening and Closing: Strategies of Information Adaptation in Society*
Rita James Simon: *Continuity and Change: A Study of Two Ethnic Communities in Israel*
Marshall B. Clinard: *Cities with Little Crime: The Case of Switzerland*
Steven T. Bossert: *Tasks and Social Relationships in Classrooms: A Study of Instructional Organization and Its Consequences*
Richard E. Johnson: *Juvenile Delinquency and Its Origins: An Integrated Theoretical Approach*
Ida Harper Simpson: *From Student to Nurse: A Longitudinal Study of Socialization*

Volumes previously published by the American Sociological Association

Michael Schwartz and Sheldon Stryker: *Deviance, Selves and Others*
Robert M. Hauser: *Socioeconomic Background and Educational Performance*
Morris Rosenberg and Roberta G. Simmons: *Black and White Self-Esteem: The Urban School Child*
Chad Gordon: *Looking Ahead: Self-Conceptions: Race and Family as Determinants of Adolescent Orientation to Achievement*
Anthony M. Orum: *Black Students in Protest: A Study of the Origins of the Black Student Movement*
Ruth M. Gasson, Archibald O. Haller, and William H. Sewell: *Attitudes and Facilitation in the Attainment of Status*
Sheila R. Klatzky: *Patterns of Contact with Relatives*
Herman Turk: *Interorganizational Activation in Urban Communities: Deductions from the Concept of System*
John DeLamater: *The Study of Political Commitment*
Alan C. Kerckhoff: *Ambition and Attainment: A Study of Four Samples of American Boys*
Scott McNall: *The Greek Peasant*
Lowell L. Hargens: *Patterns of Scientific Research: A Comparative Analysis of Research in Three Scientific Fields*
Charles Hirschman: *Ethnic Stratification in Peninsular Malaysia*

Understanding events

Affect and the construction of social action

David R. Heise

Professor of Sociology
University of North Carolina

Cambridge University Press

Cambridge
London   New York   Melbourne

95-336

To Elsa and Stephen

Published by the Syndics of the Cambridge University Press
The Pitt Building, Trumpington Street, Cambridge CB2 1RP
Bentley House, 200 Euston Road, London NW1 2DB
32 East 57th Street, New York, NY 10022, USA
296 Beaconsfield Parade, Middle Park, Melbourne 3206, Australia

© Cambridge University Press 1979

First published 1979

Printed in the United States of America
Typeset by Automated Composition Service, Lancaster, Pa.
Printed and bound by The Murray Printing Company, Westford, Mass.

Library of Congress Cataloging in Publication Data

Heise, David R.
Understanding events.

(The Arnold and Caroline Rose monograph series of the
American Sociological Association)

Includes index.

1. Social interaction – Mathematical models.   2. Social
role.   3. Affect (Psychology)   I. Title.   II. Series:
The Arnold and Caroline Rose monograph series in sociology.
HM291.H47   301.11   78–24177
ISBN 0 521 22539 6 in hard covers
ISBN 0 521 29544 0 as a paperback

Contents

Figures and tables

vii

Preface

Interpretive sociology considers the individual and his action as the basic unit, as its "atom" – if the disputable comparison for once may be permitted. In this approach, the individual is also the upper limit and the sole carrier of meaningful conduct . . . In general, for sociology, such concepts as "state," "association," "feudalism," and the like, designate certain categories of human interaction. Hence it is the task of sociology to reduce these concepts to "understandable" action, that is, without exception, to the actions of participating individual men [Max Weber, quoted in Gerth and Mills, 1958:55] .

The theory presented in this book relates to common social actions, like those of a doctor toward a patient, a judge toward a thief, a mother toward a daughter, a football tackle toward a quarterback, a policeman toward a burglar, a mugger toward a victim. According to the theory, all such events have an underlying basis in the psychology of affect. In particular, people in such relationships theoretically act to maintain established feelings, and when an event occurs that strains these feelings, the individuals anticipate and implement new events to restore normal impressions. Events cause people to respond affectively. In turn, people expect and construct new events that will cause established sentiments to be confirmed. Theoretically, event responses and anticipations both develop out of feelings about the separate components of an event – actor, act, and object in particular. For example, the affective response to "The husband complimented the wife" is a derivative from feelings about husband, wife, and complimenting; a behavioral expectation like "The judge should convict the thief" develops from feelings about judges, thieves, and convicting. Thus, social experiencing is a generative process, and almost endless qualitative variations in interaction result from a finite amount of socialization.

The ultimate goal in this work is development of an interpretive sociology formulated with mathematical rigor, grounded in empirical procedures, and permitting complex and subtle analyses of social relationships. What is presented now is far short of this. The statement of affect-control theory given here is temporary, each passing month bringing new research reports that sharpen issues and lead to improvements in conceptualization. The current mathematical model is subject to revision as experiments provide better specifications of social psychological processes and better parameter estimates for equations. The current empirical base, just adequate for the exploratory work, must be improved by large-scale social surveys employing standard sampling procedures. And though analyses of social behavior are presented here, the results are primitive, tentative, simply illustrative, meant only to suggest what might be anticipated as the theory, the model, and the data base improve. Thus, as the first full statement of affect-control theory, this monograph represents simply an announcement that a possible path toward an interpretive sociology has been found and is being tried.

The topics covered in this monograph are as follows. Chapter 1 reviews some recent developments in cognitive psychology, social psychology, and microsociology that have contributed to affect-control theory. The chapter focuses particularly on the nature of psychological control processes, on the conceptualization of affect, and on the importance of situation definitions in structuring thought and action. Chapter 2 reviews recent research on affective responses to events and presents empirically derived equations that serve as the foundation of the formal affect-control theory model. Chapter 3 presents materials showing a close relation between affective dynamics and impressions of event likelihood and then proceeds to show how the general principle of affect control allows the reaction equations in Chapter 2 to be transformed mathematically into proaction equations for the theoretical specification of maximally likely events. The same empirical equations, theoretical principles, and mathematical procedures also are used to derive other formulas defining how situations are reconceptualized following disturbing events. Chapter 4 translates the abstract mathematical model into operational procedures for qualitative analyses of social events and shows that the full model permits sensible analyses of social interactions.

Chapter 5 discusses how affect-control theory can be employed as a framework for an objective theory of roles and demonstrates the approach through analyses of roles in several institutions and role expectations in special circumstances.

An Appendix presents affective measurements for a large number of social identities and social acts and pinpoints differences in sentiments by sex and by conservatism (the latter being a traditional dimension for representing variations in sundry attitudes). These are the data used to construct illustrative theoretical analyses in Chapters 4 and 5.

The procedures involved in collecting and analyzing empirical data used in this monograph are presented in a separate technical report (Heise, 1978). That report also presents a detailed description of the program used here to conduct computer-assisted theoretical analyses. A brief synopsis of affect-control theory has been provided in Heise (1977*b*).

A one-thousand-word dictionary of semantic differential profiles (Heise, 1965) used in exploratory studies of the theory presented here was compiled in 1963 with the cooperation of Frank J. Holland, then Lt. Jg. MSC, U.S. Navy. Harry Gollob's 1965 oral presentation of his dissertation results at the American Pyschological Association meetings led to my own 1969 and 1970 papers on affective dynamics. The first public presentation of affect-control theory was made in 1971 at the University of Missouri (St. Louis) on invitation from Professor Mae Gordon. Bruce Biddle's positive response to the first written formulation of affect-control theory in 1973 sustained me while I pondered the theory and its implications. I circulated additional reports in 1974 and 1975 and received encouragement and welcome criticism from Charles Osgood, William Powers, Harry Triandis, Robert Wyer, Jr., and Norman Anderson. In 1975, Chester Cassel and Dennis Willigan committed themselves as graduate students to projects related to affect-control theory. In 1976, Beverly Aiken, Chris Proctor Averett, and D. Lynn Smith-Lovin began projects involving the theory.

The National Institute of Mental Health contributed indirectly to the development of affect-control theory through my pre- and postdoctoral fellowships and through provision of secretarial help while I administered NIMH graduate training programs at the University of Wisconsin and the University of North Carolina. New work on the theory is currently being supported directly by NIMH Grant Number 1-R01-MH29978-01-SSR. Revision of this manuscript was facilitated by a fellowship from the John Simon Guggenheim Foundation. The University of North Carolina's Institute for Research in Social Science and the UNC Computation Center have provided generous help in different aspects of data reduction and programming. Gert Rippy and Susan Hinson helped type the manuscript.

D.R.H.

1. Affect control and situated action

Behavioral events change transient feelings about people and acts, and deviations of feeling from established sentiments lead to new behaviors. Affect and behavior are linked in a causal circle or feedback loop. The notion of mutual causality was employed by Calder and Ross (1973) in reviewing literature on attitude–behavior consistency.[1] Fishbein and Ajzen (1975:15) also presented a model in which attitudes influence behaviors by contributing to behavioral intentions, whereas behaviors affect attitudes by changing beliefs about reality. Kelman (1974) stated the basic idea of mutual attitude–behavior causality as follows:

Attitude, in my view, and in the view of most attitude theorists, is not an index of action, but a determinant, component, and consequent of it. Furthermore, it is not an entity that can be separated – functionally or temporally – from the flow of action, but is an integral part of action. Attitude and action are linked in a continuing reciprocal process, each generating the other in an endless chain [p. 316].

Relationships between attitudes and behaviors usually are viewed as reinforcing – a favorable attitude disposes one to positive acts, and engaging in such acts makes one's attitude more favorable. Such relationships, however, do not necessitate a simple causal model in which an unusually favorable act toward an object generates a more positive attitude toward the object, which in turn directly leads to more favorable acts in the future. Such a model would make attitudes little more than affectual weathervanes of recent experience, leaving unexplained their stability over long periods of time and the historical evidence indicating that people work, scheme, and battle to protect established feelings about reality.

The theory presented here distinguishes between established affective associations (fundamentals) and the feelings one has in an immediate situation (transients), and the theory's basic postulate is that acts are constructed to maintain congruency between the two. In this formulation, established sentiments do positively determine behavior, and actions do positively determine immediate feelings. However, immedi-

1

ate feelings that are too favorable relative to established sentiments typically lead to less favorable subsequent acts; immediate feelings that are not favorable enough relative to established sentiments typically lead to more favorable later actions. Consequently, immediate feelings have an inverse effect on behavior, and the overall configuration of relationships forms a control system. Unusual events generate unusual feelings, and these cause the construction of subsequent corrective acts restoring normal feelings.

The theory of control systems is a rapidly expanding paradigm for the analysis of behavioral and social phenomena (see Buckley, 1968; Hawkes, 1975; Heise, 1975). A systematic application of control theory in cognitive psychology is William Powers's *Behavior: The Control of Perception* (1973). Powers suggests that perception is not a passive process: the organism brings learned expectations (reference levels) to the process of perception and actively tries to maintain incoming stimulation at these expected levels. In particular, Powers develops a model of perception as a hierarchically ordered system in which a recognition at a higher level (e.g., perception of a configuration) provides reference values for the next lower level (e.g., perception of sensations), which the organism tries to maintain by various kinds of behavior. If behavior fails to maintain these expectations, the organism shifts at the higher level and perceives something new. However, then the revised higher-order perception resets expectations at lower levels, and the organism again tries to maintain these expectations behaviorally.

Affect-control theory might be viewed as an extension of Powers's framework to levels of psychological processing that he does not consider in detail. In any case, it similarly is proposed that affective dynamics are not simply a passive process. People actively operate so as to keep their momentary feelings aligned with established sentiments, and they do this by acting so as to change what they are experiencing.

Paralleling Powers's model of hierarchical control in perception, affect-behavior dynamics are viewed as subordinate to a definition of the situation – that is, to a person's categorizations of people and objects in a scene. A definition of the situation provides a restricted domain of cognitive elements to be used in recognizing and constructing events, and because it determines which cognitive categories are salient, it retrieves appropriate established sentiments for judging immediate feelings.[2] Behavior within the situation then is directed at maintaining feelings near these fundamental values by constructing events involving the identified persons and objects.

The overall operation of the system can be indicated roughly by describing the natural history of social action in a particular setting:

1. The persons present do cognitive work to define the situation.
2. Events that are comprehensible within this definition of the situation are recognized.
3. These recognitions generate particularized feelings about the participants in the events.
4. Discrepancies between these particularized feelings and corresponding established sentiments lead to conceptualizations of the new events that would bring present feelings closer to established sentiments. If the self is the actor in such a conceptualization, a behavioral *intention* or disposition is the result; if another is the actor, the result is an *expectation* for the other's behavior.
5. Behavioral intentions are implemented when feasible, creating new events and looping the process back to step (2).
6. If for some reason established sentiments cannot be confirmed behaviorally, higher-order feedback causes redefinition of the situation on the basis of the most recent event, thereby helping to stabilize the process.

Such a model reflects the classical sociological insight that action occurs within a definition of the situation (see the succinct review by Berger et al., 1977:12-15). Moreover, because a situation is usually resilient once defined, and subsequent cognitive activity mainly involves recognition and construction of events, the implication is that action is the major procedure by which people control their experience of reality. Of course, a person can be engaged in social action as actor, object, or observer and so need not be continually creating events: "One of the most neglected observations of philosophers and early psychologists is the fact that we participate directly and overtly in the behavior of others" (Church, 1961:31).

Definition of the situation

Definitions of situations depend partly on the space-time coordinates of a given setting and on the setting's material organization (e.g., Barker and Wright, 1955, were able to census a small town's situations mainly on a physical basis). The materialistic basis of situations is important from a sociological standpoint, because it implies that a community's ecology constrains the definable situations to some degree. Thus shifts in commercial services, building and remodeling of structures, and changes in scheduling all can modify the range and nature of situational definitions available to a populace. Physical anchoring of situations also is significant from a psychological standpoint, because it implies that defining a situation must be largely a perceptual process.

Defining a situation involves registering information about a setting and organizing it into a cognitively sensible whole (Heider, 1958). Work on perception (see Reed, 1973) suggests that the process is partly a matter of feature recognition; for example, a blue uniform, visored hat, badge, and weapon are characteristic paraphernalia of urban policemen, and perceiving the conjunction of such "features" allows us to infer that someone is a policeman, whereupon we react to the person in a unique way (Bickman, 1974). Models of feature analysis have been applied mostly to recognition of simple figures (e.g., trying to define the combination of colors, angles, and other visual qualities that characterize a badge). However, inferences at one level of perception might be viewed as features at the next higher level in the perceptual hierarchy (Powers, 1973; Palmer, 1975; Minsky, 1975) – an idea that is congruent with anthropologists' studies of cognitive organization (Werner and Fenton, 1970) – and so recent advances in understanding the process of feature analysis might apply over a broad range of perception. Theory and empirical research (e.g., Tversky, 1977; Fillenbaum and Rapoport, 1971) suggest that informants' judgments of object similarities, analyzed via nonmetric scaling procedures, might provide a method for identifying critical features distinguishing objects.

However, perception goes beyond passive registration – we fill in gaps and create good forms, as Gestaltists have long pointed out (Köhler, 1969) – and models of feature analysis do not really represent this active aspect of perceptual processing. Generative models of perception (e.g., those of Leeuwenberg, 1971; Fu, 1974; Palmer, 1975) and the related "artificial intelligence" approach to scene definition (e.g., see Minsky, 1975; Schank and Abelson, 1977) relate to this kind of operation. Instead of defining an object as a configuration of features, an object is defined as a construction from rules and formulas (as a rough example, a policeman might be characterized by a set of rules and formulas that, if followed conscientiously, would allow one to draw a picture of a policeman). Accordingly, perception becomes an active process: perception of features cues a mental construction of a hypothetical object, which is accepted as a recognition if consequent expectations fit subsequent perceptions reasonably well, allowing that one may have to fill in some gaps with imaginings or default assumptions. Such a model seems especially well adapted to describing the final stages in the process of defining a situation when active interpretation is necessary.

In defining social situations, the assigned identities of persons have to fit together in an interpersonal gestalt that defines sensible relations for various pairs of actors. Roughly speaking, this means that identities are chosen to represent a single social institution – all participants become part of a family scene, a courtroom scene, a hospital scene, and so on, with presence in a particular setting frequently determining what identities can be allocated (Schank and Abelson, 1977: 49). Sacks's (1972) "categorization device" refers to any set of related identities (e.g., male and female) that can be applied to a group of persons to yield a definition of the situation. Sacks observes that multiple devices are always available for categorizing any person. However, for a situation to be meaningful, everyone must be classified by the same device (or else there must be some understanding of how identities provided by different devices, like judge and father, circumstantially relate to one another – e.g., the defendant's father). Consequently, the search for an appropriate device narrows to just those that can be projected on all the persons present.

Hierarchical-control theories of perception (Powers, 1973; Minsky, 1975) propose that perception is not only cognitively active but behaviorally active, too. Behavioral closure is an important idea in considering definitions of situations, because people often arrive at a definition of a situation that does not really fit the immediate setting, whereupon they go on to *shape* the setting so that it does fit (Frake, 1964). Scene setting may involve just moving about to confirm that all required parts of a scene are present, or it may involve assembling required paraphernalia or mustering human participants, or it may involve locomoting to a setting where a required situation exists intact. Additionally, the configuration of "cultural things" (Harris, 1964) that compose a given situation may require certain recipe behaviors (Schank and Abelson, 1977). For example, routine exchanges of greetings and other courtesies are required to validate many everyday situations; if these are withheld, the situation is not adequately defined, and the possibility of normal interaction is foreclosed (Garfinkel, 1964). Rituals constitute more elaborate scripted behavior patterns that define situations, making possible certain kinds of other events; for example, Frake (1964) observed that, within the tribal group he studied, the occurrence of a scheduled ceremony not only signaled an expected unfolding of events but was necessary if anticipations of future events were to be fulfilled. Thus rituals are elaborate "cultural things" that must be assembled to establish special situations in which ordinary persons and objects acquire identities with unusual powers. (Weekly religious services, for example, sanctify priest and temple, providing holy presences within the community for the week ahead.)

People readily accept definitions of situations provided verbally by others (Kohn and Williams, 1956). That is one way of interpreting Milgram's (1974) experiments, in which subjects delivered what they believed to be gruesome punishments to other persons simply because they accepted the idea that they were in an experiment with a researcher who demanded that they do so. McHugh (1968), working explicitly on the problem of situation definitions, found a similar phenomenon: subjects accepted the experimenter's suggestion that they would experience meaningful psychotherapy via an intercom, and they held to this definition of the situation until overwhelmed by the meaninglessness of random responses from the machine. The fact that much of the time – perhaps most of the time – people are operating with situational definitions that have been provided by others implies that all people probably do not give equal attention to problems of defining situations. It also suggests that individuals might be able to manipulate others by the presentation of artificial or inauthentic definitions, a possibility that has captured the attention of some social scientists (e.g., Goffman, 1959).

Sociologists (e.g., McCall and Simmons, 1966; Lofland, 1969; Collins, 1975) recently have given considerable attention to the kinds of negotiation and power plays that arise when people disagree in their definitions of a situation. These analyses are particularly relevant when the disagreement results from a clash in subcultural perspectives: for example, a person stopped for speeding may see himself as citizen, whereas the policeman, operating within a legal subculture, sees a violator. In such cases, the imposition of one form of consciousness over another seems to be largely a matter of power and coercion. However, an element of constructiveness may also be involved, as pointed out by Edward Bruner in the following anecdote. Soon after beginning field work among the Batak of Sumatra, he had to report the theft of two stoves and four tins of chicken to village elders, the village headman, and the Indonesian police.

The head police officer shortly after his arrival in the village stated that he was a member of the same clan that had adopted my wife as daughter. Therefore, she was to address him as *amang* (father) and I was to call him *tulang* (mother's brother). There were further conversations between the other policeman and the village elders after which everyone in the group used Batak kinship terms in both address and reference even though all conversations were in the Indonesian language . . . [This use of kin terms] created a means of encompassing everyone – an American anthropologist and his wife, three policemen, three village elders, and the headman – within one familiar frame of reference . . . Every time I spoke to the head policeman I called him father and he responded to me as son, which had an impact on the relationship [Bruner, 1973:226-7].

In this case, a situation that might have been defined as a confrontation between police, village leaders, and Americans was turned into something more like a family gathering, and possible conflicts were thereby avoided.

Negotiations often arise because people arrive in a situation with dispositions to take on some identities rather than others: such a disposition may arise from having special information about the self, like knowledge of illness or other morbidity (Sacks, 1972): If I decide I'm ill, then in the right setting, I prefer to be a patient and see a particular other as a physician. A predisposition to take on a particular identity may also exist because a person previously, in another situation, has generated a behavioral intention that must be implemented by entering this setting instrumentally, in order to obtain some specific outcomes (Schank and Abelson, 1977:49). Because the intent is to have events in the immediate situation recursively contribute to the other event-in-process, the acceptable identity for the self is predetermined, and others must be convinced to adopt identities that are institutionally compatible, so that meaningful action can occur (Sacks, 1972). Berger et al. (1977:105) consider predefined tasks central in the definition of many situations. Moreover, as Minsky (1975) has pointed out, settings typically are organized as elements within larger or more general settings – for example, a room in a building on a campus in a city. Ordinarily, we have a definite sense of where we are, which inclines us to categorize a given setting as a situation implied by our location. This, too, provides predispositions for certain identities – the ones associated with our personal understanding of where we are.

People have a strong disposition to retain a definition once it has been adopted: "given a particular way of defining a situation, individuals then act in ways that confirm that definition because the definition itself governs the subsequent behavior. To all outward appearances, therefore, the structure is very stable" (Berger et al., 1977:10). McHugh (1968) originally supposed that his subjects would soon reexamine their definitions of the situation when confronted with meaningless events, but he found instead that they worked to bolster and elaborate their current definition. Only when the current definition became completely untenable did they reexamine the scene. In a theoretical essay, Emerson (1970) emphasized that people are reluctant to redefine a situation – a fact that frequently allows deviants to maintain normal identities if others can be reassured that nothing unusual is happening. Such resilience of situational definitions is to be expected within the perspective offered here. If the definition of a situation is high up on the perceptual hierarchy, then it is protected by other psychological activity and by behavior and will be abandoned only when maintaining it becomes impossible.

By narrowing attention just to immediately relevant persons and objects, a definition of the situation has the crucial effect of simplifying experience to manageable proportions. For example, if the United Nations, or a spider in a corner, is not part of one's definition of the situation at a given moment, then events involving the United Nations or the spider are not salient, at least until there is a shift in the definition of the situation: The complexity of reality is drastically reduced by having a small window for viewing it. Moreover, a definition of the situation selects a particular social identity for each person who is present from that person's large collection of possible identities (the status set), including not only the ascribed and achieved statuses traditionally emphasized by social scientists, but also many common identities that can be assigned to essentially anyone (e.g., pedestrian, stranger, lover). By drawing out some of these identities rather than others, the definition of the situation reduces possible confusion in interpreting events.

Event recognition

Analyzing events in terms of an actor, an act, an object of action, an instrument of action, and encompassing circumstances parallels the *W* formula used by journalists: Who did what to whom, where, when, why, and how? Similar approaches to analyzing action have appeared in sociology (Parsons and Shils, 1951), psychology (Barker and Wright, 1955), and anthropology (Harris, 1964). An English sentence with its subject, verb, direct object, indirect object, and prepositional phrases provides a parallel framework (Chafe, 1970; Osgood, 1970, 1977; Miller and Johnson-Laird, 1976). Indeed, Schank (1973; Schank and Abelson, 1977) provides a system that analyzes language as a code for describing actions. Moreover, subjects, verbs, and objects are components of sentences in all languages (Greenberg, 1963), which suggests that some such framework is used universally by humans in analyzing events. Here both event recognitions and event constructions are analyzed within this general framework. In particular, a simple event is conceived as a syntactically ordered conjunction of cognitive elements (usually culturally defined) designating actor, act, and object.

A definition of the situation identifies the setting and the relevant persons and objects that are present; so it preselects the actors and objects that can be combined into recognition of events in that situation. In fact, a definition of the situation ordinarily limits attention to such a relatively small number of persons and objects that even the number of permutations of these elements can be viewed as fairly small. This is clearest for dyads: There are only so many ways of combining identified persons into actor–object combinations. In groups there are more possible permutations, but still the number is distinctly limited; for example, a five-person group yields twenty ordered pairs of persons. In situations where there are masses of persons or great numbers of different objects, the definition of a situation partitions them into relatively few types (e.g., professor and students in a lecture hall), so that the number of possible permutations still is effectively bound (Lofland, 1976:27).

This finiteness, not only of the elements of situations but also of their permutations, allows the initial stage of event recognition to be analyzed as a process in which a person scans actor–object combinations, examining the potential of each as a frame for a possible event. Such a procedure is actually feasible because there are a relatively small number of possibilities.[3] Furthermore, many of these can be rejected with only cursory examination. In particular, an event with P as actor and O as object can be occurring only if P's behavior, whatever it is, is coordinated with O's physical presence (Kendon, 1973). If there is no coordination then the *P-O* permutation can be eliminated immediately as a possible event, and consideration can move to other possibilities. Eye movements, voice volume, body posture, and positioning movements are common cues for discerning coordination.

Coordinated activity focuses attention on a specific actor-object combination and raises the question of what behavior the actor is engaging in. This can be decided largely by observing the actor's motions and their effects. A competent person engaging in a particular act moves various body parts in an organized, predictable sequence, often producing intermediate environmental effects, and thus displaying a kinesic "message" that observers can interpret. These elementary motions and effects probably are registered initially by feature analysis (Newtson, Engquist, and Bois, 1977; also, Powers, 1973: chaps. 10 and 11 deal with the perception of transitions and sequences). Moreover, because acts have to be comprehended while they are in progress – much like a spoken message, except that information is received visually and tactilely as well as audibly – theories of speech comprehension (e.g., see Osgood, 1963 and 1977; Winograd, 1972; Schank and Abelson, 1977) also may provide insights in the study of event recognition.

Within a given definition of the situation we readily solve the problem of what is going on around us. The process is so automatic that we assume it is objectively determined by reality, so that everyone must see events as we do. (In fact, social phenomenologists have pointed out that this is one of the necessary presumptions for meaningful social interaction: See Schutz and Luckman, 1973; Cicourel, 1974.) Research also seems to support the objectivity of event recognitions. For example, Fishbein and Ajzen (1975) reviewed a variety of research and concluded that

there is practically no evidence to support the notion that a person's own beliefs, attitudes, or personality characteristics have any systematic effects on descriptive beliefs based on direct observation. This should not be taken to mean that all types of beliefs are unaffected by such variables; on the contrary, some of them play an important role in the formation of beliefs that go beyond direct observation; i.e., they will tend to affect the inference process [p. 143].

Nevertheless, there often comes a point in event recognition when perceived activity can be viewed in different ways. For instance, a given behavior might be interpreted with equal accuracy as "teasing" someone or as "coercing" someone; and the final choice here is inferential rather than just descriptive (Heider, 1958). Indeed, subjectivism may be the rule rather than the exception in the last stages of event recognition.

Work on generative semantics and disambiguation of texts seems relevant in dealing with the stage where an observer disambiguates an act, choosing one interpretation over another. For example, a set of motions might be interpreted as "having a drink" until we learn that the fluid is medicine; then another definition of the act is required (taking medicine); if a person is angry and seems to be coordinating as object with respect to a machine, we might conclude that the machine is frustrating him, but not that it is teasing him; a child turning the steering wheel and moving the gearshift in a stationary car must be playing, though this interpretation would not be attributed to a chauffeur. In recognizing an event, as in comprehending a sentence, "projection rules" (Katz, 1972) constrain the kinds of acts that can be combined with a given actor and object.

Wilks (1972 and 1973), who represents projection systems by lists of abstract "template" sentences defining culturally permissible combinations, gives the following example of his own symbol conventions and of the general approach:

|⟨*ANI⟩⟨FEEL⟩⟨*MAR⟩| ... says that, for bare templates whose middle action element is FEEL, the first (agent) element must be from the class *ANI. Similarly, the object element must come from the element class *MAR ... All of which is to say that only animate things can feel, and that what they feel (since the notion of tactile feeling is covered by SENSE, not FEEL) are internal states, and acts, or their written equivalents [1973:126].

A given type of actor and a given type of object can be sensibly combined only with certain acts. Thus projection rules allow people to reject some interpretations of an event, reducing the alternative ways in which the event can be defined. Beckmann (1972:chap. 6) developed a computer program for generating English sentences within the constraints of a set of simplified projection rules, using a small lexicon of nouns and verbs, and his results demonstrate the power of this approach. Osgood (1970), Rubenstein (1973), and Szalay and Bryson (1974) have considered some of the issues that can arise empirically in defining the syntactic features that might be employed in projection systems. At the sociological level, projection rules relate to institutional frameworks for action (e.g., medicine, kinship): "Social institutions consist of shared expectations about what sets of actions and attributes should go together in a particular type of situation" (Cancian, 1975:80).

Logical and causal thinking is usually supposed to begin after events have been recognized, as part of the response to events rather than part of event recognition. Sometimes, in fact, events can be identified early on, so that their later consequences can be inferred. However, logical and causal analyses frequently are also part of deciding what has occurred, rather than of figuring out what is implied next. Harris (1964) argued that actions are naturally segmented in their environmental effects and that recognition of an act must depend heavily on observing the effects the behavior has. McHugh's (1968) concept of emergence in people's thinking about the flow of activity emphasizes directly the retrospective aspects of event recognition, and he describes the need for the concept as follows:

> What is there in the nature of being that makes it necessary to recast the past, and, in so doing, to change the meaning of the present and future as well?
>
> Simply put, it is because an unanticipated change in the present requires a change in the assessment of the past and anticipated future . . . The development of novelty, surprise, or the unexpected is the impetus to the reconstruction of what already has happened [p.27] .

Hanson (1958:86) described retroductions as follows: (1) some surprising phenomenon P is observed; (2) P would be explicable as a matter of course if H were true; (3) hence there is reason to think that H is true. Hanson also pointed out that many verbs – the names given to actions – are causally loaded, in the sense that certain consequences are routinely anticipated once the name is applied (for example, to poison someone implies death or illness). Together these points imply that retroduction frequently must be important in event recognition. The identification of an act explains what is caused, and a final identification of an act often requires waiting until we know what needs explaining.

Final interpretations of acts also are influenced by what is thought probable. Smith, Shoben, and Rips (1974) distinguished between "defining" features and "characteristic" features in analyzing how semantic information is processed to make logical decisions, and the same kind of distinction seems appropriate here in analyzing how acts are identified to form a credible combination of actor, act, and object. The kinds of restrictions on events provided by projection rules and causal knowledge have to do with the basic definitions of actor, act, and object. Selection among alternative interpretations according to likelihoods has to do with notions about what kinds of happenings are characteristic for the given actor and for the given object – judgments that may be heavily influenced by opinions and attitudes. For example, even if a threatening act is perceived, it would seem unlikely that a bride is coercing her groom, not because it is illogical (i.e., incompatible with projection rules or knowledge of causality) but because such an act seems so uncharacteristic of the relationship between bride and groom. Thus we ordinarily would decide that some other interpretation (teasing, taunting, seducing) is more likely and would settle on that as our interpretation of the event. Objective conditions restrict the possibilities of interpretation; estimations of likelihood further narrow the possible selections.

As will be shown in Chapter 3, the estimation of event likelihoods can be viewed partly as an outcome of affective dynamics (the interpretation "Bride coerces groom" seems improbable because it so seriously conflicts with our established sentiments about brides and grooms). Thus the likelihood factor entering the final stages of event recognition can be treated as an operation that maintains or restores established feelings about actor and object as much as possible within the objective facts of perception. Given a set of different events to recognize or several possible interpretations of one event, the recognition that achieves maximal restoration (or minimal disturbance) of fundamental affects would be the one finally selected. This same point can also be viewed from another perspective. As will be seen, persons almost always are anticipating some particular event once a situation and the circumstances are well defined. Then, as long as others act in accordance with our expectations, event recognition amounts to confirmation of an idea already formed.

Recognizing events and defining a situation conceptually are two different processes, but it is worth emphasizing how dependent event recognition is on the way the situation is defined. The definition of the situation narrows attention to a small band in the stream of change surrounding us, provides a manageable set of definite entitites for cognitive manipulation, and evokes feelings that allow us to assess the relative likelihoods of various formulations of events, so that we can settle on a single interpretation.

Affective response

The vast body of crosscultural studies in more than twenty nations by Charles Osgood and others working with the semantic differential (see Osgood, May, and Miron, 1975; Snider and Osgood, 1969) indicates that humans of all kinds react to stimuli of all kinds according to three different dimensions of response: *evaluation* (good versus bad); *potency* (strong versus weak); and *activity* (lively versus still). These dimensions have been identified as aspects of affect by researchers investigating words for emotions, they arise in theoretical and empirical studies of facial expression, and they correspond somewhat with neurological mechanisms believed to be involved in affect (Osgood, 1962; Izard, 1971:chap. 5). Thus evaluation, potency, and activity are viewed here as dimensions of variation in affective responses. Evaluation, potency, and activity associations are readily measured, and the Appendix in this book presents numerous examples of such measurements. (Semantic differential measurement procedures are discussed in the Osgood references just given and in Heise, 1969*b* and 1978.)

Some social psychologists prefer to characterize ratings of goodness, potency, and activity as measurements of "impressions" (e.g., Gollob, 1968). Such a perspective is not antithetical to the present work. The term "affect" emphasizes the relation of this work to the extensive literature on experimental and survey analysis of attitudes (the evaluation dimension – see note 1 to this chapter); the term "impression" would relate the work more to studies of psychological information processing (e.g., Wyer, 1974). It will be seen later that both orientations indeed are involved in the theory. Use of the word "affect" leads to the name Affect-Control Theory for the general theory presented here. Reference instead to Impression Control or Management Theory would emphasize more explicitly the theory's correspondence to other work in microsociology (e.g., Goffman, 1959; Lofland, 1969) and social psychology (e.g., Schlenker and Schlenker, 1975; Snyder, Tanke, and Berscheid, 1977).

Fundamentals and transients

Hovland (1959) observed that attitudes about established issues seem resistant to change when they are observed in natural situations where people exercise normal control over communications and events. However, attitudes seem changeable – even mercurial – when experiences are imposed on people and they have no opportunity to respond actively.

Results from survey research suggested to Hovland the conception of attitudes as stable dispositions. Studies of attitude change over long periods of time provide additional evidence suggesting that attitudes are stable. For example, Capel (1967) reported test–retest correlations over a thirty-year period for a sample of 100 women whose attitudes were measured using Thurstone scales during their college years in the 1930s. The long-term correlations for various attitude objects were as follows: Negro, .68; Sunday Observance, .67; Church, .61; War, .51; Law, .46; Patriotism, .46; Birth Control, .43. Kelly (1955) retested 368 subjects twenty years after their initial testing in the 1930s. Measurements at the two times on Remmers' Generalized Attitude scales correlated as follows (the figures have been read from graphs): Gardening, .35; Housekeeping, .33; Church, .32; Entertaining, .30; Rearing Children, .15; Marriage, .06. These long-term stabilities reported by Capel and Kelly certainly are not so high as to suggest that peoples' attitudes do not change at all over time, but they are high enough to suggest that short-term stabilities should be very high indeed. For example, the average test–retest correlation over thirty years as reported by Capel is .55. If this were the product of a simple change process in which attitude variance remained the same with some random shifts added each year, then the long-term stability coefficient might be specified in terms of a one-year stability coefficient as follows: $r_1^{30} = .55$, where r_1 is the test–retest correlation over one year. Solved for r_1, this formula suggests that the one-year correlations would be about .98. Kelly's average stability coefficient over a twenty-year period is .25 – substantially lower than Capel's, possibly because of lower measurement reliabilities. Nevertheless, the same calculation (now the formula is $r_1^{20} = .25$) yields a one-year test–retest correlation of .95. Moreover, no shifts in direction (that is, from positive to negative or vice versa) were found by either Capel or Kelly for any of the attitudes they examined, and about half of the mean over-time shifts in attitudes were not even statistically significant, though the measurements were separated by several decades during which there was substantial social change.

As Hovland observed, a finding of high stabilities in attitudes contradicts the impression one receives from experimental research. Experiments have shown repeatedly that a message, even a single sentence, can dramatically affect people's feelings about something. Additionally, actual longitudinal measurements of short-term stability also provide a different picture. Kelly, for example, reported an average one-year test–retest correlation of about .75 – much lower than what seems to be implied by his long-term correlations. DiVesta and Dick (1966) reported a .78 test–retest correlation for attitude measurements made a few weeks apart among seventh graders. Averaging test–retest correlations given by Boshier (1969) yields a similar figure, .75, for adults.[4]

Thus it is as if two different kinds of attitude arise in social psychological research, one persistently resitant to change even over long periods of time, the other mercurial and responsive to immediate stimuli. Kelman (1974) concluded that such results imply that there are two different aspects to any attitude – "In general, . . . it can be said that both stability and change are parts of the essential nature of attitudes" (Kelman, 1974:317) – and that both aspects must be taken into account in attitude research.

Anderson and Farkas (1973) presented a model of attitudes involving such a conceptualization in the course of reporting experiments on primacy and recency effects in attitude change. They found that the first few messages concerning an unfamiliar object are quite important in forming a basic attitude about the object. Thereafter, the most recent message causes additional change, but only as a deviation from the established base-line attitude. They used the terms "basal" to refer to the base-line attitude and "surface" to refer to the attitude manifested after any particular later message: "The surface component represents an immediate but readily reversible reaction to the information just presented . . . The basal component develops underneath and almost independent of the surface component. Once developed the basal component is very resistant to change" (Anderson and Farkas, 1973:91). A more neutral terminology will be adopted here to eliminate the anatomic connotations of "basal" and "surface." The relatively stable component of an attitude can be called the *fundamental* attitude. This is in accord with other scientific usage where a fundamental designates "that component of a periodic oscillation that has the lowest frequency." The attitude that is actually manifest at any given time is called the *transient* attitude to designate its "brief; fleeting; momentary" nature.[5]

A fundamental is essentially a kind of adaptation level:

The theory we propose assumes that all behavior is adaptive in nature and is referable to internal norms that are products of all relevant environmental and internal stimuli. These norms have proven to be weighted averages of focal, background, and residual stimuli in a variety of experimental situations ranging from psychophysical judging situations to interpersonal interactions . . . Instead of taking absolute thresholds or so called effective thresholds, or complete lack of physical stimulation as representing behavioral zero, we take the adaptation level (AL) as the zero or neutral of function. Since values of AL are nonzero and positive, stimuli above AL have qualities and magnitudes opposite to those below AL, whereas stimuli near AL are either neutral or ineffective. From this formulation the bipolar nature of all types of behavior immediately follows, especially affective and emotional responses whose bipolarity has long been recognized . . . Concretely, whether a stimulus is sensed and reacted to as loud or soft, bright or dim, beautiful or ugly, simple or complex, novel or hackneyed, and so on, depends upon its relation to prevailing ALs [Helson, 1973:169].

Hovland (1959) suggested that one reason experimentalists find change rather than permanence in attitudes is that they frequently focus on relatively unformed attitudes or on attitude shifts occurring immediately after a manipulatory message. This explanation fits the findings of Anderson and Farkas (1973): Fundamental attitudes are readily molded during the early period of attitude formation, and transient attitudes always are considerably influenced by the most recent stimulation. On the other side, Hovland suggested that survey researchers find attitude stability in part because they focus on attitudes that are important to respondents and well established; correspondingly, Anderson and Farkas find that mature fundamentals are very stable.

Hovland observed that another reason why attitudes do not change much in natural situations is that people ordinarily are free to maintain their fundamental feelings through processes of message selection, counterargument, bolstering, and other mechanisms of defense. Experimental studies confirm that an opportunity to respond immediately in order to deal with tensions and restore original attitudes does reduce net changes in attitudes following manipulations (Kenrick, Reich, and Cialdini, 1976; Osterhouse and Brock, 1970; Thibaut and Coules, 1952). Moreover, the idea of active control explains why a fundamental attitude – which is a weighted average of past transients in the Anderson and Farkas model – does not ultimately regress to neutrality as a person gains a variety of experiences with the attitude object. Once formed, a fundamental attitude begins to shape activities so that the transient attitudes deriving from experiences become selected and nonrandom, producing a stable, nonregressive average over time.

Although this discussion is phrased in terms of "attitudes" and therefore strictly relates only to the evaluation dimension of affect, it is assumed henceforth that the distinction between fundamentals and transients applies also to potency and activity associations. Relevant data, where they are available for these other two dimensions, show the same general patterns as discussed in considering evaluations.

Semantic differential ratings assess transient feelings about the stimulus at the time of the rating. Ideally, fundamental feelings would be assessed by averaging repeated measurements of transients. However, as a practical compromise, a cross section of ratings by numerous people from a homogenous culture can be averaged, allowing the transient deviations of different individuals to cancel, so that the common fundamental is revealed (the logic is discussed further in Heise, 1975: chap. 6).

Affective dynamics

Recognition of an event affects feelings about the persons and objects involved. For instance, mothers in general are viewed positively, but seeing a mother abuse her baby would cause most people to feel repulsed; gangsters ordinarily evoke negative feelings, but seeing a gangster honor his father would perhaps generate admiration. The transient feelings associated with people and things shift fluently as we observe events.

Work on affective dynamics by Harry Gollob and D. Heise using Gollob's SVO research design (see Chapter 2) has provided powerful, empirically based formulas for the prediction of impression formation. For example, given the statement "The mother abused her child," one's new attitude toward the mother is predicted from general attitudes toward "mother" (the sentence subject), "abuse" (the sentence verb), and "child" (the sentence object), the three being combined in ways specified by the relevant prediction formula. The Gollob–Heise research shows that new evaluation transients for subject, verb, and object derive directly from the old transients for the subject and verb and from a multiplicative interaction involving the old verb and object transients. Roughly, the implications are as follows. First, events produced by good actors are felt to be somewhat nicer than those provided by bad actors. Second, a good act produces a positive impression and a bad act a negative impression, regardless of other considerations. Third, outcomes are also a function of what can be recognized as a balance principle: Goodness comes from good acts on good objects or from bad acts on bad objects; whereas negative impressions result from good acts on bad objects or bad acts on good objects. To illustrate: "The mother abused her baby" produces a slight positive effect because mother is initially good; however, the net outcome is overwhelmingly negative because she engages in a bad act and moreover acts very badly toward a good object (the baby).

The impression of an actor's potency is a function of the prior potency of both actor and object to some degree; however, the new potency transient for the actor depends largely on the potency of the act that has been committed. Similarly, the new potency of an act changes a bit depending on its interpersonal context, but generally behavior potencies are stable, predictable largely from their own past values. In the case of objects, the old potency transients for actor and act are remarkably uninfluential in the outcome. The object in an event loses potency merely by being the object. Additionally, the original potency of an object, whether positive or negative, tends to be drawn toward neutrality. The most interesting implications of these dynamics come when we turn to event constructions: For example, a person trying to maintain a high-potency identity generally must initiate events (to avoid being the object of others' acts) and must behave in powerful ways.

Activity transients for actor, act, and object change in parallel, each dominated by the initial activity for the subject but influenced also by the old activity transients for act and object. In general, the more lively the actor is initially, the more active that person's events seem to be, though fast acts on alive, "young" objects also contribute to such an impression. Though the response dynamics for activity transients are simple in form, they may become highly significant in sequences of constructed events. For example, the activity transient for an act changes markedly with its occurrence, which may make that act less suitable for continued use in tension-reduction events.

The formulas presented in Chapter 2 are interpreted here as describing the affective reactions that occur with event recognition. Recognition of an event, establishing that a specified actor has engaged a particular object with a certain kind of activity, acts as a psychological operator transforming current feelings. That is, the affective associations last associated with the actor, act, and object are combined as specified by the formulas to form a set of new transients that replaces the old. New transients produced by event recognition become the prevailing feelings for subsequent psychological operations. In particular, these are the transients that are weighed for consistency with fundamental sentiments and that serve as parameters for constructing expectations about new events. Furthermore, when a later event is recognized, these transients in their turn take on the role of "old" transients, combining within the syntax of the later events to generate still another set of new transients.[6]

Construction of expectations

Because discrepancies between immediate feelings and established sentiments arise from recognizing events, people frequently plan and implement new events to return feelings to normal. Constructing restorative events inverts the operations involved in recognizing events. Whereas affective dynamics are among the final outcomes of event recognitions, they are wellsprings of event conceptualizations, generating key specifications for future acts. Additional restrictions on the acts that can be organized into an event are provided by projection rules, and the definition of the situation remains important in limiting possible combinations of actors and objects.

Consider the problem facing a person when a particular actor and a particular object are given and an act must be chosen to create an event that would transform present transient feelings into new transients maximally close to fundamental sentiments. Theoretically, this problem can be converted to a mathematical formulation: The present transients for the actor and object are known quantities; the fundamentals for actor and object (which serve as target values) also are known; equations describing how an event transforms old transients into new transients are available; so the only unknown is the affective profile for the act that would effect the transformation. Because the act must produce an optimal transformation, minimization techniques from calculus can be used to obtain equations that define the required profile in terms of the fundamentals and present transients for the given actor and object. Following this logic, we obtain a mathematical model describing the psychological operation of finding an act to combine with the given actor and object in order to create a restorative event.

Though the assumption is made here that actor and object for the new event are given, ordinarily there would be at least several different possibilities concerning who might be actor and who (or what) might be the object in a next event, with no way to prejudge the desirability of one combination over another. However, the operation outlined here could be applied to every permutation in turn, and the event producing optimal restoration of feelings then could be selected. Conceptualization of an event, like event recognition, operates within the definition of the situation, and the finiteness of that definition limits the number of event frames that need to be considered, here as in event recognition. Thus, to complete our model, we assume that a person tries each possible actor–object combination in a situation, testing which would provide maximum tension reduction when linked by an optimal act.

The affective profile for an act linking a particular actor and object in an optimal event, as generated by these operations, has no substantive quality and therefore still must be turned into conceptualization of an actual act. This is a matter of recalling appropriate possibilities from memory. We can think of the affective profile as acting like a template in testing retrievals from memory or, perhaps more realistically, as specifying the coordinates in memory space of a location where conceptualizations of more or less appropriate acts are stored. Additionally, retrievals from memory must be tested against projection rules, as only acts that make sense with the given actor and object are to be accepted. The same projection rules that constrained recognition of actual events now also constrain conceptualization of anticipated events.

Although these operations specify the basic processes of event construction, some complications have to be added for completeness. In particular, a presumably optimal event may be subsequently rejected as a person thinks through its required instrumental acts and likely responses from others, defining a sequence of events that altogether may be more disturbing than it is restorative. Implementing an event involves use of a script or series of scripts (Schank and Abelson, 1977), and these may require undesirable acts. For example, intending to visit mother may involve getting time off from work, buying a ticket, and riding a plane. However, a man may imagine that in trying to get time off from work he will have to act as a supplicant with his boss, and he may dread the flying because he is frightened of planes. So the process of elaborating the plan could generate disturbances that cause reassessment of the original intention. "Thinking through" an intended act allows one to assess the net affective restoration at the end of a predictable sequence; and if the net restoration is much less than the immediate restoration, the act may be discarded as actually nonoptimal.

The more detailed specification of event construction provided in Chapter 3 makes extensive use of a construct called "affective deflection." Deflection is mathematically defined as the squared difference between a transient and its corresponding fundamental. Summing deflections over all nine of the affective components influenced by a simple event (i.e., evaluation, potency, and activity of actor, act, and object) indicates the total amount of affective dislocation that exists following an event. Deflection is important in the theory mainly for mathematical reasons – it is the quantity that is minimized in order to obtain the proaction formulas defining event constructions. However, empirical evidence presented in Chapter 3 indicates that the deflection is subjectively manifested by a sense of unlikelihood: Events that generate large affective deflections seem improbable. Thus constructing events to minimize deflections creates events that seem probable, and such constructions can be identified as anticipations, intentions, and expectations.

Behavioral implementations

Intentions

Hypothetical intentions generated in imagined situations and circumstances ordinarily do not predict behavior very well, unless the imagined circumstances are rather precisely realized (Fishbein and Ajzen, 1975). However, an intention generated in response to an immediate real situation usually involves persons and objects that are actually perceived; the required circumstances are what generated the intention, so that it has a nonhypothetical here-and-now quality; and it defines an event that the person believes should occur, must occur, will occur next. Indeed, once the anticipation of an event in the immediate situation has been generated, that event has already begun occurring psychologically. The anticipation establishes a reference idea that is waiting to be realized perceptually.

Consequently, if we ask what causes a person to begin implementing a behavioral intention generated by immediate circumstances, the implication is that, in fact, there are no additional conditions other than the behavioral intention itself. As soon as a person finds that an event with the self as actor is the one that will best confirm sentiments in the circumstances, that act has begun psychologically, and behavioral implementation follows as a matter of course unless interrupted. (This explanation suggests the traditional concept of ideomotor action, but it is more accurate to think in control theory terms, following Powers, 1973: The anticipation establishes reference signals, which the organism begins realizing perceptually through action.)

Behavioral intentions (and other expectations) ordinarily begin in abstract form, corresponding roughly to imperative kernel sentences like "Mother, reprimand son" or "Thief, beg judge." The actual implementation of acts like reprimand or beg can take a variety of forms, depending on the substantive context – both symbolic and material – that exists at the moment; for example, a reprimand might be a whisper in church, a yell at home; and the notion of begging leaves open what the thief should beg for. Moreover, every act requires the actor to do some preparatory maneuvering in order to coordinate with the object, so that the act will "take" in a causal sense (Schank and Abelson, 1977). Additionally, many acts – like defeating, influencing, training – require elaborate and resourceful planning and may have to be implemented in a sequence of tightly organized behavioral steps. Thus a behavior intention in a sense establishes a puzzle that has to be solved by thinking up a more or less detailed plan for realizing the intention, using available resources and meeting standard conditions of causality. Some of the procedures people use to solve puzzles in general are discussed by Newell and Simon (1972).

Miller, Galanter, and Pribram (1960) described how the process of action can be analyzed in terms of hierarchical-control systems. Their central thesis was that every action begins with a general intention, like the simple self-commands just discussed; this intention in turn generates a hierarchy of goals (the plan) that has to be completed before the act is finished. In the process of enactment, each goal – a conceptualization or "image" drawn from memory – serves as a reference for judging whether perceived reality has attained a particular state. If not, behavior continues to be directed at attaining that state. When a state is attained, behavior begins to be directed at fulfilling another goal. The completion of a pattern of lower-order goals is the condition that fulfills a higher-order goal, and completion of all lower-order goals constitutes execution of the original intention. Rather similar ideas are elaborated in the artificial-intelligence literature (Goldstein and Papert, 1977), with the important elaboration that a plan often involves routinized programs or scripts that have been learned previously (Schank and Abelson, 1977).

Intentions are implemented in exactly the same system as is involved in the perception of reality (Powers, 1973). Whereas perception involves "accommodating" higher-order conceptualizations to sensory inputs, executing actions involves changing reality so that sensory inputs are "assimilated" within higher-order concepts. Stretching Piaget's (1970) notions of accommodation and assimilation, the general theory proposed here might be reworded as follows: People first accommodate to settings, developing a definition of the situation; then they make events that assimilate their later experiences within this definition.

The complexity and enduringness of intended acts spans a continuum ranging from "impulsive" behaviors (like punching someone) to events permeating many situations and perhaps unrealizable in a lifetime (like honoring one's country, pleasing one's parents, or actualizing the self). Miller, Galanter, and Pribram (1960:chap. 8) pointed out that the existence of enduring plans supports a sense of normality and meaningfulness in life (see also Schank and Abelson's [1977] discussion of "life themes"). Indeed, one's sense of self may be largely determined by long-term plans that are in the process of being implemented; each plan corresponds to some intended event in which the self is acting in a particular identity, and the identities involved in "what am I doing?" can be named to describe "who I am." Although it is not yet clear why people develop long-term goals, as opposed to intentions for concrete acts, a few points can be mentioned. First, even if adoption of enduring goals were an unusual occurrence, most people eventually would end up with some of these goals, because, once adopted, they persist. Second, the continuum from impulsive acts to enduring goals parallels a dimension of character variously named "ego development" (Loevinger and Wessler, 1970) or "moral development" (Kohlberg and Kramer, 1969); thus it is possible that selecting concrete or more abstract acts is a disposition varying from one individual to another.

Intentions may be generated that cannot actually be implemented for any of several reasons. First, they may violate projection rules, including the irregular forms we call taboos. For example: A parent may have the impulse to heal a diseased child but may reject direct action on the child's body because therapy, medication, and cures are the province of healers; or, because it is senseless, we reject any impulse to reason with an infant, just as we would reject an impulse to diaper an adult; or family members other than spouses may have sexual impulses toward one another but reject them because of incest taboos, and similarly we reject most impulses to manipulate physically adult actors who are not intimates. Sometimes acts are simply materialistically impossible, so that the impulse has to be abandoned; for instance, an off-duty policeman may wish he could handcuff an arrested thief, but he has no handcuffs; or one may want to return a dropped object to someone who has already vanished into a crowd. Also, a person may conceptualize an act while not having the competence to perform it; for example, one may want to swim, sail, and dance with another but not have any of the skills. Thus logic (in any of a variety of guises) sometimes demands that intentions generated in the service of attitude maintenance be replaced by other, less than optimal, events.

Expectations

The event associated with a behavioral expectation (as contrasted with a behavioral intention) also begins psychologically with its conception, but now the very definition of the act requires another to be the actor, and the observer must simply wait for the event to be executed. If the designated actor has the same event anticipation, then the event generally will be realized, because it is also that actor's behavioral intention. If, however, the designated actor has not generated the corresponding behavior intention, then the observer's anticipation is interrupted in one way or another. The designated actor may do nothing or may implement another event, carrying it out before the observer intervenes, so that the observer is confronted with an unanticipated event and new circumstances. The new event may be recognized as its originator intended it, or the observer, with his own expectation in mind, may interpret the new event in an idiosyncratic way (e.g., if a greeting is expected from someone who instead rushes to an elevator, the act may be interpreted as "He snubbed me").

Often an observer judges that a behavioral expectation is not being realized by another because the designated actor does not fully comprehend the situation at the moment. The designated actor may have missed a conditioning event (e.g., by facing the wrong way) or may have missed a key element in it (e.g., a side wink that made ridicule out of deference), or the designated actor may simply be seen as too insensitive an observer to have properly registered the event (e.g., a child, a novice, a dullard, a boor). In any of these cases, the designated actor's failure to begin implementing an expectation is likely to stimulate a verbalization of the expectation that the observer holds. Such verbalizations sometimes seem almost automatic, as at a movie when the crowd begins shouting instructions to a hero or heroine on the screen. Even so, they remain definite acts being implemented by the observer, and their tone is adjusted, in line with the affect-confirmation principle, to fit the relative statuses of observer and designated actor as well as the existing deflections prevailing in the immediate circumstances. Thus these verbalizations, or instructions, range from forceful commands (do *X!*) to polite requests (please do *X*) to indirect suggestions (shouldn't *X* be done?). Skinner (1957) provided the term "mand" to refer to all kinds of verbalizations of expectations for another's behavior.

Manding vocalizations correspond approximately to the traditional notion of "prescriptions for behavior." However, in the present formulation, it is readily understood that these do not reflect consensual norms but, rather, occur only when people are not generating the same expectations. If an actor's behavioral intention is the same as others' event expectations, then the actor implements the expected act, and the others will not be impelled to mand. Mands and statements of behavioral prescriptions occur only where this matching does not occur. Thus the sounding of prescriptions is characteristic of situations where there is conflict of one form or another. Similarly, the formalization of mands into laws also implies conflict, not universal ethical principles.

A mand has suggestive power in the sense that it registers as a definition of a possible event and competes with other possible behavior intentions being generated internally. As Miller, Galanter, and Pribram (1960) noted, the literature on hypnosis (e.g., see Weitzenhoffer, 1953 and 1957; Hilgard, 1965) provides important information about suggestibility and the adoption of behavioral intentions defined by others. Several points from that literature are worth noting here. First, suggestibility is a general phenomenon occurring under normal conditions, not just in hypnosis; therefore, it is relevant in ordinary interaction circumstances. Second, there are important individual differences in suggestibility, so that there should be corresponding differences in people's responsiveness to mands. (However, suggestibility is uncorrelated with usual conceptions of conformity and in fact is correlated positively with field independence [Hilgard, 1965]). Third, the heightening of suggestibility through hypnosis, sometimes characterized as relaxation of the "critical faculty," might be viewed as detachment from one's own reactions to and anticipations of events, so that received suggestions have less to compete with. This explanation suggests that the entire mechanism for generating event anticipations can be switched into what Powers (1973:220) calls "passive observation mode" and that certain circumstances (perhaps sensory overload and "crowd psychology" as well as hypnosis) generate this condition, producing unusual responsiveness to mands. Finally, if reactions to mands parallel hypnotic phenomena, then there should be a rather long response latency to a mand; repetitions should increase a mand's effect; and successful manding should create a relationship between mander and receiver that makes acceptance of later mands more likely (Weitzenhoffer, 1953 and 1957).

Viewing verbalized rules sociologically, Cancian wrote:

Norms are . . . rules that inform persons and groups that if an individual does certain things or has certain attributes then he or she is a particular kind of person. More precisely, norms are collective prescriptions or beliefs about what actions or attributes will cause others to validate a particular identity. Individuals conform to norms in order to validate an identity [1975:137].

A statement by another or a person's own inference that a manded behavior confirms the person's current identity may increase the suggestive power of the mand. This seems most likely to occur when the person lacks confidence in the appropriateness of his or her own disposition, as when enacting a new or esoteric role for which stable fundamentals have not yet been developed.

Mands have an additional impact, outside the psychology of suggestibility: They bind a receiver into a compounding of relationships that almost inevitably changes the optimality of events. To respond to a mand is to realize the manded act but also to acknowledge, follow, obey, and so on, the mander; not to respond is to leave the manded act unrealized, but the nonresponse also becomes an act itself – of ignoring, disengaging from, or disobeying the mander. Thus, once a mand has been voiced, its referent act cannot be weighed for just its affect-control potential: It must be weighed in a recursive interpersonal context. Similarly, all alternative acts become recursively embedded in the interpersonal act of *not* responding to the mander, and their affect-control potential must be assessed in this compounded form.

Roughly speaking, ignoring the expressed wishes of high-status persons disturbs our feelings more than ignoring the mands of weak and disliked persons; consequently, the mands of high-status persons more often are realized by others, and their expectations tend to prevail. The compellingness of mands from high-status persons seems phenomenalistically like coercion, because we give content to the affective deflections arising from disobedience by anticipating dire consequences. Theoretically, however, the compellingness arises simply because we are psychologically organized to confirm our sentiments about others, and so we tend to do the bidding of high-status persons in order to confirm their status, regardless of whether there would be material repercussions.

Thus mands affect a receiver in two different ways: by the mechanism of suggestion and by the mechanism of interpersonal recursion. Suggestibility is heightened as a person disengages from personal event constructions, allowing externally received mands to be determiners of behavior, and persons who avoid the tensions of complex interpersonal situations by disengaging their "critical faculty" respond to mands by the mechanism of suggestibility. On the other hand, interpersonal recursions arise from elaborated event constructions, and people who avoid suggestibility may become more subject to a sense of interpersonal coercion. Either way – whether by suggestion or by coercion – the effectiveness of mands is supported, and therefore mands are powerful forces shaping the behavior of individuals in accordance with others' stated expectations.

Sometimes a person realizes that others in a setting have different definitions or sentiments, and the matter is nonnegotiable. Then the person may attempt to identify and remember the others' viewpoints in order to see events from their perspectives (Foa, 1958). This attempt to remember is particularly important just before implementing a behavioral intention. The imminent event can be tested by recalling the others' viewpoints, reconstructing the event as they will experience it. Experiencing a disturbance while operating in another's perspective signals that the intended act may have undesirable consequences. Others may mand a different act, in which case one's own act takes on the meaning of *not* being something, rather than keeping the meaning it was supposed to have. Or if one completes the act before manding can occur, then the others may have to restore their own sentiments with return acts that regenerate affective deflections for the self. On the other hand, such elaborated testing of events is redundant when others share one's own viewpoint. Then one's intentions routinely are the same as others' expectations, and the additional analysis from others' viewpoints is unnecessary (such sharing of viewpoints may occur especially in intimate relationships).

Some people may fail to work through events in almost all situations because they lack the skill to "read" others' viewpoints and feelings (Davitz, 1964) or because they lack the capacity to store, process, or integrate the outcomes of multiple viewpoints. Because working-through activity frequently causes suppression of impulses in consideration of others, this, too, seems to be closely related to notions of ego and moral development (Loevinger and Wessler, 1970; Kolberg and Kramer, 1969). Judging from research on these topics, most people appear to operate with a fairly simple system. Those in the modal category of "conformists" perhaps deal with only their own viewpoint and that of a "generalized other."

Control mechanisms

Behavior

Behavior closes the affect-control loop. Implemented intentions and expectations provide new events for recognition, and in turn these recognitions generate new feelings and anticipations of still other events. The process continues until the present definition of the situation is replaced by a temporally or logically sequential situation or, perhaps, by a previously interrupted situation involving the same persons in different identities (Deutsch, 1968, provides a brief overview of research on the salience of interrupted processes).

The fact that we often are recognizing events that already have been anticipated suggests that reality might be bypassed entirely and the control loop closed intrapsychically. Such short-circuiting is one way of viewing fantasy: When operating in this mode we just imagine that sentiment-confirming events occur (Powers, 1973:222–8). However, a real reduction in affective dislocation seems to require a high level of intensity and conviction in event recognitions of the kind that is produced only in perception of real events, dreaming or hallucinations. Hypothetically, the control loop might be closed just as well by hallucinations as by behavior, but in fact humans do not usually operate that way.

Redefinitions

Earlier, it was proposed that some events may lead to redefinitions of the situation rather than to corrective actions and that, in particular, this may happen when an event is so disturbing it is deemed incredible – for example, a mother kills her baby – or when projection rules are violated – a tree moves, for example. The case of redefinition because of affective deflections is of particular interest here, because it is an alternative mode of reducing deflections that can be invoked when construction of new events fails, and thereby it provides a higher-order control mechanism in the affect-control system.

If a recent event increased deflection beyond an individual's tolerance limit, the individual may redefine the actor or object in that event so as to provide a new set of fundamental sentiments that feasibly can be maintained in the circumstances. It is possible to model this process in the same way the event-construction process was modeled. Now we suppose that a perceived act is accepted as an undeniable given (e.g., killing of a baby), and the identity of the actor is to be changed so that the overall event is maximally plausible, which is to say that the actor's identity is to be changed so that the event generates as little deflection as possible. Mathematically, fundamentals associated with "killing" and "baby" are knowns; formulas defining the transients produced by the event are available; and calculus can be used to obtain equations that transform the act and object fundamentals into a definition of the affective profile for an actor identity that would reduce to a minimum deflections produced by this event. Once the required profile is obtained, it serves as a template (or address) for retrieving an appropriate actor identity from memory, additional selection being imposed by projection rules and by the perceived characteristics of the actor (e.g., female and adult).

Attribution research (Regan and Totten, 1975) indicates that observers generally are inclined to interpret strange events by adjusting their notion of the actor. However, the general problem also could be formulated so that it is the object's identity that is to be respecified (e.g., "Rosemary, the mother, killed something, but what?"). In particular, actors might interpret their own odd acts situationally by adjusting their notion of the object. Affect-control theory also can provide a model for this kind of reidentification. The logic is the same as that just presented, but we would solve for an object profile rather than an actor profile.

Such reidentification processes may abort if the required identity shift is so drastic that it creates more tension than was produced by the last event without reidentifications (Emerson, 1970). For example, an immense amount of affective deflection would be necessary before we would be willing to accept that someone who was believed to be good, strong, and lively now has a foul, shallow, and withdrawn identity. Moreover, a reassessment of someone else's identity may reverberate to one's own identity ("This man is a mugger; I must be the victim") or to the identities of others, both on and off the scene (e.g., "How can this boy be a worthless do-nothing when his parents are sound people and my friends?"). The reverberatory tensions arising from reidentification also must be considered in the assessment of whether the reidentification is acceptable.

It is important to emphasize that projection rules and perceived characteristics do impose strong constraints in redefinition processes. For example, numerous identities with negative affective profiles exist for males, but in the "Mother kills baby" example a tension-reducing reidentification specifically has to apply to an adult female, and so selection has to be made from the smaller set of negative identities for females. Also, there are interpersonal factors involved in redefinitions, as emphasized by sociologists interested in societal reaction to deviance, in particular the labeling process (e.g., see Lofland, 1969; Hawkins and Tiedeman, 1975; Gove, 1975). A reidentification usually comes to be shared with others only after some amount of communication, persuasion, and negotiation, and someone tempted to redefine a person's identity may be dissuaded by that person or by others on the scene.

The whole point of reidentification is to provide a more tolerable assessment of an event that already has happened. Thus, following a reidentification, the instigating event is reassessed using the new identity for the actor or object, and the historical event takes on a new sense ex post facto in much the way that McHugh (1968) proposed with his principle of emergence. The reidentification provides a new set of fundamental sentiments to be confirmed by subsequent events, and the reassessed event gives a new set of transient feelings that lead to the construction of new anticipations.

Other controls

Occasions do arise when events are increasing affective deflections, and adjusting the definition of the situation is impossible because too much tension is produced by the primary and secondary reidentifications or because suitable alternate identities do not fit the features of the characters involved. In such circumstances, fundamental sentiments sometimes can still be protected by instrumental actions that materially change the setting so that it no longer supports the problematic definition of the situation. Many acts, possibly most of them, have effects on only minor details of a situation. However, some – like escape, break, find, build – have major consequences for settings, in that the acts can hardly be contemplated apart from the changes in situational definitions that they imply. If such acts are being generated affectively, one might now select them as a way of changing the scene. Settings can be reconstructed, say by introducing fences, walls, or locked doors, so as to disassemble the unwanted scenes and prevent them from reoccurring in the future. Similarly, acts might now be chosen, like killing, or deifying, that change the basic features of other humans so that a new definition of the situation becomes possible.

Interpersonal expansions

Behavior extrudes a person's psychological processes into reality, where the perceptions and reactions of others create new feedbacks with delayed effects. For example, an act on another modifies one's own transient feelings, but it may also stimulate the other to construct a return act modifying one's transient feelings again later. In larger groups, some circuits of reaction could involve several persons, return effects could be delayed by several events,[7] and the whole process might easily escape awareness.

Thus individual control systems link together into a group system when individuals perceive and respond to one another's actions (Heise, 1977a). Face-to-face gatherings of persons constructing events that involve one another are the most common basis for the development of group systems, but linkages between actors might also arise via communication media (telephone, letters, publications). Observers at a scene also may link into a group system: the actions of others affect observers' transient feelings and lead to the construction of expectations that the observers may verbalize. Furthermore, even if observers have adopted extremely passive roles, they retain a potential for action and so may add additional feedbacks to the system in some circumstances.

Whereas individual psychological systems are organized to control immediate feelings, the larger interpersonal system often operates as an amplifier. That is, though we each work to confirm our own fundamental sentiments in interactions with others, the concert of events sometimes causes a drift toward disconfirmation, generating more and more affective dislocation (which might produce a sense that an interaction is becoming an increasingly unique experience). In fact, an interpersonal system perhaps can be unstable, ultimately generating unmanageable dislocations and forcing individuals to resort to one of the higher-order psychological control mechanisms. Such instability is likely when there is no initial consensus in defining a situation; failure to agree at the beginning may force later redefinitions of the situation, reconstruction of the setting, or termination of the scene. Amplifications and instabilities in interpersonal relations are often nonintuitive: For instance, a person may initiate an unstable relationship because it appears to be a way of confirming fundamental sentiments, without realizing that the relationship is destined to self-destruct.

Association networks

Once a situation is defined so that all the persons at a scene have definite identities, networks of relationships begin to evolve, giving structure to the group system. This happens partly because some identities cannot be brought together into an event frame without generating substantial deflections. For example, any act by a judge on a thief creates deflection by threatening the judge's dignity, and an act by a thief on a judge is worse; thus, as they operate to minimize deflections, neither judge nor thief ordinarily seeks out the other for events. Even within a courtroom the judge should prefer to interact with attorneys, jurors, and clerks, and the thief should prefer his lawyer and other defendants. Outside the courtroom the disassociation is more complete: Judges and thieves segregate and operate in different settings.

Propensities for association or avoidance are not always symmetric. For example, an ordinary citizen in a courthouse has few satisfactory interaction partners, so that a policeman may be selected as the best of the lot. For a policeman, however, interactions with other policemen, lawyers, or clerks permit more confirmation of fundamental sentiments than do interactions with ordinary citizens. Thus citizens in a courthouse may approach policemen, but policemen do not ordinarily seek interactions with citizens.

Disassociation from others might occur to avoid events in which the self is not a direct participant. To an anarchist, courtroom events might seem incredible; he might try to avoid observing them simply to avoid the large affective dislocations implied by "incredible events." Back, Bunker, and Dunnagan (1972) found withdrawal from interactions when participants in a group maintained different sentiments about key concepts in discussions.[8] Similarly, a classic experiment by Schachter (1951) showed that persons are rejected and ignored once it is firmly ascertained that they are maintaining deviant attitudes.

Thus several general principles govern the formation of association networks. People seek associations with some persons and avoid associations with others in order to experience events confirming fundamental sentiments. The relevant sentiments may be those associated with the self and others' identities, or they may be sentiments about other objects of action or conversation. Preferences need not be reciprocated: In a given setting, the interactions that are optimal for one person may not be optimal for the chosen interaction partner. Finally, when there is freedom of choice and movement, preferences for association and disassociation tend to materialize into patterns of segregation.

The association network that arises and links specific individuals in a group is a complex product of the situation as defined (including the composition of characters) and of the fundamental sentiments being maintained by the persons present. Thus the same factors that generate substantive events also generate the larger interpersonal system that processes these events. Moreover, as completed events change affective transients, preferences for events with others might change also, shifting the form of the association network. Thus an association network may be a nonstationary phenomenon, complexly dependent not only on the scene and its definition, but also on the course of recent events.

Verbal communication

Speech and other media for delivering symbolic messages expand individuals' thinking capacities by giving access to others' memories, reasoning abilities, and perceptions. However, speech also provides linkages between persons that short-circuit the usual action system, linking individual psychologies at the higher-order symbolic level and further complicating a group system by greatly increasing the density of interpersonal feedback. At the strictly symbolic level communication feedback operates in such a way as to accentuate convictions about a shared cognition or so as to magnify the apparent difference in discrepant cognitions. Moreover, because speech is fast, these effects tend to occur before the control processes of social action really have a chance to operate. This is essentially another way of saying that situations and events are socially defined – discussed and negotiated – before action takes place.

One type of verbalization, mands, already has been discussed, and it was hypothesized that these occur when perceptions of immediate events are not conforming to expectations. Similarly, it seems likely that "tacts" (the other major class of verbalizations proposed by Skinner, 1957) occur when a question is raised concerning the recognizability of situations, people, actions, things, processes, and so on, or the applicability of projection rules, or the proper form of a salient belief (Fishbein and Ajzen, 1975) defining fundamental sentiments. This kind of communication is analyzed extensively in the artificial-intelligence literature (Goldstein and Papert, 1977).

As noted in the discussion of mands, verbal communications themselves are actions, and so their general structure and even their content should be partly shaped by the principles of action discussed previously. In particular, communications presumably unfold from kernel intentions indicated by verbs like tell, explain, report, brief, hint, and so on (or, alternatively, ask, query, interrogate, etc.); and the selection of one of these styles of communication rather than another presumably is a function of the affect-control principle applied to the self-identity, the identity of others, and the circumstances generated by recent events. Additionally, the selection of topics and the construction of these should be matters subject to constraints of affect control. For example, a husband may choose to "report" to his wife as a means of minimizing deflections in that relationship. He furthermore may select from alternative topics the one that minimizes affective deflections, and, moreover, he should construct the sentences that he speaks in such a way as to achieve such minimization. Consequently, communicatory acts often are fairly intricate compound events requiring construction simultaneously at the level of relationships and circumstances (e.g., "I, weary husband, will report to my cheerful wife") and at the level of discourse ("on that arrogant boss of mine and how I'm going to fix him").

Affect-control theory bears on communication acts in principle, but explicit analyses cannot be attempted now because of the lack of empirical affective-reaction formulas applicable to the recursions routinely involved in speech acts (i.e., "*A* tells *B* that *X* does *Y* to *Z*"). Instead, communication processes are treated in the traditional way in terms of references to discussion and negotiation.

Relations to other theories

The essentials of the symbolic interaction perspective in social psychology have been summarized by Stryker (1977:150).

a. Behavior is premised on a "named" or classified world, and "names" or class terms carry meaning consisting of shared behavioral expectations emergent from the process of social interaction. One learns, in interaction with others, both how to classify objects with which one comes into contact and how one is expected to behave towards these objects. The meaning of the classifications one constructs resides in the shared expectations for behavior the classifications invoke.

b. Among these class terms are symbols used to designate the stable, morphological components of social structure usually termed "positions," and it is these positions which carry the shared behavioral expectation conventionally labeled "roles."

c. Actors within this social structure name one another, in the sense that they recognize each other as occupants of positions, and in naming one another they invoke expectations with respect to one another's behavior.

d. Actors within this social structure name themselves as well – it is to these reflexively applied positional designations that the concept of self is typically intended to refer – and in so doing they create internalized expectations with regard to their own behavior.

e. Social behavior is not, however, given by these expectations (either reflected or internalized). That behavior is the product of a role-making process initiated by expectations but developing through a subtle, tentative, probing interchange among actors in given situations that continually reshapes both the form and the content of the interaction.

The theory outlined in this chapter has these features and can be considered a version of symbolic interactionism. In fact, development of the overall framework has been strongly guided by several key works in symbolic interactionism, especially Secord and Backman (1965), McCall and Simmons (1966), and Rose (1962). Similar theoretical work by Heider (1958) also has been influential.

The theory presented here does differ in two ways from prior symbolic interaction formulations. First, this theory is grounded in control-system theory, and an accurate application of control theory in symbolic interactionism has not been achieved previously. Moreover, the mathematization and strong determinism implied by such an approach seem to contrast with the humanistic leanings of many symbolic interactionists. Second, fundamental sentiments and transient feelings are pivotal concepts in the present theory, whereas traditional symbolic interactionism has been criticized for neglecting affect.

Affect-control theory can be viewed as a development in sociological theories of action (see Lazarsfeld's [1972] history of action theories). However, affect-control theory provides a generative framework for analyzing social interaction, in contrast to the inventorial frameworks that dominate much of the traditional and recent literature on normative behavior. The generative and normative approaches are compared in Chapter 5.

Although this is not a field theory of action, the influence of Kurt Lewin is obvious in the repeated references to his students' work throughout this volume. Lewin's insight that action is generated by "tension" dynamics operating within a cognitive representation of a social setting is reproduced here. Moreover, this theory depends on the idea that people generate action from their psychological representation of circumstances at the moment, as Lewin said:

behavior depends neither on the past nor on the future but on the present field. (This present field has a certain time-depth. It includes the "psychological past," "psychological present," and "psychological future" which constitute one of the dimensions of the life space existing at a given time.) This is in contrast both to the belief of teleology that the future is the cause of behavior, and that of associationism that the past is the cause of behavior [1951:27].

A human preference for consistency has been a key element in attitude theory at least since Heider (1946) proposed a consistency principle as one of the basic propositions in his theory. However, the systems perspective taken here differs from past suggestions in at least one important way: The proposal is that consistency is sought between the transient and fundamental components of the same attitude, rather than among different attitudes that are cognitively linked. This change in perspective creates subtle but profound shifts in emphasis. For example, consider the following scenario: A likes B, B insults A, and in return A insults B. A traditional analysis would say that the situation after the first insult is unbalanced,

$$A \overset{+}{\underset{-}{\rightleftarrows}} B$$

but A's insult restores balance by creating mutual dislike:

$$A \overset{\rightarrow}{\underset{\leftarrow}{=}} B$$

However, the control perspective emphasizes the restorative nature of events. Before the first insult, A's attitudes toward the self and the other presumably are both positive and consistent with fundamentals; after the first insult attitudes toward both the self and the other presumably are negative and inconsistent with fundamentals; finally, the second insult operates on these negative transients correctively – that is, A's insult is a corrective restoring the normal state of liking. Whereas the traditional analyst might expect further hostile acts from A to B, reflecting the new hostility, the control analyst might expect A's future behavior to be friendly (providing that A's return insult actually was an adequate "sanction"). Thus the understanding of what has happened is entirely different in the two perspectives.

In general, the present theory places an emphasis on action that is largely lacking in other attitude theories. Here we see "imbalanced" situations as usually instigating event constructions, rather than as invoking defense mechanisms: Corrective behavior is the first resort, rather than the last resort. Even when action fails to confirm attitudes, it is proposed that relatively ordinary backup operations are used to regain control (redefinition of the situation or reconstruction of the setting); and psychopathologies (e.g., repression, projection, hallucinations) would be proposed as confirmation mechanisms only in extraordinary circumstances or for abnormal individuals. The traditional emphasis on attitude change as a response to "imbalanced" cognitive structures is retained here, but in a special way. The rather ephemeral transient attitudes are readily influenced by cognitions, but then ordinarily actions are generated to undo the changes. Fundamental sentiments are viewed as relatively inaccessible for change because of the protections provided by behavior and cognitive processing.

The traditional framework for studying attitudes and attitude dynamics (e.g., Krech, Crutchfield, and Ballachey, 1962:139–147) suggests that attitudes are learned stimuli that dispose people to certain typical behaviors.[9] In the control perspective, fundamental attitudes are learned and serve as reference points for interpreting transient attitudes – the affective responses to present experiences. Then together the two generate actions that help undo recent disturbing events. Because behavior is not generated directly from either fundamental or transient attitudes but rather from the discrepancies between the two, an attitude as such does not ordinarily generate any typical behavior. Typical behaviors might be associated with a particular type of discrepancy between fundamental and transient attitudes, but that is a more complicated specification of attitude–behavior relations, which requires analyzing not only a person's fundamental attitudes but also the kinds of events that could produce a particular configuration of discrepant feelings.

The traditional paradigm views attitude as a mediating variable in a one-way chain of causation by which external stimulation produces behavioral responses. Fishbein and Ajzen's (1975) more sophisticated formulation recognizes that behavior changes the environment one experiences and thus may have a return effect on attitudes. However, the formulation presented here proposes that feedback from behavior to attitudes is not just incidental or accidental. Fundamental attitudes and momentary feelings generate behaviors *designed* to create new feelings that confirm fundamental attitudes.

Beyond these points, affect-control theory depends on the argument that behavior is a function not just of attitude dynamics but of affective dynamics. Consideration of potency and activity associations, as well as of evaluations, is essential in the affect-control model.

2. Affective reactions

Basic principles of attitude dynamics were extracted from the writings of Spinoza by Fritz Heider (1946). According to Heider: "A balanced configuration exists if the attitudes toward the parts of a causal unit are similar" or "if entities with different dynamic character are segregated from each other. If no balanced state exists, then forces toward this state will arise. Either the dynamic characters [i.e., attitudes] will change, or the unit relations will be changed through action or through cognitive reorganization. If a change is not possible, the state of imbalance will produce tension" (pp. 107–8). Heider discussed how such principles favor consistent orientations toward others – for example, someone who is liked tends to be respected. Moreover, Heider pointed out that the balance principle underlies a sentiment like "My enemy's enemy is my friend." The speaker of such a statement presumably has a negative attitude toward his enemy and a positive attitude toward the third person, and these attitudes are in balance because the enemy and the friend are dissociated. Heider discussed how balance principles influence interpersonal behavior and concluded that "a good deal of interpersonal behavior and social perception is determined – or at least co-determined – by simple cognitive configurations" (p. 111).

The Heider paper served as the threshold for a highly productive period in the development of attitude theory. Theodore Newcomb (1953) developed a "theory of communicative acts" that paralleled Heider's theory in many ways but that was addressed more explicitly to comprehending group dynamics in terms of individual attitudinal processes. Cartwright and Harary (1956) provided an influential mathematization of Heider's theory according to linear graphs, thereby increasing the precision of the theoretical statement. Abelson and Rosenberg (1958) defined "psychologic," a form of thinking that operates on affectively loaded verbal assertions. They identified sentences as "cognitive units" and observed that, in this case, cognitive relations are defined by the verbs in an assertion (e.g., helps, uses, opposes). Also, Abelson

40

and Rosenberg focused special attention on how people generate new assertions or expectations from a set of existing beliefs about objects.

Osgood and Tannenbaum's Congruity Theory (1955) implicitly invoked balance principles in attempting to account for attitude changes following fairly complex messages and events. Their formulation included an incredulity factor (too much tension may cause a message to be discounted) and an assertion constant (the source is less affected than the object of a message). However, Congruity Theory is most notable for its attempt to make quantitative predictions about attitude change. Osgood and Tannenbaum proposed a set of formulas predicting attitude changes when two entities are cognitively associated or dissociated. The following single formula is equivalent to the set of formulas they presented:

$$\Delta x = w(ry - x) \tag{1}$$

where x is the original attitude toward one of the objects being cognitively linked (measured on a 7-point good–bad rating scale) and Δx is the change in this attitude; y is the original attitude toward the other object (again measured on a 7-point good–bad scale); r is the value of the cognitive linkage; +1 for association; – 1 for dissociation; and w is a weight depending on the intensities (absolute values) of the attitudes:

$$w = \frac{|y|}{|x| + |y|} \tag{2}$$

(The same formula can be used to predict changes in attitude toward the other object simply by interchanging the definitions of x and y.) In this formula, Δx is the predicted change in the attitude toward x. If x' is the new value of attitude x after a message or event, then $\Delta x = x' - x$, and the above formula can be rewritten as:

$$x' = wry + (1 - w)x \tag{3}$$

In this alternative formulation, the first term on the right can be identified as a balance effect: A negative relation combined with a negative y attitude helps to generate a new attitude toward x that is positive. The second term represents a stability factor: The new attitude toward x still is partly a function of the old attitude toward x.

Heider himself published another article (1967) two decades after his original report in which he, like Abelson and Rosenberg, treated sentences as cognitive units. He also reported measuring attitudes toward verbs (or acts) on good–bad rating scales, just as Osgood and Tannenbaum had measured attitudes toward objects. His experimental results seemed to suggest that the balance principle could be reconceptualized as a multiplicative interaction between attitudes toward behaviors and attitudes toward the objects of the behaviors.

Evaluation dynamics

The attitude-change studies mentioned above established that attitudes do change when evoked together in cognitive structures, that sentences describing events can act as cognitive operators effecting attitude change, and that algebraic equations might describe attitude dynamics, including peculiar balance effects. More recent research has built on these findings, yielding fairly precise formulas for predicting attitude change.

Harry Gollob (1968) designed an experiment specifically to determine whether attitudinal changes produced by assertions about an event could be predicted from attitudes associated with the actor (A), behavior (B), and object (O) in the event.[1] He created three sets of 192 event descriptions (the sets served as replications). Each event was specified by a sentence of the form "The *adjective* man *verbs* the *object*" (e.g., "The evil man reassures the neighbors"). Gollob varied the events in each set by systematically combining positive and negative adjectives for the subject, positive and negative behaviors, and positive and negative objects. Then he analyzed respondents' evaluative ratings on a good–bad scale of the "man" in the various sentences, to determine whether outcome attitudes could be predicted from configurations of input attitudes.

Analyzing the mean ratings for the elements in each sentence (averaged across twenty-four subjects in each set), Gollob was able to account for 86 percent of the variance in outcome attitudes, using a regression model. The same model explained 74 percent of the variance when applied to less reliable individual ratings. The formula producing these results is:

$$A'_e = -.26 + .39A_e + .48B_e + .25B_eO_e \tag{4}$$

in which A'_e stands for the outcome evaluation of an actor; A_e is a measure of the original attitude toward the actor (i.e., the adjective-man) obtained apart from the stimulus sentence; B_e is an attitude measure of the behavior out of context; and O_e is a measure of the attitude toward the object rated in isolation. [In formula (4), Gollob's original regression coefficients have been rescaled to apply to seven-point good–bad rating scales, rather than the eleven-point scales Gollob used. This change is made to maintain continuity with other results presented later.]

Gollob's formula indicates that the outcome attitude toward the "man" in each event was formed as a composite from the original attitude toward the actor (e.g., an "evil man"), the original attitude toward the behavior (e.g., "reassures"), and the arithmetic product of the original attitudes toward the behavior and toward the object (e.g., "neighbors"). Suppose, for example, that an "evil man" is rated -2.0; "reassuring" is $+1.0$, and "neighbors" is $+.8$. Then the predicted attitude toward an evil man who reassures neighbors is:

$$A' = (-.26) + (.39)(-2.0) + (.48)(1.0) + (.25)(1.0)(.8) = -.4 \qquad (5)$$

The evaluation of the man improves (though not into the positive range). This improvement represents the idea that a man who reassures neighbors – who does good things and to good people – cannot be so very bad.

The A_e term in the Gollob formula acts much like a stability effect. That is, an event may exert pressure for change on the actor attitude, but the net change is damped somewhat in the direction of the original actor attitude. The B_e term indicates that the action specified in a sentence is an important basis for evaluating the actor. Gollob (1968:348) observes: "A man who, say, hates tends to be thought of as a 'hater'; and similarly, a man who, say, helps tends to be thought of as a 'helper.' " The $B_e O_e$ term represents the balance effect. Goodness arises from doing good unto good or doing bad unto bad. A negative impression results from doing good unto bad, or doing bad unto good. Note that the formula does not include a direct effect from the original object attitude, nor does it allow for any additional interactions. Including these additional terms in the equation yielded only trivial improvements in predictions.

Gollob also examined an analysis-of-variance model, which essentially infers the input attitudes from the data on outcomes, rather than using independent measurements of the event's attitudinal components. This approach involved estimating many more parameters than the regression approach, but about 97 percent of the variance in event outcomes is explained with a model using just A_e, B_e, and $B_e O_e$ components.

Multiplying B_e and O_e ratings, as was done in the regression analysis, is a simple way of representing interaction effects between behavior and object attitudes. However, Gollob noted that this simple procedure does not completely represent the complex interactions occurring between behaviors and objects. This is the main reason that the regression equation is somewhat less efficient in accounting for results than the analysis-of-variance model. Gollob considered the complexities of the behavior–object interaction in considerable detail. However, his analyses are not reviewed here because they do not suggest yet a better way of predicting outcomes from independent measurements of input attitudes than the regression equation having a simple multiplicative behavior–object interaction.

Behavior and object resultants

Gollob's equation predicted only attitudinal outcomes for the actors in events. However, formulations of balance theory had proposed that any of the attitudes in a cognitive unit might be liable to change. Thus it seemed plausible that formulas might be defined describing attitude changes for both of the persons in a social event. Because the positivity or negativity of cognitive linkages was known now to correspond to behavior attitudes, it also seemed reasonable to allow for a formula predicting changes in behavior attitudes.

Heise (1969a) constructed a corpus of twenty-three event sentences from nouns and verbs presumed to have either positive (+) or negative (–) evaluations. Different words were entered in the subject, verb, and object positions to create sentences representing all major *ABO* attitudinal configurations (+++, ++–, +–+, etc.). Then attitudinal measures on the elements were made, using seven-point rating scales.

In one part of the study, respondents rated the elements out of context, each element being presented in a minimal context to show whether it was a person or thing (e.g., "The enemy was there") or a behavior (e.g., "It helped them"). In the second part of the study, the event sentences themselves were presented with one word underlined (e.g., "The enemy surrounded the church"), and respondents were instructed to rate the underlined word, taking the whole event into account. These data were converted to two sets of mean evaluation ratings. One set contained the mean ratings for all of the elements out of context, thereby defining the attitudinal inputs for each event. The second set – the mean ratings of elements in context – defined the attitudinal outcomes of each event for actor, behavior, and object. With event as the unit of analysis, regression equations were obtained for predicting the mean evaluation ratings in context (A_e', B_e', O_e') from the mean ratings out of context (A_e, B_e, O_e).

A number of models, including some with numerous interaction terms, were tried. None of the examined models did appreciably better than the model already suggested by Gollob's work. The obtained equations for this model were:

$$A_e' = -.15 + .37A_e + .55B_e + .07O_e + .25B_eO_e \tag{6}$$

$$B_e' = -.24 + .23A_e + .60B_e + .07O_e + .25B_eO_e \tag{7}$$

$$O_e' = -.13 + .17A_e + .40B_e + .36O_e + .30B_eO_e \tag{8}$$

Symbols are the same as those used in presenting Gollob's equation.

The analyses yielding equation (6) constitute a replication of Gollob's analyses, and the formula bears a resemblance to the one that Gollob obtained. The constants in equations (4) and (6) are negative and within .11 units of each other. The other coefficients in the equations differ by no more than .07 units. (Gollob deleted the object term – that is, set its coefficient to zero – because the term contributed negligibly. The same thing could have been done here, except that the object term is required in equation (8) for predicting object outcomes.) This convergence in formulas occurred despite different subject populations (Yale students and University of Wisconsin summer school students) and despite somewhat different methodologies (e.g., ratings on a single eleven-point scale versus average ratings on three seven-point scales). Moreover, Gollob's sentences described only interpersonal events, whereas some of Heise's sentences were impersonal (e.g., "The farms saved the nation"). Thus it appears that the Gollob and Heise subject formulas can be viewed as essentially the same and that such a formula applies under fairly general conditions.[2]

The first of the three Heise equations (6) shows that the outcome attitude toward the actor is a composite made up of a small negative constant, a component representing the original attitude toward the actor, a component representing the original attitude toward the behavior, and a "balance" component formed from the product of the original behavior and object attitudes. (The contribution of the O_e term in equation (6) is almost negligible.) Equation (7) shows that outcome attitudes toward the behavior are composed similarly, but the components are weighted somewhat differently. Equation (8) shows that outcome attitudes toward the object also are formed similarly, except, again, weights are different and, additionally, the original attitude toward the object does make an appreciable direct contribution. Examination of these equations suggested that roughly the same equation seems to be involved, whether predicting A'_e, B'_e, or O'_e, except that in each equation extra weight is given to the original attitude for the element being predicted. This conclusion in turn suggested that the outcome attitude for any word in an event sentence (W'_e) might be represented as the sum of a general resultant (R_e) and the original attitude for that word (W_e):

$$W'_e = R_e + eW_e \quad \text{where}$$
$$R_e = k + aA_e + bB_e + dB_eO_e \tag{9}$$

(A direct contribution from O_e is not shown in the R_e formula, because such an effect is appreciable only when predicting O'_e, and in that one case the O_e effect would be simply the stability effect, eW_e, represented in the first formula.) Of course, this model really consists of a single equation, because R_e in the first equation can be expanded by using the second equation.

The data sets for predicting A'_e, B'_e, and O'_e separately were pooled (giving a total of sixty-nine cases), and a regression analysis was conducted to estimate the various coefficients in the Heise (1969) model. Results were as follows (representing the model as a single equation):

$$W'_e = -.19 + .16A_e + .44B_e + .28B_eO_e + .24W_e \tag{10}$$

This simplified model accounted for 67 percent of the variance in all outcome attitudes. The mean proportion of variance explained by the three separate equations for predicting A'_e, B'_e, and O'_e was .71. Thus, for heuristic purposes, the model consisting of one equation can reasonably be considered equivalent to the first *ABO* model stated in three equations.

To clarify this model of attitude dynamics, consider the example sentence "A gypsy cheats a soldier." Estimates of the original evaluations of the actor, behavior, and object are, respectively, $-.4$, -2.1, and $+1.5$ (the figures are from the dictionary provided as an appendix in Heise, 1978). The sentence resultant is calculated as follows:

$$R_e = (-.19) + (.16)(-.4) + (.44)(-2.1) + (.28)(-2.1)(1.5)$$
$$= -2.06 \tag{11}$$

The final predicted A'_e, B'_e, and O'_e attitudes then are:

$$A'_e = (-2.06) + (.24)(-.4) = -2.2 \tag{12}$$

$$B'_e = (-2.06) + (.24)(-2.1) = -2.6 \tag{13}$$

$$O'_e = (-2.06) + (.24)(1.5) = -1.7 \tag{14}$$

These results suggest that an observer would devalue a gypsy who cheats a soldier (from $-.4$ to -2.2). This is a familiar kind of result that would be predicted by most balance theory formulations. The results also indicate that an observer would devalue the soldier dramatically (from $+1.5$ to -1.7). Although this conclusion would not be predicted by most balance theory formulations, subjects would presumably tend to rate the soldier in this way when presented with the event sentence, as the prediction equation is derived from similar sentences. Moreover, exactly such a phenomenon has been identified in other social psychological research; persons who see an innocent person victimized frequently do devalue that person (Lerner, 1971; Lincoln and Levinger, 1972; Aderman, Brehm, and Katz, 1974).

These results also indicate that the behavior attitude would decline slightly (from -2.1 to -2.6). That is, momentarily after the event, cheating someone seems fouler than usual. The possibility of such changes in attitudes toward actions seems not to have been considered in previous formulations of attitude theory.

Comparison with other formulations

This empirically based model of attitude change contains a term representing the classic attitude-balance principle. Now, however, the balance effect is seen to be essentially a multiplicative interaction of original attitudes toward the behavior and the object of an event. This finding means that specification of balance phenomena no longer needs to depend on researchers' subjective assessments of positive or negative linkages. Instead, one identifies the appropriate formulation of an event from the subject's point of view and then employs attitude measurements for the behavior and object to define the nature of the balance effect. The $B_e O_e$ term in the model also fully quantifies the balance effect for the first time. Both behavior attitudes and object attitudes can take on a continuous range of positive and negative values, and because the balance effect is the product of these attitudes, it, too, can take on a range of positive and negative values. Additionally, it now is clear that some cognitions may yield no balance effect at all – as, for example, when the object attitude is completely neutral. This is a possibility that had been anticipated but not demonstrated by Abelson and Rosenberg (1958).

The single-equation formulation of Congruity Theory – equation (3) – contains two terms: one for the balance effect and another representing stability in attitudes. The *ABO* model contains parallel terms: one for the balance effect, as noted above; and the eW_e term, which indicates that an outcome attitude is constrained to some degree in the direction of its original value. In this sense, the *ABO* model incorporates Congruity Theory.

However, the Congruity Theory formulation proposes that the terms should be weighted according to the relative intensity of input attitudes. A regression analysis with polarization weights added to each term in the *ABO* model provided no improvement in predictions (Heise, 1969:n. 4). Additional (unpublished) analyses of the Heise data, using various weighting schemes like those proposed in Congruity Theory, also have led to no improvements. Moreover, the actual Congruity Theory predictions (with incredulity corrections) for the seventeen Heise events that have clearly nonneutral behaviors yield predictions correlating .66 with the obtained subject outcomes. Predictions from the *ABO* model correlate .92 with subject outcomes in this same subset of sentences. Thus, in fact, there seems little reason to believe that the relative weights of the components in the prediction equation vary as Congruity Theory proposes. (However, Gollob, 1968, found that the relative weights for components may vary somewhat across subjects.)

Congruity Theory also proposes that dissociations should cause attitudes to be polarized in opposite directions – one positive and one negative. The Heise data show no evidence of bipolarization in the case of dissociations. Moreover, the gravest errors in the Congruity Theory predictions for the Heise data often arise because of this factor. For example, according to Congruity Theory, "The father shot the uncle" should lead to attenuation of both attitudes, but with father somewhat positive and uncle somewhat negative. The actual results (approximately predicted by the *ABO* model) were extreme negative evaluations of both father and uncle.

Osgood and Tannenbaum's results (1955:table 3) did show some evidence of bipolarization as a result of dissociation. Perhaps the explanation is that Osgood and Tannenbaum did not use single-event sentences as stimuli but rather "highly realistic newspaper stories including positive or negative assertions involving the experimental source-concept pairs." Such a manipulation, being lengthy and complex compared to presentation of a single sentence, might have generated additional conditions besides mere association or dissociation. That such complications could affect results is indicated by the recent work on "derogation of victims." For example, Lincoln and Levinger (1972) showed subjects either a picture of a policeman attacking a black man with dogs or else the same picture with the dogs cropped out, so that no aggression was evident. The aggression picture led to devaluation of both the victim and the policeman, compared to the ratings with the nonaggression picture. However, when subjects also were told that their responses would be important in a commission investigation and would be shown to the policeman and the black man, then they rated the victim of unjustified aggression more positively and devalued only the policeman. Lerner (1971) found that the amount of devaluation of a victim depended on whether the suffering was undeserved (more devaluation) or compensated for by payments. Aderman, Brehm, and Katz (1974) found devaluation of victims under a variety of conditions but sometimes found enhancement of the victim when the observer was instructed to "imagine how you yourself would feel." Thus innocent victims usually are devalued, as predicted by the Heise (1969) elaboration of the *ABO* model, but conditions can be complicated so that this is not the case.

Directionality in cognitive linkages has been a somewhat confused issue in traditional formulations of balance theory. Abelson and Rosenberg (1958) assumed that a linkage is symmetric – that *xry* is essentially equivalent to *yrx*. Osgood and Tannenbaum (1955) assumed symmetric linkages and then added the qualification that a "source" may be less affected by a message than is the "concept" to which it is linked. In contrast, Cartwright and Harary's (1956) formalization of Heider's theory explicitly allowed for asymmetry, so that *xry* does not necessarily imply *yrx*. The *ABO* model also is asymmetric, predicting quite different outcomes for such pairs of events as "The policeman shot the rapist" and "The rapist shot the policeman."

When symmetry is assumed theoretically, the stated or unstated premise is that asymmetries are unbalanced, and so ultimately they will be changed to symmetries. Thus the assumption of symmetry relates to the net outcome of a structure after it has been both cognized and restructured in accordance with balance principles. In contrast, the *ABO* model focuses just on the attitudinal dynamics produced by a single event. The directionality of action – who is actor and who is object – is crucial in determining attitudinal outcomes of a single event, and one cannot presume that *xby* is the same as *ybx*. Actions and restructurings resulting from attitudinal deflection are left as topics for further analysis in the *ABO* formulation.

ABO research depends on rating-scale measurements of attitudes. Such scales provide reasonably accurate measurements of attitudes (Heise, 1969*b*). More important, they serve the function of generalized attitude scales, allowing attitudes toward stimuli of all kinds to be measured on a single metric (Osgood, Suci, and Tannenbaum, 1957:195-8). Heise (1965) and Heider (1967) demonstrated that such scales could be used to measure attitudes toward acts as well as attitudes toward actors and object. The work of Gollob (1968) and Heise (1969*a* and 1970) demonstrated further that such rating scales provide a mathematically coherent metric, so that attitudes toward the different parts of an event can be combined in a single formula giving precise predictions of attitudinal outcomes. The traditional methodology of deriving a different scale for every attitude stimulus could not have led to a parallel mathematical model, partly because of the prohibitive expense of developing scales for a multitude of stimuli, and partly because attitude measurements on the usual Thurstone, Likert, or Guttman scales are fundamentally incomparable and hence cannot be added and multiplied in meaningful ways.

Potency and activity dynamics

Cognitions might instigate more than just the evaluation dynamics that have been the focus of traditional balance theories. Heise (1969*a* and 1970) explored this possibility by extending the *ABO* experimental framework to the potency and activity dimensions.

Potency

Heise (1970) generated a corpus of fifty-four event sentences[3] containing all major configurations of potency in the *A*, *B*, and *O* positions (+++, ++-, +-+, etc.). Measurements of actor, behavior, and object potencies were obtained by averaging ratings on three scales: powerful-powerless, strong–weak, and big–little. First these ratings were made when the elements were presented out of context, and then another set of ratings was obtained when the elements were presented within the context of the stimulus sentences. Multiple regression analyses were used to determine how best to predict the in-context ratings of the elements in each event from out-of-context ratings.

Equations predicting outcomes A'_p, B'_p, and O'_p from out-of-context potency ratings of the actor, behavior, and object explained 60 percent or more of the outcome variances. This level of prediction was obtained without interaction terms, and the level of prediction could be improved only minutely by including statistically significant interactions in equations (one appeared in data from males; another in data from females). Thus the following equations involve only the A_p, B_p, and O_p main effects:

$$A'_p = -.14 + .33A_p + .53B_p + .15O_p \tag{15}$$

$$B'_p = -.17 + .09A_p + .70B_p + .17O_p \tag{16}$$

$$O'_p = -.29 + .08A_p + .28B_p + .45O_p \quad \text{(males)} \tag{17}$$

$$O_p = -.33 + .12A_p + .11B_p + .44O_p \quad \text{(females)} \tag{18}$$

Symbols are the same as used in presenting the equations for evaluation dynamics, except that here letters refer to potency measurements rather than to evaluation measurements. Two equations – one for males and one for females – are given for predicting potency outcomes at the object position. The two equations are similar, but they indicate that males weight behaviors more heavily than females in developing the object outcome. (The first two equations are based on pooled data from males and females, as the formulas were similar across sexes.)

Equations (15) and (16) approximately fit the model of a single resultant plus a stability factor – a notion already introduced in the section on evaluation dynamics. Such a formula was not presented by Heise (1970), but an approximation can be derived from the results shown:

$$W'_p = -.16 + .11A_p + .51B_p + .16O_p + .21W_p \tag{19}$$

In this formula, W_p and W'_p refer to potency ratings for the actor or for the behavior, depending on which is being predicted. The formula does *not* apply for objects.

Equation (19) indicates that impressions of an actor's potency depend heavily on the potency of that person's acts. Additionally, an actor seems more powerful if engaged with powerful objects, but the impact of this factor is relatively small compared to the effect produced by the behavior itself. For example, a person who controls another tends to be seen as strong, whereas one who betrays another tends to be seen as weak, and the particular object in the event adjusts these results only somewhat. The last item in the formula indicates that potency impressions (like evaluations) also have a certain inertia, in that the actor's resultant potency is partly a function of the initial potency.

Potency outcomes at the object position – whether defined by the male or by the female formula – cannot be incorporated within the same dynamic that describes actors and behaviors. The object equations contain negative constants that are larger than those in the actor and behavior equations, and the behavior effect is smaller in the object equations than in the actor and behavior equations. Thus an event yields one impression of potency for the actor and behavior and another, different impression for the object.

Although the formulas predicting object outcomes are somewhat different for males and females, the male and female results are similar enough so that a single averaged formula might be used heuristically. Equation (20) (unreported in Heise, 1970) was obtained by running the regression analysis over the pooled set of male and female data (i.e., over 108 units rather than 54):

$$O'_p = -.31 + .10A_p + .18B_p + .44O_p \tag{20}$$

The sizable negative constant in this formula implies that potency impressions of entities in the object position are forced generally in the direction of "slightly weak." The effect of the event's actor is nearly negligible. The potency of the behavior spills over somewhat to the object, but the effect is small compared to the behavior effect for actor and behavior outcomes. Also, the behavior effect is of less consequence than the effect of the original impression of object potency. The coefficient for O_p is largest of all those in the formula, yet even it is less than the .5, indicating that merely being the object of an event causes potency impressions of an entity to attenuate. Overall, the formula indicates that if an object was initially strong, it loses potency dramatically merely by being in the object position; if initially it was slightly weak, then it stays about the same; something extremely powerful gains slightly in potency by being objectified.

As an example of potency dynamics, suppose college students are confronted with the isolated information that "the thief controlled the judge," and their initial impressions of A_p, B_p, and O_p potencies are $-.4$, 1.6, and 1.6, respectively (these are the values obtained from males in the Heise, 1970, study). Substituting these values in the summary formulas gives:

$$W_p' = (-.16) + (.11)(-.4) + (.51)(1.6) + .16(1.6) + .21W_p$$

$$= .87 + .21W_p \tag{21}$$

$$A_p' = (.87) + (.21)(-.4) = .78 \tag{22}$$

$$B_p' = (.87) + (.21)(1.6) = 1.20 \tag{23}$$

$$O_p' = (-.31) + (.10)(-.4) + (.18)(1.6) + (.44)(1.6) = .64 \tag{24}$$

The outcome impression of the thief's potency is predicted to be .78 (the Heise, 1970, respondents actually gave an average value of 1.4). The thief gains in potency because he engaged in a strong act (and also to some degree because he acted on a powerful object). It is predicted that the judge's potency declines to .64 (.2 was the value obtained empirically). The judge loses potency simply because he has been made an object. Note that the thief's identity has almost nothing to do with the judge's loss. Moreover, the fact that the judge submits to a strong act rather than a weak one is of only marginal importance in avoiding potency loss.

A loss of potency for the object of a sentence was found also by Johnson (1967). In one experiment, he created thirty-six sentences whose subjects and objects were nonsense syllables (e.g., NIJ, GAQ), these being linked by twelve ordinary English verbs matched so that their average semantic differential ratings averaged to about zero. On being presented with these sentences, respondents rated the syllables in the object position as significantly less potent than those in the subject position. Johnson designed a second experiment, in which twenty-four sentences were phrased in the active voice (e.g., the NIJ hurt the GAQ), and an additional twenty-four sentences were constructed in the passive voice (e.g., the GAQ was hurt by the NIJ). Again, the object of action generally was seen as less potent than the subject, regardless of voice. (On the other hand, Johnson found no significant mean difference in the evaluations of subjects and objects in his sentences.[4])

Evaluation effects in potency dynamics

Gollob and Rossman (1973) created another experiment to examine potency dynamics within the *ABO* framework. However, they anticipated that potency impressions for subjects of sentences would be a function of behavior evaluations as well as the *ABO* potencies:

It seems likely that an actor described as doing a bad act to a powerful person would be seen as relatively powerful because he risks retaliation, whereas an actor described as doing a bad act to a weak person would be seen as relatively weak because he is taking advantage of or victimizing a weaker person. On the other hand, an actor described as doing a good thing for a powerful person might be seen as being relatively weak because the actor might well be attempting to appease or ingratiate a more powerful other; whereas an actor described as doing a good thing for a weak person may be judged as relatively powerful and humanitarian because it is unlikely that the weak person would be able to offer much to repay the favor [p. 393].

To examine these ideas, Gollob and Rossman created 128 sentences of the form "Bill *verbed* the *object*" (the personal name was varied across items). Behaviors and objects were chosen to provide a balanced set of combinations (++, +−, −+, −−) on both the potency and evaluation dimensions. In-context measurements of the actor's potency were obtained by ratings on an eleven-point yes–no scale in answer to the question "Is Bill powerful and able to influence others?" Out-of-context potency ratings were obtained using a similar format ("Mark is a child. Is Mark powerful and able to influence others?")

Stepwise regression was used to define the best equation for predicting in-context potencies from the independent variables B_e, O_e, B_p, and O_p and all first-order products of these. The result was:

$$A'_p = -.19 + .77B_p + .35B_eO_e - .15B_eO_p \tag{25}$$

(Again, for the sake of continuity, the coefficients have been rescaled to apply to seven-point scales, rather than the eleven-point scales used by Gollob and Rossman.) This equation accounted for 74 percent of the variance in the potency ratings of sentence subjects.

The Gollob–Rossman result indicates that evaluations of acts may be involved in potency impressions, and, in particular, the B_eO_p term defines a process similar to what they had described verbally. The B_eO_e term adds still another factor: More potency is attributed to a person whose acts are evaluatively congruent with the object of the act.

Heise (1970) also had obtained out-of-context good–bad ratings for words used in his corpus of sentences. He reported an analysis in which the evaluation sentence resultant was added to potency analyses, and no effect was found (p. 53). This finding seems to contradict the Gollob–Rossman results, as the B_eO_e term is an important component of R_e, and one would expect R_e to predict potencies if B_eO_e is predictive. However, to provide a more straightforward parallel to the Gollob–Rossman study, the Heise data for males were reanalyzed, adding just the extra terms that Gollob and Rossman found to be significant. This process resulted in the following:

$$A_p' = -.11 - .11B_eO_e + .06B_eO_p + .31A_p + .56B_p + .14O_p \quad (26)$$

Here the coefficients for the two interaction terms are statistically non-significant. Moreover, their values are opposite in sign to what Gollob and Rossman reported.

Gollob and Rossman's theorizing about the impact of behavior evaluations in potency dynamics was explicitly interpersonal, depending on the possibility of return acts by the person in the object position. Moreover, they pointed out that only a few of the sentences in the Heise (1970) corpus were strictly interpersonal, with a social actor in both the actor and object positions. Thus perhaps the original Heise corpus is not appropriate for finding the kinds of effects they postulated. To allow for this possibility, the male data from the Heise study have been analyzed once more, this time using two subsamples from the original corpus. One sample consists of thirty sentences with a social actor in the subject position but not in the object position. The second sample consists of ten completely interpersonal sentences like Gollob and Rossman's. (Fourteen sentences with nonhuman subjects have been deleted.) This time the results are as follows:

Impersonal objects,

$$A_p' = -.09 + .06B_eO_e + .22B_eO_p + \mathbf{.27}A_p + \mathbf{.37}B_p + \mathbf{.30}O_p \quad (27)$$

Personal objects,

$$A_p' = -.30 + .11B_eO_e - .25B_eO_p + .30A_p + \mathbf{.82}B_p + .15O_p \quad (28)$$

(Boldface coefficients are significant at the .05 level. The coefficient for B_eO_e in the second equation is almost significant at the .05 level.)

These new results are based on small samples of sentences, and the predictor variables have rather high colinearity, confounding regression analyses. Nevertheless, a pattern emerges. In the interpersonal sentences, the B_eO_p term has a large (almost significant) negative coefficient, just as Gollob and Rossman found. In the sentences with impersonal objects, a significant coefficient for the B_eO_p term emerges, but now it is positive in value – the opposite of what Gollob and Rossman found. The results for the interpersonal sentences are consistent with the Gollob–Rossman findings. Additionally, though, the results suggest that the effect of behavior evaluations on potency dynamics may be conditioned by whether the object is a social actor or an impersonal entity.

Gollob and Rossman did not examine potency outcomes at the behavior and object positions. However, the required formulas were obtained in the course of reanalyzing the Heise data. As in the original Heise study, behavior outcomes appear to involve essentially the same dynamics as actor outcomes. That is, the behavior formulas are roughly the same as the actor formulas (now including the B_eO_e and B_eO_p effects), except that, as usual, the original actor potency is weighted less and the original behavior potency is weighted more. Parallelism holds in both samples of sentences (i.e., those with personal objects and those with impersonal objects).

The new object formulas differ from the actor–behavior formulas; their structure is different for personal objects as opposed to impersonal objects; and the new results contrast in some important ways with the original object formulas for males discussed in the previous section. Thus it is of some interest to examine the results, despite the fact that the samples are small and that now there is no other study for comparison:

Personal objects,

$$O'_p = -.41 + .14B_eO_e - .11B_eO_p + .01A_p + .06B_p + .34O_p \quad (29)$$

Impersonal objects,

$$O'_p = -.28 - .15B_eO_e + .06B_eO_p + .04A_p + .38B_p + .62O_p \quad (30)$$

Here again the interaction terms change sign depending on whether persons or impersonal entitities are in the object position, and the signs correspond to those reported by Gollob and Rossman only in the case of personal objects. The B_eO_e consistency effect reported by Gollob and Rossman appears to be sizable in these formulas (it was not significant in any of the actor or behavior formulas). On the other hand, the B_eO_p

term seems to be of diminished importance. Aside from the interaction terms, the formula for potency of persons as objects shows only two major effects: a large negative constant and a moderate stability coefficient for O_p. Thus potency impressions of personal objects would change largely as was discussed in the previous section, except for the added effect from B_eO_e. On the other hand, the formula for impersonal objects involves a moderate negative constant, a moderately large coefficient for B_p, and a large stability coefficient for O_p. This finding implies that the potency impression for an impersonal object is more affected by acts received than is that for a human object, and at the same time the potency of a thing is less attenuated than is that of a person by serving as the object of someone's action.

Two major points emerge from the Gollob and Rossman study and these reanalyses of the Heise (1970) data. First, affective dynamics in discerned events may be dependent on the human–nonhuman distinction for objects. Second, the dynamics of one dimension of response may be influenced by responses on other dimensions.

Activity

Formulas for predicting the activity impressions produced by an event were derived by Heise (1969a) through the usual experimental design of obtaining mean ratings of words presented both in context and out of context. A regression analysis over twenty-four event sentences included the main effects of A, B, and O and the effects of all multiplicative terms. However, interaction effects were found to be negligible in this case, and a set of final prediction equations was obtained using main effects only:

$$A_a' = .16 + .79A_a + .29B_a + .26O_a \tag{31}$$

$$B_a' = .02 + .44A_a + .41B_a + .31O_a \tag{32}$$

$$O_a' = .06 + .37A_a + .18B_a + .43O_a \tag{33}$$

(Symbols are the same as in previous sections, except that now A, B, and O refer to activity ratings averaged over three scales: fast–slow, lively–still, noisy–quiet.) Equation (31) predicts 75 percent of the variance in impressions of actor activity, formula (32) accounts for 64 percent of the behavior outcomes, and formula (33) explains 67 percent of the variance in activity impressions of objects.

An example of activity dynamics is provided by the sentence "The boy forgot the letter." Mean out-of-context activity ratings (from the Heise, 1969, subjects) are 1.3, -.5, and -.7 for A, B, and O, respectively. Formula (31) predicts that the impression of the boy's activity should decline to .86 (the observed in-context value was .7) – a loss in liveliness because he acted so passively toward a "dead" object. The predicted value for the letter is .15, which suggests that it should seem livelier even by indirect association with the boy (the obtained in-context value for the letter was -.3).

Thus activity dynamics are relatively simple: Resultants are just linear composites of the inputs, though the weights are somewhat different for actor, behavior, and object. The formulas account for about two-thirds of the variance in activity outcomes, a respectable figure but somewhat less than has been achieved in predicting evaluation outcomes. At present, it cannot be ascertained whether this lower figure is the result of lower reliabilities for activity measurements (a frequently noted problem) or the result of some complications in activity dynamics left unspecified in the model. The possibility of relations between activity outcomes and dynamics on other dimensions is suggested by the Hayes and Sievers (1972) finding of a parabolic relation between evaluations and the amount of "participation" implied by adjectives describing persons (too much or too little participation correlates with unfavorable evaluations).

Current formulas

The affective-reaction formulas given in preceding sections served to parameterize the formal model of affect-control theory for an earlier report (Heise, 1977). A new study provides improved formulas for this monograph. The procedures are described in detail elsewhere (Heise, 1978), and therefore only the general design of the study and results are outlined here.

Twenty-six person identities and twenty-three interpersonal behaviors were combined to define sixty-nine interpersonal events. *EPA* ratings of the identities and behaviors were obtained out of context and within the context of the event sentences from seventy-eight undergraduates in sociology classes at the University of North Carolina. Ratings were obtained on a single evaluation scale contrasting "good, helpful, nice, sweet" at one pole with "bad, unhelpful, awful, sour" at the other pole. A single potency scale contrasted "strong, powerful, big, deep" with "weak, powerless, little, shallow," and a single activity scale contrasted "hurried, alive, noisy, fiery, young" with "slow, dead, quiet, stiff, old." Each scale offered eight rating positions labeled "infinitely," "extremely," "quite," or "slightly," plus a middle position labeled "neither or neutral." (These are the same scales used to obtain the profiles reported in the Appendix.)

Regression analyses of mean ratings replicated the main results discussed in previous sections, and structural relationships were found to be approximately the same for males and females. An analysis employing LISREL (Jöreskog and Sörbom, 1976) – a full-information, maximum-likelihood procedure – was used to estimate equation parameters, with the results shown in Table 2.1. Each column of Table 2.1 gives a formula for predicting outcome impressions after an event from prior impressions. For example, the impression of the actor in an event is defined by the coefficients in the first column:

$$A_e' = -.094 + .351A_e + .031A_p - .035A_a + .425B_e + .162B_p$$
$$- .233B_a - .059O_e + .039O_p + .056O_a + .203B_eO_e \qquad (34)$$

where symbols are the same as in previous sections.

The figures reported in Table 2.1 have a looser correspondence with prior results than can be obtained through regression analyses of the

Table 2.1. *Coefficients for affective-reaction equations*

Coefficient for	Coefficients for predicting								
	A_e'	A_p'	A_a'	B_e'	B_p'	B_a'	O_e'	O_p'	O_a'
Constant	-.094	-.139	.077	-.136	-.036	.267	-.069	-.430	-.113
A_e	.351	.060	-.010	.234	.065	.007	.137	.160	.083
A_p	.031	.268	-.050	.016	-.007	-.071	.012	.008	-.017
A_a	-.035	.034	.415	.019	.100	.233	-.014	-.003	.065
B_e	.425	.062	-.113	.535	.052	-.049	.166	.117	.018
B_p	.162	.401	.191	.128	.437	.055	.063	.074	.052
B_a	-.233	-.089	.372	-.118	.051	.526	-.091	-.059	.126
O_e	-.059	-.108	-.016	-.134	-.112	.005	.306	.000	.012
O_p	.039	.009	.021	.028	.013	.013	.015	.306	.013
O_a	.056	.009	-.002	.037	.010	.001	.022	.025	.400
B_eO_e	.203	.117	.008	.169	.097	-.002	.079	.083	.037

same data, but the general pattern of the LISREL results still is comparable to that obtained in past work. Replications are fairly close in the case of evaluation equations (remembering that the coefficient for the B_eO_e term must be smaller for nine-point scales than for seven-point scales). Replications are less close in the case of potency, but still the main patterns discussed previously appear here again. Continuity is least in the case of activity formulas, several of the coefficients in Table 2.1 being substantially smaller than those reported previously. Nevertheless, the idea that activity dynamics build up from just linear relationships remains accurate.

Table 2.1 provides new information on cross-dimension effects, and two points stand out. First, there now is evidence of some simple linear effects across dimensions. Notably, Table 2.1 shows that evaluations of actors are affected by the potency and quietness of their behaviors, and activity impressions of actors are affected by behavior badness and powerfulness. Second, the previous finding of a B_eO_e effect in potency impressions is replicated, and such an effect is found influencing impressions of actors, behaviors, and objects (however, in the full model displayed in Heise, 1978, object impressions are affected only via their dependency on transient actor and behavior impressions). Gollob and Rossman's (1975) B_eO_p effect did not attain significance in the LISREL model. However, its coefficient had the predicted sign, and it could be a significant factor in studies of larger samples of sentences.

The specifications and estimations of impression-formation equations represented in Table 2.1 still are not definitive, and a study of 515 event sentences is underway at the time of writing to provide better information. However, the figures in Table 2.1 do serve as parameters for the current formal model of affect-control theory used in the exploratory work reported here.

The complexity of affective reaction

Research by Charles Osgood and his colleagues demonstrated that, regardless of a person's native language or culture, the impressions associated with different stimuli tend to vary along the three underlying dimensions of evaluation, potency, and activity, and in general a stimulus's value on one dimension cannot be predicted from its position on either of the other two. Research in the *ABO* framework has shown that evaluation, potency, and activity associations enter into highly determinate dynamics when they are linked in cognitive structures, and changes in response to events and communications often produce curious outcomes that are predictable only by taking into account both the content and the organization of cognitions.

The discovery of different dynamics for the three dimensions indicates that the statistical independence found in factor analytic studies reflects something more than just the presence of three different pieces of information about any stimulus. Cognitions cause operations of one sort on evaluation associations, operations of another sort on potency associations, and operations of still another sort on activity associations. Thus there appear to be three distinct psychological subsystems for processing the different types of associations, and affective response is not simply a multidimensional process: It is additionally a multifunction process. The balance principle does *not* apply to potency or activity associations (except for the evaluation spillovers affecting potency). Meanwhile, potency dynamics yield almost unrelated outcomes for actor and object, and activity dynamics involve simple linear resultants of input associations.

Evaluation, potency, and activity correspond to commonly cited dimensions of social identities and interpersonal relations. (For example, Burke and Bennis, 1961, identified evaluation with friendliness, potency with dominance, and activity with participation; see also Kemper, 1972; Bales, 1970.) Thus the fact that the dynamics of the affective dimensions are different may mean that corresponding interpersonal dynamics are different, too. In particular, we probably should not expect the balance principle to operate in interpersonal networks except for friendliness. On the other hand, we might expect dominance relations to relate to patterns of initiative, because an initiator – the actor of an event – can maintain an impression of high potency, whereas the recipient of an act – the object – suffers attenuated potency. The implications of the various formulas for social interaction are considered in detail in later chapters.

Fundamentals

Fundamental sentiments are very stable, as indicated by substantial test-retest correlations for individual attitudes measured twenty and thirty years apart (Kelly, 1955; Capel, 1967), by near-perfect correlations obtained over short periods when fundamentals are estimated by group means (Heise, 1969*b*), and by analyses that explicitly correct test-retest correlations for transient variations (Wheaton et al., 1976). Thus fundamentals have been discussed as if they were completely static, their only temporal variations occurring during a developmental period that is of little concern, as the focus here is on mature attitudes. However, the attitude-change literature (e.g., see the review by Fishbein and Ajzen, 1975), including dramatic recent experiments worked out by Rokeach (1971; Greenstein, 1976), indicates that fundamentals may change in maturity, and so some attention to the static assumption is warranted.

Equation (35) constitutes a general model defining fundamentals according to their transient origins:

$$F_t = \sum_{i=1}^{t} w_i T_i \tag{35}$$

F_t stands for the fundamental sentiment of interest, measured on evaluation, potency, or activity at a time t; T_i stands for the transient evaluation, potency, or activity (chosen to correspond to the measurement of F_t) that existed at some time i between t and time one – the point at which the person began to experience impressions of the attitude object. The coefficient, w_i (probably a positive fraction), represents the weight that T_i has in contributing to the definition of F_t. Thus the formula formalizes the proposition that a fundamental is some weighted summation of past transients.[5]

Such a formulation encompasses a wide range of ideas about attitude formation, depending on how the weights, w_i, are defined. For example, with a pure "primacy" model, all weights after, say, the first half dozen would be practically zero, as in the following illustrative pattern:

$$w_1 = .50, \quad w_2 = .25, \quad w_3 = .12, \quad w_4 = .06, \quad w_5 = .03,$$
$$w_6 = .02, \quad w_7 = .01, \quad w_8 = .00, \quad w_9 = .00, \ldots \tag{36}$$

In this formulation, mature fundamentals would be totally unaffected by transients after the development period. In an "averaging" model, such as Anderson and Farkas (1973) propose, all weights are assumed equal to $1/t$, so that a fundamental at a particular time is a linear combination of all past transients weighted equally. The peculiarity of the averaging model is that the weights themselves are time-varying, becoming smaller as a person has more experiences with an attitude object; therefore, as a fundamental matures, the most recent transient contributes less and less to its definition, as in a primacy model. A "recency" theory would employ a rising pattern of weights, constant in value over time, but moving forward with t as follows:

$$w_{t-7} = .00, \quad w_{t-6} = .01, \quad w_{t-5} = .02, \quad w_{t-4} = .03,$$
$$w_{t-3} = .06, \quad w_{t-2} = .12, \quad w_{t-1} = .25, \quad w_t = .50 \tag{37}$$

In this case, recent transients contribute significantly to the current definition of a fundamental, and the fundamental typically will not have a static value, though it will be less variable over time than the transients. Innumerable other weighting patterns (including some with negative weights) are possible in principle, but not all of them would correspond to a recognized psychological theory.

Weighting patterns can be identified empirically, using experimental procedures like those of Anderson and Farkas (1973) and time-series analytic techniques (Jenkins and Watts, 1968; Box and Jenkins, 1970). Anderson and Farkas's results support an averaging model, but the issue is not settled, particularly for longer sequences than Anderson and Farkas examined.

3. Event construction and retroduction

According to the theory outlined in Chapter 1, when events disturb an individual's feelings away from fundamental values, the individual anticipates a new event that will restore more appropriate feelings. This chapter develops a formal model to represent the event-construction process. The general thesis is that descriptions of past-becoming-present can be converted into further descriptions of present-becoming-future. In particular, reaction formulas from Chapter 2, describing how people respond to events, will be transformed here into proaction equations specifying how anticipations of new events are generated.

First a construct of "deflection" is defined to treat fundamental-transient differences in a precise way. Next empirical data are reviewed, demonstrating that deflections produced by hypothetical events correlate negatively with the perceived probabilities of those events: an event producing small deflections tends to be seen as likely; one that produces large deflections tends to be seen as unlikely. In the third section, algebraic expressions for the deflections that would be produced by a future event with a given actor and object are mathematically minimized, yielding formulas that define sentiment-confirming acts in evaluation–potency–activity profiles. An event specified by means of these formulas minimizes deflections, and so it should be seen as maximally likely under the circumstances. Finally, in the fourth section, the same deflection-minimization procedure is extended to reidentification processes, yielding formulas for an evaluation–potency–activity profile that defines the most plausible actor in a past event involving a given act and object, thereby providing a model of retroduction processes.

Deflection

In principle, the values of both fundamental and transient feelings can be defined on quantitative scales, so that the differences between the

64

two can be conceptualized as actual quantitative measures, and the process of confirming fundamental sentiments can be viewed as minimizing these differences in event constructions. What is minimized, however, is not the algebraic difference carrying a positive or negative sign but rather the absolute discrepancy between the fundamental and the transient. The algebraic differences can easily be converted into measures that are always positive, just by taking their absolute value (Heise, 1969a; Gollob and Fischer, 1973). However, for purposes of theoretical analysis, it is best to remove the sign by squaring, because squared differences are subject to powerful mathematical manipulations, and squaring gives relatively less weight to small inconsequential differences.

Even the simplest event transforms nine different affective transients at once – evaluation, potency, and activity of the actor, act, and object – and so nine differences must necessarily be treated in theoretical analyses of event construction. These can be defined quantitatively as follows, employing the notion of squared differences between transients and fundamentals:

$$(\mathbf{A}_e - A_e')^2 \quad (\mathbf{B}_e - B_e')^2 \quad (\mathbf{O}_e - O_e')^2$$
$$(\mathbf{A}_p - A_p')^2 \quad (\mathbf{B}_p - B_p')^2 \quad (\mathbf{O}_p - O_p')^2 \tag{1}$$
$$(\mathbf{A}_a - A_a')^2 \quad (\mathbf{B}_a - B_a')^2 \quad (\mathbf{O}_a - O_a')^2$$

A', B', and O' respectively represent transient feelings about the actor, behavior, and object of an event after an event has been recognized. The same letters in boldface, $\mathbf{A}$, $\mathbf{B}$, and $\mathbf{O}$, represent fundamental sentiments. Subscripts, e, p, and a, indicate which dimension of affect is under consideration.

The quantities in (1) will be called *deflections* to suggest that they measure the extent to which a specified event moves transient feelings toward or away from fundamental values.

Deflection measurement

The deflections generated by an event could be measured by using essentially the same logic as has been developed for *ABO* attitude research. The fundamental sentiments associated with the event's actor, act, and object would be measured as the mean ratings for these stimuli when presented out of context. The transients resulting from the event would correspond to the new ratings of actor, act, and object when seen together within the event's syntactic structure.[1] Then a deflection could be quantitatively assessed by subtracting a transient from its corresponding fundamental and squaring.

This procedure for measuring deflections has the disadvantage of requiring a set of affect measurements immediately after an event has occurred. However, an alternative assessment procedure can be defined in which the deflections produced by an event are estimated from quantities existing prior to the event's realization. The fundamental sentiments are the same either before or after an event, and the values of transient feelings resulting from an event can be predicted from measurements of transients existing *before* the event by using the formulas represented in Table 2.1. The affective-reaction equations can be symbolized as follows:

$$A'_\partial = k_{A\partial} + a_{A\partial 0}A_e + a_{A\partial 1}A_p + a_{A\partial 2}A_a + a_{A\partial 3}B_e + a_{A\partial 4}B_p$$
$$+ a_{A\partial 5}B_a + a_{A\partial 6}O_e + a_{A\partial 7}O_p + a_{A\partial 8}O_a + a_{A\partial 9}B_eO_e \quad (2)$$

$$B'_\partial = k_{B\partial} + a_{B\partial 0}A_e + a_{B\partial 1}A_p + a_{B\partial 2}A_a + a_{B\partial 3}B_e + a_{B\partial 4}B_p$$
$$+ a_{B\partial 5}B_a + a_{B\partial 6}O_e + a_{B\partial 7}O_p + a_{B\partial 8}O_a + a_{B\partial 9}B_eO_e \quad (3)$$

$$O'_\partial = k_{O\partial} + a_{O\partial 0}A_e + a_{O\partial 1}A_p + a_{O\partial 2}A_a + a_{O\partial 3}B_e + a_{O\partial 4}B_p$$
$$+ a_{O\partial 5}B_a + a_{O\partial 6}O_e + a_{O\partial 7}O_p + a_{O\partial 8}O_a + a_{O\partial 9}B_eO_e \quad (4)$$

where $\partial = e$, p, or a, depending on which dimension is being considered.

Using these general forms of the prediction equations, each of the nine affective deflections generated by an event can be respecified in terms of fundamentals and transients existing prior to the event's realization. Formula (5), specifying evaluative deflection for the actor and employing parameter estimates given in equation (34) in Chapter 2, illustrates the idea:

$$(A_e - A'_e)^2 = (A_e + .094 - .351A_e - .031A_p + .035A_a - .425B_e - .162B_p$$
$$+ .233B_a + .059O_e - .039O_p - .059O_a - .203B_eO_e)^2 \quad (5)$$

Of course, there actually are nine such equations. However, using expressions (2), (3), and (4), they all can be represented as follows:

$$(A_\partial - A'_\partial)^2 = (A_\partial - k_{A\partial} - a_{A\partial 0}A_e - a_{A\partial 1}A_p - a_{A\partial 2}A_a - a_{A\partial 3}B_e - a_{A\partial 4}B_p$$
$$- a_{A\partial 5}B_a - a_{A\partial 6}O_e - a_{A\partial 7}O_p - a_{A\partial 8}O_a - a_{A\partial 9}B_eO_e)^2 \quad (6)$$

$$(\mathbf{B}_\partial - B'_\partial)^2 = (\mathbf{B}_\partial - k_{B\partial} - a_{B\partial 0}A_e - a_{B\partial 1}A_p - a_{B\partial 2}A_a - a_{B\partial 3}B_e - a_{B\partial 4}B_p$$
$$- a_{B\partial 5}B_a - a_{B\partial 6}O_e - a_{B\partial 7}O_p - a_{B\partial 8}O_a - a_{B\partial 9}B_eO_e)^2 \qquad (7)$$

$$(\mathbf{O}_\partial - O'_\partial)^2 = (\mathbf{O}_\partial - k_{O\partial} - a_{O\partial 0}A_e - a_{O\partial 1}A_p - a_{O\partial 2}A_a - a_{O\partial 3}B_e - a_{O\partial 4}B_p$$
$$- a_{O\partial 5}B_a - a_{O\partial 6}O_e - a_{O\partial 7}O_p - a_{O\partial 8}O_a - a_{O\partial 9}B_eO_e)^2 \qquad (8)$$

Equations (6), (7), and (8) estimate deflections generated by an event from information existing prior to the event's realization. In the next section the equations are adapted to estimating the deflections produced by discerned events, assuming that transients equal fundamentals beforehand. However, the major significance of these equations is theoretical: they define the deflections produced by a future event from relevant fundamental sentiments and from the transient feelings toward actor, behavior, and object that exist in the present.

Deflections and likelihoods

In affect-control theory, expected events are constructed by a series of operations that serve to minimize affective deflections. Because expected events are those seen as "certain or probable" in the near future,[2] the operation of minimizing deflections would seem to correspond to maximizing likelihoods, and a relation between deflections and the perceived likelihood of an event is implied if the theory is correct.

Blumstein (1973) published mean out-of-context evaluation ratings for the subjects and predicates of fifty-four event sentences and also provided mean likelihood ratings for the events described by the whole sentences. The two evaluation measures can be used to derive a measure of the attitudinal deflection generated by each sentence, using Gollob's (1968) subject–predicate formula. The measure is only a rough indicator of the overall deflection: It does not include deflections arising in the potency and activity dimensions; and the whole predicate contributes only a single term, rather than separate act and object components. Even with these deficiencies, however, the estimates of deflections for the event sentences correlate $-.64$ with the averaged perceived likelihoods of the events. This is a substantial figure, suggesting that events producing greater amounts of deflection are perceived as relatively unlikely and events producing less deflection are judged more probable.

Gollob (1974*a*) published data that permit another, somewhat different, kind of analysis. He presented subjects with such stimuli as "Bill is *optimistic*. How probable is it that Bill *helps physicians?*" The italicized words were varied to generate stimuli with the standard eight *ABO* evaluation patterns, and likelihood ratings were obtained on a 15-point probable–improbable scale. Gollob's published data do not permit analyses of potency and activity deflections, and he did not present actual evaluation measurements for the components of the sentences. However, we can now average the probabilities for each *ABO* evaluation pattern over sixteen replications, and, accordingly, the mean probabilities should be relatively unaffected by unsystematic potency and activity deflections within stimuli. Also, Gollob attempted to construct stimuli with strong and essentially uniform contrasts on the evaluation dimension, and so we can adopt a single number, varying its sign, as the typical value for each transient input in a stimulus in order to estimate the evaluation deflections. The value of 2.1 on a 7-point scale is used; this is the average evaluative polarization of those words in Gollob's experimental stimuli that could be found in the Kirby and Gardner (1972) adjective dictionary or in Heise (1978: app. B). We assume that transient feelings toward actor, behavior, and object typically equal fundamentals in an experimental design like Gollob's, where events are offered without circumstantial elaboration; thus $A_e = \mathbf{A}_e$, $B_e = \mathbf{B}_e$, and $O_e = \mathbf{O}_e$. The three evaluative deflections (D) for a sentence were defined by the following formulas (based on equation [10] of Chapter 2):

$$D_{Ae} = (.60A_e - .44B_e - .28B_eO_e + .19)^2 \tag{9}$$

$$D_{Be} = (.32B_e - .16A_e - .28B_eO_e + .19)^2 \tag{10}$$

$$D_{Oe} = (.76O_e - .16A_e - .44B_e - .28B_eO_e + .19)^2 \tag{11}$$

Evaluation deflections for the various patterns are obtained by substituting +2.1 or -2.1 for A_e, B_e, and O_e in these formulas. Results of the calculations are shown in Table 3.1.

The mean likelihoods in Table 3.1 were regressed on the A, B, and O deflections, yielding the prediction formula:

$$L = .864 - .047D_{Ae} - .077D_{Be} - .007D_{Oe} \tag{12}$$

The predicted values, using formula (12), are given in the last column of Table 3.1. The predicted and obtained ratings correlate .98. Of course,

Table 3.1. *Approximate deflections and average perceived likelihoods for eight evaluation patterns*

Pattern of ABO evaluations	Deflection associated with			Perceived likelihood	
	Actor	Behavior	Object	Empirical[a]	Predicted
+ + +	.50	.50	.50	.85	.80
− − +	1.19	1.19	18.33	.58	.59
− − −	1.91	1.91	1.91	.55	.61
+ + −	3.10	3.10	2.05	.50	.47
+ − −	1.30	4.21	4.21	.43	.45
− + −	.58	5.92	.58	.39	.38
− + +	10.43	.00	.00	.35	.37
+ − +	13.02	.17	13.02	.18	.15

[a]Gollob's (1974a) measures of likelihood have been converted to a scale ranging from 0 (extremely improbable) to 1.0 (extremely probable).

the degree of correspondence is exaggerated, because the weights in (12) were themselves estimated from the data. Some idea of the degree of exaggeration can be obtained by considering two additional data sets Gollob (1974a) presented, using data from other subjects. His Study 2 (1974a) reproduced all the key features of the first study except that it structured presentation of stimuli somewhat differently and it involved eleven replications rather than sixteen. The perceived likelihoods obtained in this study (averaged over the eleven replications) correlate .97 with the predictions from formula (12). Gollob's Study 3 (1974a) differed substantially from the other two. Subjects were mostly black third-grade children of low socioeconomic status (as compared to college students in the first two studies). They were told to imagine that they themselves were friendly or mean and then asked whether they would help, tease, and so on, a friendly boy, a friendly man, a mean boy, or a mean man. For example, to generate an item with a (−++) pattern, a child might be asked to imagine that he was a mean boy and then asked if he would help a friendly man. The proportion of "yes" responses (averaged across males and females and over events with boy or man as object[3]) correlates .84 with the likelihood predictions provided by (12).

Thus reanalyses of both the Blumstein and the Gollob data support the idea that affective deflections generated by an event contribute to impressions of unlikelihood: Events causing extreme deflections are sensed to be improbable, rare, or incredible.[4] This relation between deflections and perceived likelihoods may occur partly because fundamental sentiments reflect previous experiences with and beliefs about reality (Bem, 1968; Fishbein and Ajzen, 1975); for example, those who are always being punished must be bad; those who are always being dominated must be weak; those who are always interacting must be lively; and in each case we expect the people involved to continue that way. Also, however, conceptualizations of events that minimize deflections theoretically become plans that the self and similar others ordinarily operationalize in reality. Thus not only do deflections index the degree to which current events deviate from regularities of the past, but also, when we are with others whose pasts are similar, then events generating little deflection really are probable, because everyone is acting to recreate the common past, or at least to confirm the affective residues from it.

Gollob (1974*a* and 1974*b*) developed an alternative model relating *ABO* variables to impressions of likelihood, with particular stress laid on the contributions of different kinds of attitudinal balance. For example, in his own analysis of his 1974 data, he found that predictive rules giving precedence mainly to actor–behavior balance (*AB*), behavior–object balance (*BO*), and "Heiderian balance" (*ABO*) predicted the likelihood rankings of the stimuli quite well. Gollob's approach does not necessarily conflict with the formulation just presented in terms of deflections. In fact, expanding the expressions for deflections (9), (10), and (11) yields formulas in which deflections are expressed in terms of various kinds of attitudinal balance (plus some higher-order terms that Gollob does not consider). Summing the expressions for actor, behavior, and object deflections, with weights proportional to those in (12), gives the following expression for the total attitudinal dislocation (*D*) produced by a sentence (terms with coefficients less than .04 have been dropped for the sake of simplicity):

$$D_\Sigma = -.24AB - .14BO - .07ABO + (.15A^2 + .14B + .08B^2O^2 + .04A)$$

$$(13)$$

This expression reveals that the balance terms that Gollob identified as particularly important also turn out to be key components of attitudinal dislocation, which in turn has an inverse relation to perceived likelihoods. Indeed, *AB* balance would appear to be the most important balance component in expression (13), and Gollob found empirically that AB balance is most related to perceived likelihoods. Expression (13) also suggests that different kinds of balance should contribute differentially, depending on the values of the A, B, and O attitudes; for example, relatively extreme O attitudes would increase the contributions of the BO and ABO terms. Additionally, expression (13) suggests that perceived likelihoods also should vary with the absolute polarizations of attitudes (as represented by the terms with squares).

Gollob's approach of focusing on "biases" and balance effects offers the promise of providing detailed understanding of processes involved in likelihood assessments, and it could help refine the mathematical specification of deflection, which after all is only presumed to be a squared difference. On the other hand, deflection variables are appropriately related to subjective probabilities, and they are valuable in providing quantities subject to powerful mathematical manipulations.

Optimal acts

A limited number of actor-object frames for the construction of events are given by a person's current definition of the situation, and, in the model of event construction outlined in Chapter 1, each different frame is examined in turn in order to compare the consequences of different possible events. However, the frames alone are not sufficient to define these consequences. An act has to be added to an actor-object frame before it constitutes an event, and because potential events are to be compared for their optimality, the selected act itself must be optimal in the sense of creating an event that produces maximum sentiment confirmation within the constraints of the given frame. Because any actor might engage in hundreds of conceivable acts toward any object, it is implausible that a person considers all these possibilities one by one. Theoretically, it seems that there must be a proactive system for choosing acts that will reduce deflections within a given actor-object frame, just as there is a reactive system determining affective responses to completed events.

The problem can be stated formally as follows. An event is to be constructed with person a as actor and person o as object. The fundamentals for these entities are available – A and O – as are their transients existing at the present moment – A and O. Moreover, equations (6), (7), and (8) allow us to predict how much deflection would be generated by a future event with this actor and object from **A**, *A*, **O**, and *O*, along with the fundamentals and present transients for the act that completes the event – **B** and *B*. For example, according to (6), and according to equation (10) of Chapter 2, actor deflection on the evaluation dimension would be:

$$D_e = (A_e + .19 - .16A_e - .44B_e - .28B_eO_e - .24A_e)^2 \qquad (14)$$

Of course, the appropriate act is not a given, and so the values of **B** and *B* are unknowns in these expressions. However, whatever act ultimately is chosen, it theoretically should be the one that best confirms fundamental sentiments and thus minimizes the deflections specified. Mathematical procedures for minimizing such algebraic expressions are well known: the expressions are differentiated with respect to their unknown quantities, and the derivative expressions, set equal to zero, are solved to specify values for the unknown quantities (in terms of known quantities) whose substitution would reduce the original expression to its lowest magnitude. In this particular case, the evaluation–potency–activity profile for the act constitutes the set of unknowns, and so we differentiate the deflection expressions with respect to these, set the derivative expressions equal to zero, and solve them so as to define the unknown behavior profile in terms of the known fundamentals and transients for actor and object.

We must treat actor, behavior, and object deflections together, trying to define a solution that minimizes all three of these quantities at once. A behavior that minimizes actor deflection may not minimize object deflection, and vice versa; and an event that reduces actor and object deflections might strain feelings about the act that is involved. Accordingly, it is the summed actor, act, and object deflections that will be minimized. Because the analyses relating deflections to likelihoods indicated that actor, act, and object deflections may contribute in different amounts to cognitive functioning (see equation [12]), we allow for a weighted sum.

Mathematical derivations

Affective reaction equations obtained from *ABO* research can be formulated in matrices as follows:

$$\hat{\imath} = \mathfrak{D}\imath \qquad (15)$$

where

$$\hat{\imath}' = [A_e'\ A_p'\ A_a'\ B_e'\ B_p'\ B_a'\ O_e'\ O_p'\ O_a'] \qquad (16)$$

$\mathfrak{D}$ is the matrix of coefficients for predicting in-context values from out-of-context values, and $\imath$ is the vector of variables contributing to the predictions. Entries in $\mathfrak{D}$ and $\imath$ depend on particulars of specification and estimation in ABO research. In the work reported here, $\mathfrak{D}$ consists of the values shown in Table 2.1 (the values in the table are organized as $\mathfrak{D}'$ – the transpose of the $\mathfrak{D}$ matrix), and $\imath$ is composed as follows:

$$\imath' = [1\ A_e\ A_p\ A_a\ B_e\ B_p\ B_a\ O_e\ O_p\ O_a\ B_eO_e] \qquad (17)$$

The total amount of affective deflection existing after an event is defined by the following formula:

$$T = w_1(\mathbf{A}_e - A_e')^2 + w_2(\mathbf{A}_p - A_p')^2 + w_3(\mathbf{A}_a - A_a')^2$$
$$+ w_4(\mathbf{B}_e - B_e')^2 + w_5(\mathbf{B}_p - B_p')^2 + w_6(\mathbf{B}_a - B_a')^2 \qquad (18)$$
$$+ w_7(\mathbf{O}_e - O_e')^2 + w_8(\mathbf{O}_p - O_p')^2 + w_9(\mathbf{O}_a - O_a')^2$$

where the ws are the weights for summing the separate deflections. Here the normalized values of the coefficients in equation (12) are used: .36, .59, and .05 for actor, behavior, and object deflections. These quantities are partitioned equally over evaluation, potency, and activity, giving .12, .12, .12, .19, .19, .19, .02, .02, and .02 for w_1 to w_9.

Equation (18) can be expressed as the matrix product shown in equation (19).

$$T = [1\ 1\ 1\ 1\ 1\ 1\ 1\ 1\ 1\ 1]$$

$$\cdot \begin{bmatrix} \mathbf{A}_e & & & & & & & & \\ & \mathbf{A}_p & & & & & & & \\ & & \mathbf{A}_a & & & & & & \\ & & & \mathbf{B}_e & & & & & \\ & & & & \mathbf{B}_p & & & & \\ & & & & & \mathbf{B}_a & & & \\ & & & & & & \mathbf{O}_e & & \\ & & & & & & & \mathbf{O}_p & \\ & & & & & & & & \mathbf{O}_a \\ -A_e' & -A_p' & -A_a' & -B_e' & -B_p' & -B_a' & -O_e' & -O_p' & -O_a' \end{bmatrix}$$

$$
\begin{bmatrix}
w_1 & & & & & & & & \\
 & w_2 & & & & & & & \\
 & & w_3 & & & & & & \\
 & & & w_4 & & & & & \\
 & & & & w_5 & & & & \\
 & & & & & w_6 & & & \\
 & & & & & & w_7 & & \\
 & & & & & & & w_8 & \\
 & & & & & & & & w_9
\end{bmatrix} \tag{19}
$$

$$
\cdot
\begin{bmatrix}
\mathbf{A}_e & & & & & & & & & -\mathbf{A}_e' \\
 & \mathbf{A}_p & & & & & & & & -\mathbf{A}_p' \\
 & & \mathbf{A}_a & & & & & & & -\mathbf{A}_a' \\
 & & & \mathbf{B}_e & & & & & & -\mathbf{B}_e' \\
 & & & & \mathbf{B}_p & & & & & -\mathbf{B}_p' \\
 & & & & & \mathbf{B}_a & & & & -\mathbf{B}_a' \\
 & & & & & & \mathbf{O}_e & & & -\mathbf{O}_e' \\
 & & & & & & & \mathbf{O}_p & & -\mathbf{O}_p' \\
 & & & & & & & & \mathbf{O}_a & -\mathbf{O}_a'
\end{bmatrix}
\begin{bmatrix}
1 \\ 1 \\ 1 \\ 1 \\ 1 \\ 1 \\ 1 \\ 1 \\ 1 \\ 1
\end{bmatrix}
$$

Let $\mathfrak{L}_{10}'$ be a vector of ones with ten elements, $\mathbf{d}_f$ a 9×9 diagonal matrix with the *ABO* fundamentals in its nonzero cells, and $\mathbf{d}_w$ a 9×9 diagonal matrix with the summation weights in its nonzero cells. Then (19) can be rewritten as:

$$
T = \mathfrak{L}_{10}' \begin{bmatrix} \mathbf{d}_f \\ -\hat{\mathbf{\imath}}' \end{bmatrix} \mathbf{d}_w [\mathbf{d}_f \ -\hat{\mathbf{\imath}}] \, \mathfrak{L}_{10} \tag{20}
$$

Equation (15) can be used in place of $\hat{\mathbf{\imath}}$, giving the following alternative:

$$
T = \mathfrak{L}_{10}' \begin{bmatrix} \mathbf{d}_f \\ -\mathbf{\imath}'\mathfrak{D}' \end{bmatrix} \mathbf{d}_w [\mathbf{d}_f \ -\mathfrak{D}\mathbf{\imath}] \, \mathfrak{L}_{10} \tag{21}
$$

This expression now can be reformulated into the following:

$$T = [\ell'\ \imath']\ \begin{bmatrix} \mathfrak{I} \\ -\mathfrak{D}' \end{bmatrix}\ d_w[\mathfrak{I}\ -\mathfrak{D}\ ]\ \begin{bmatrix} \ell \\ \imath \end{bmatrix} \tag{22}$$

where $\mathfrak{I}$ is a 9×9 identity matrix. All of the variables in the equation now are factored to the outside in the supervector:

$$\begin{aligned}[\ell'\ \imath'] = [&A_e\ \ A_p\ \ A_a\ \ B_e\ \ B_p\ \ B_a\ \ O_e\ \ O_p\ \ O_a \\ &1\ A_e\ \ A_p\ \ A_a\ \ B_e\ \ B_p\ \ B_a\ \ O_e\ \ O_p\ \ O_a\ \ B_eO_e]\end{aligned} \tag{23}$$

The internal part of equation (8) is a 20×20 square matrix defined entirely in terms of model parameters – the reaction-equation coefficients and the summation weights. Representing this part as $\mathfrak{K}$ for convenience, equation (8) becomes:

$$T = [\ell'\ \imath']\mathfrak{K}\begin{bmatrix} \ell \\ \imath \end{bmatrix} \tag{24}$$

Vector $[\ell'\ \imath']$ contains a product term, B_eO_e (and in general it might contain more than one such term). Further analysis requires representing this term in another way, so that the vector itself consists only of first-order terms. Specifically, in this case, B_e is to be left in the vector and O_e is to be moved inward, where it can be treated as a constant while a B profile that minimizes total deflection is found. Accordingly, a matrix $\mathfrak{I}_{Oe}$ is defined as a 20×20 identity matrix with the value of O_e substituted in its bottom diagonal cell:

$$\mathfrak{I}_{Oe} = \begin{bmatrix} \mathfrak{I} & \mathcal{O} \\ O & O_e \end{bmatrix} \tag{25}$$

Now $\mathfrak{z}_{Oe}$ is defined as a new vector of variables like $[\ell'\ \imath']$, but without the interaction term:

$$[\ell'\ \imath'] = \mathfrak{z}'_{Oe}\mathfrak{I}_{Oe} \tag{26}$$

Thus equation (10) can be rewritten as:

$$T = \mathfrak{z}'_{Oe}\mathfrak{I}_{Oe}\mathfrak{K}\mathfrak{I}_{Oe}\mathfrak{z}_{Oe} \tag{27}$$

In general, matrices like $\mathfrak{z}_{Oe}$ and $\mathfrak{I}_{Oe}$ can be defined as needed so that the outside vector of variables always consists only of first-order terms, as in equation (27).

Affect-control theory proposes that events are constructed or reconstructed by choosing values for elements in $[f'\ t']$ such that T is minimized. In the case of choosing an act in given circumstances, it will be assumed that the act is recalled from memory with transients equal to fundamentals:

$$B_e = \mathbf{B}_e, \quad B_p = \mathbf{B}_p, \quad B_a = \mathbf{B}_a \tag{28}$$

The given circumstances define the values of A_e, A_p, A_a, A_e, A_p, A_a, O_e, O_p, O_a, O_e, O_p, and O_a. Thus the problem is to find values for B_e, B_p, and B_a that minimize T. Mathematically, the solution is obtained by differentiating T with respect to the Bs, setting each derivative equal to zero, and solving these equations to define the optimal values of the Bs in terms of known quantities.

Equation (27) is a quadratic form, with the understanding that O_e is treated as a constant so that the outside vector of variables is defined without powers or product terms in the Bs. Thus (27) provides the basis for differentiating T by using the formula for matrix differentiation of a quadratic form (Goldberger, 1964:42). In particular, the derivative of T with respect to each element in $\mathbf{z}_{Oe}$ is as follows:

$$\frac{\partial \mathbf{z}'_{Oe} \mathbf{\mathfrak{I}}_{Oe} \mathcal{H} \mathbf{\mathfrak{I}}_{Oe} \mathbf{z}_{Oe}}{\partial \mathbf{z}_{Oe}} = 2 \mathbf{\mathfrak{I}}_{Oe} \mathcal{H} \mathbf{\mathfrak{I}}_{Oe} \mathbf{z}_{Oe} \tag{29}$$

The overall derivative of T with respect to B_e is the sum of all the derivatives in expression (29) that are associated with a B_e or B_e in vector $\mathbf{z}_{Oe}$. Premultiplying the result in equation (29) by the vector

$$\delta'_{Be} = [0\ 0\ 0\ 1\ 0\ 0\ 0\ 0\ 0\ 0\ 0\ 0\ 0\ 1\ 0\ 0\ 0\ 0\ 0\ 1] \tag{30}$$

selects and sums the proper entries. Thus the minimization equation obtained by differentiation with respect to B_e is:

$$\delta'_{Be} \mathbf{\mathfrak{I}}_{Oe} \mathcal{H} \mathbf{\mathfrak{I}}_{Oe} \mathbf{z}_{Oe} = 0 \tag{31}$$

Similarly, the equations obtained by differentiation with respect to B_p and B_a are:

$$\delta'_{Bp} \mathbf{\mathfrak{I}}_{Oe} \mathcal{H} \mathbf{\mathfrak{I}}_{Oe} \mathbf{z}_{Oe} = 0 \tag{32}$$

where

$$\delta'_{Bp} = [0\ 0\ 0\ 0\ 1\ 0\ 0\ 0\ 0\ 0\ 0\ 0\ 0\ 0\ 1\ 0\ 0\ 0\ 0\ 0] \tag{33}$$

and

$$\delta'_{Ba} \mathbf{\mathfrak{I}}_{Oe} \mathcal{H} \mathbf{\mathfrak{I}}_{Oe} \mathbf{z}_{Oe} = 0 \tag{34}$$

where

$$\delta'_{Ba} = [0\ 0\ 0\ 0\ 0\ 1\ 0\ 0\ 0\ 0\ 0\ 0\ 0\ 0\ 0\ 1\ 0\ 0\ 0\ 0] \tag{35}$$

All three equations can be represented in a single matrix-formulation:

$$\delta'_B \mathbf{J}_{Oe} \mathbf{H} \mathbf{J}_{Oe} \mathbf{\overline{z}}_{Oe} = 0 \tag{36}$$

where

$$\delta_B = [\delta_{Be}\ \ \delta_{Bp}\ \ \delta_{Ba}] \tag{37}$$

To complete the solution, equation (36) has to be algebraically manipulated to a form that expresses the act profile, $\mathcal{B}' = [\mathbf{B}_e\ \mathbf{B}_p\ \mathbf{B}_a]$, as a function of other quantitites. The selection vectors δ_{Be}, δ_{Bp}, and δ_{Ba} indicate which terms in $\mathbf{\overline{z}}_{Oe}$ can be identitified as $\mathbf{B}_e$, $\mathbf{B}_p$, or $\mathbf{B}_a$, respectively. A new vector, $\mathbf{\mathcal{g}}_{-B}$, is defined to assemble all of the other terms:

$$\mathbf{\overline{z}}_{Oe} = \delta_B \begin{bmatrix} \mathbf{B}_e \\ \mathbf{B}_p \\ \mathbf{B}_a \end{bmatrix} + \mathbf{\mathcal{g}}_{-B} = \delta_B \mathcal{B} + \mathbf{\mathcal{g}}_{-B} \tag{38}$$

Now equation (36) can be expressed in the following form:

$$\delta'_B \mathbf{J}_{Oe} \mathbf{H} \mathbf{J}_{Oe} (\delta_B \mathcal{B} + \mathbf{\mathcal{g}}_{-B}) = 0 \tag{39}$$

or

$$\delta'_B \mathbf{J}_{Oe} \mathbf{H} \mathbf{J}_{Oe} \delta_B \mathcal{B} = -\delta'_B \mathbf{J}_{Oe} \mathbf{H} \mathbf{J}_{Oe} \mathbf{\mathcal{g}}_{-B} \tag{40}$$

or

$$\mathcal{B} = -(\delta'_B \mathbf{J}_{Oe} \mathbf{H} \mathbf{J}_{Oe} \delta_B)^{-1} \delta'_B \mathbf{J}_{Oe} \mathbf{H} \mathbf{J}_{Oe} \mathbf{\mathcal{g}}_{-B} \tag{41}$$

which is the required solution.

Formulas for reconstructing events by defining a new and optimal actor profile, $\mathcal{A}' = [\mathbf{A}_e\ \mathbf{A}_p\ \mathbf{A}_a]$, or object profile, $\mathcal{O}' = [\mathbf{O}_e\ \mathbf{O}_p\ \mathbf{O}_a]$, are obtained similarly. For heuristic purposes, in this monograph, it is assumed that transients are set equal to fundamentals during reconstruction processes, as represented by equations (28) plus (42):

$$\begin{aligned} A_e &= \mathbf{A}_e, \quad A_p = \mathbf{A}_p, \quad A_a = \mathbf{A}_a \\ O_e &= \mathbf{O}_e, \quad O_p = \mathbf{O}_p, \quad O_a = \mathbf{O}_a \end{aligned} \tag{42}$$

Then the formula for an optimal actor profile for a given act on a given object is:

$$\mathcal{A} = -(\delta'_A \mathbf{J}_{Oe} \mathbf{H} \mathbf{J}_{Oe} \delta_A)^{-1} \delta'_A \mathbf{J}_{Oe} \mathbf{H} \mathbf{J}_{Oe} \mathbf{\mathcal{g}}_{-A} \tag{43}$$

where

$$S'_A = \begin{bmatrix} 1 & 0 & 0 & 0 & 0 & 0 & 0 & 0 & 0 & 0 & 1 & 0 & 0 & 0 & 0 & 0 & 0 & 0 & 0 & 0 \\ 0 & 1 & 0 & 0 & 0 & 0 & 0 & 0 & 0 & 0 & 0 & 1 & 0 & 0 & 0 & 0 & 0 & 0 & 0 & 0 \\ 0 & 0 & 1 & 0 & 0 & 0 & 0 & 0 & 0 & 0 & 0 & 0 & 1 & 0 & 0 & 0 & 0 & 0 & 0 & 0 \end{bmatrix} \tag{44}$$

and

$$\mathfrak{z}_{Oe} = S_A \, \mathfrak{a} + \mathfrak{g}_{-A} \tag{45}$$

The matrices $\mathfrak{z}_{Oe}$ and $\mathfrak{z}_{Oe}$ may be used in the solution for the optimal actor profile as well as in the solution for the optimal act profile, because the current affective-reaction equations contain no interaction terms involving A_e, A_p, or A_a.

Though not used in this monograph, the formula defining an optimal object profile for a given act by a given actor would be:

$$\mathfrak{O} = -(S'_O \, \mathfrak{z}_{Be} \, \mathcal{H} \, \mathfrak{z}_{Be} \, S_O)^{-1} S_O \, \mathfrak{z}_{Be} \, \mathcal{H} \, \mathfrak{z}_{Be} \, \mathfrak{g}_{-O} \tag{46}$$

where

$$S'_O = \begin{bmatrix} 0 & 0 & 0 & 0 & 0 & 0 & 1 & 0 & 0 & 0 & 0 & 0 & 0 & 0 & 0 & 0 & 1 & 0 & 0 & 1 \\ 0 & 0 & 0 & 0 & 0 & 0 & 0 & 1 & 0 & 0 & 0 & 0 & 0 & 0 & 0 & 0 & 0 & 1 & 0 & 0 \\ 0 & 0 & 0 & 0 & 0 & 0 & 0 & 0 & 1 & 0 & 0 & 0 & 0 & 0 & 0 & 0 & 0 & 0 & 1 & 0 \end{bmatrix}$$

and

$$\mathfrak{z}_{Be} = \begin{bmatrix} \mathfrak{z} & O \\ O & B_e \end{bmatrix} \qquad \begin{bmatrix} \mathfrak{p} \\ \mathfrak{t} \end{bmatrix} = \mathfrak{z}_{Be} \, \mathfrak{z}_{Be} \tag{47}$$

and

$$\mathfrak{z}_{Be} = S_O \, \mathfrak{O} + \mathfrak{g}_{-O} \tag{48}$$

Here it is necessary to define the new matrices in (47), because the affective-reaction formulas do contain interaction terms involving O_e. Hence the $[\mathfrak{p}' \; \mathfrak{t}']$ vector has to be refactored, leaving O_e among the variable quantities.

Proaction equations

Substituting parameter estimates in equation (41) yields the following formulas defining the *EPA* profile for an ideal behavior. Here the equations are written in ordinary algebraic form:

$$\mathbf{B}_e = [O_e(.41A_e + .23A_p + .13A_a + .03O_e + .03O_p + .02O_a$$
$$- .33A_e - .09A_p - .04A_a + .17O_e - .05O_p - .06O_a) + 1.03A_e$$
$$+ .23A_p - .17A_a + .07O_e + .05O_p + .01O_a + .05A_e - .10A_p$$
$$+ .20A_a] / [(.5O_e)^2 - .10O_e + 1.30]$$
(49)

$$\mathbf{B}_p = [O_e^2(.02 + .03A_e + .13A_p + .09A_a - .01A_e - .04A_p$$
$$- .01A_a - .01O_e) + O_e(.01 - .04A_p - .02A_a - .03A_e$$
$$+ .01A_p - .01A_a + .03O_e) + .10 + .31A_e + .71A_p$$
$$+ .45A_a + .02O_e + .02O_p + .02O_a - .08A_e - .20A_p$$
$$- .02A_a - .06O_e - .02O_p - .02O_a] / [(.5O_e)^2 - .10O_e + 1.30]$$
(50)

$$\mathbf{B}_a = [O_e^2(.08 - .04A_e + .02A_p + .20A_a + .01O_a + .01A_e$$
$$- .02A_p + .01O_e) + O_e(.03 + .19A_e + .05A_p - .09A_a + .01O_e$$
$$+ .01O_p - .04A_e - .02A_p + .02A_a - .01O_e - .01O_p - .01O_a)$$
$$- .42A_e - .05A_p + .91A_a - .03O_e - .20O_p + .05O_a + .29A_e$$
$$- .04A_p + .03A_a - .07O_e + .04O_p + .03O_a + .27]$$
$$/ [(.5O_e)^2 - .10O_e + 1.30]$$
(51)

The basic structures of the equations can be seen more clearly by eliminating terms with near-zero coefficients (between $-.07$ and $+.07$). In the case of the potency and activity formulas, cancellations have been carried out on the basis of near equality in terms:

$$\mathbf{B}_e = [.17O_e^2 + O_e(.41A_e + .23A_p + .13A_a - .33A_e - .09A_p)$$
$$+ 1.03A_e + .23A_p - .17A_a - .10A_p + .20A_a]$$
$$/ [(.5O_e)^2 - .10O_e + 1.30]$$
(52)

$$\mathbf{B}_p = .53A_p + [O_e^2(.13A_p + .09A_a) + .31A_e + .45A_a - .08A_e$$
$$- .20A_p + .10] / [(.5O_e)^2 - .10O_e + 1.30]$$
(53)

$$\mathbf{B}_a = .73A_a + [.08O_e^2 + O_e(.19A_e) - .42A_e + .29A_e + .27]$$
$$/ [(.5O_e)^2 - .10O_e + 1.30]$$
(54)

The simplified evaluation formula is a function just of the actor's fundamental and transient *EPA* profiles, conditioned by transient evaluation of the object. More on the general character of the function can be seen in Table 3.2, which gives the predicted behavior profiles for selected variations in actor and object evaluations (throughout the table, the potency and activity of actor and object have been set at the values for an "adult"). The table also shows the two behaviors in the Appendix having *EPA* profiles most similar to each predicted profile, after eliminating behaviors with significant sex or conservatism differences.

Table 3.2 shows that actors identified as fundamentally good should act generally more positively than those with fundamentally neutral identities, and fundamentally neutral actors should act less negatively than fundamentally bad actors. Transient actor evaluation, A_e, and transient evaluation of the object, O_e, interact in determining behavior. The more an actor is feeling bad, the more positively he or she should behave toward someone who seems nice. However, the worse an actor feels, the more negatively he or she should behave toward someone who seems bad. In normal circumstances, a fundamentally good actor will be transiently good as well, and the table shows that such a person then should engage almost solely in positive behaviors, whatever the object. Also, the behavior of fundamentally neutral persons should be mostly positive or evaluatively neutral. If it is assumed that a fundamentally bad actor feels transiently bad in most circumstances, then the table shows that his or her behavior should be approximately neutral toward very good or very bad others, but should be negative toward neutral others (say, a stranger).

Predictions for B_e can be viewed from a different standpoint by treating A_e and A_e as constants and O_e as a variable. For example, suppose that the actor, a fundamentally good person ($A_e = 1.5$), has been mortified ($A_e = -2.5$) and is now engaged with a person who initially is seen as good ($O_e = 2.5$) but who loses face through a series of debasement events. The actor's predicted impulse in these circumstances is to do something very good to the other at first, and this impulse continues even as the other begins to lose goodness. However, in the range $O_e = .5$ to $O_e = -.5$, the actor's behavior is delicately balanced and might appear mercurial – extremely positive one moment and almost neutral in the next. Once the other has gone well beyond being evaluatively neutral, the actor's inclination to do good turns finally into impulses for unfriendly acts. (The O_e variable might be interpreted instead in terms of differential impulses toward different people: then a good person who has been mortified would be predicted to act unusually positively toward favored others – say, family and friends – and negatively toward disvalued others – say, deviants or the one who caused mortification.)

A fundamentally neutral actor (e.g., someone who identifies as a sophisticate) is predicted to have somewhat similar impulses under mortification, beginning with less positivity and ending with more negativity. Having been cloyed ($A_e = 2.5$), such a person is predicted to have joking impulses toward nice people (such as the cloying other) and perhaps libidinous impulses toward deviants or those who have been debased by events.

Someone who adopts a fundamentally negative self-identification is predicted to be particularly hostile toward nice others when transient self-evaluation is too high, as might be the case, for example, after the person has been "cleansed" by chastisement. Then the actor is predicted to have very negative – even dangerous – impulses toward good people (like the chastiser, perhaps), whereas negative others should be the objects of somewhat friendly impulses.

In a new situation, actor and object transients should tend to be at about their fundamental values, but on the average transients tend to move closer to zero after the first few behaviors. Thus, if a good actor is interacting with a good object, there often would be movement from the behaviors at the upper left of Table 3.2, Part A, to those in the middle of the same chart. If two fundamentally bad persons were interacting, there would be movement from the lower right of Table 3.2, Part C, to the middle of the same chart. The implication is that two persons with fundamentally good identities should maintain positivity in their behaviors, whereas two persons with fundamentally bad self-identifications should drift from neutral or slightly negative behaviors to more negative behaviors. Empirical observations of interacting youths by Raush (1965) confirm these ideas to some degree. He found that boys with behavior problems begin interactions in a somewhat friendly way but progressively degenerate into more negativity, as is predicted here for actors with fundamentally negative self-attitudes. Normal boys maintain positivity, as predicted here for actors with fundamentally positive self-attitudes.

The predicted potency of behavior varies largely with the actor's fundamental potency, as revealed by the first term in equation (53). A term in the second part of the equation indicates that the behavior

82

Table 3.2. *Predicted EPA profiles for acts when varying fundamental evaluation of actor, transient evaluation of actor, and transient evaluation of object (with the two behaviors that best fit the profile)*

Value of	Values of $O_e/O_p/O_a$					
	2.5/0.4/1.2	1.5/0.4/1.2	0.5/0.4/1.2	-0.5/0.4/1.2	-1.5/0.4/1.2	-2.5/0.4/1.2
A. Values of $A_e/A_p/A_a$ are 1.5/0.4/1.2						
A_e						
2.5	1.1/0.7/1.4 hail squeeze	1.3/0.8/1.3 coach hail	1.3/0.8/1.2 coach cue	1.2/0.9/1.1 cue engage	1.0/0.9/1.1 exalt engage	0.9/0.9/1.1 exalt glorify
1.5	1.4/0.8/1.2 acclaim coach	1.5/0.8/1.2 acclaim bathe	1.4/0.9/1.0 inform flatter	1.1/0.9/0.9 glorify engage	0.8/0.9/0.9 glorify exalt	0.6/0.9/0.9 entice glorify
0.5	1.7/0.8/1.1 acclaim bathe	1.8/0.8/1.2 acclaim bathe	1.5/1.0/0.8 adorn inform	1.0/0.9/0.7 initiate glorify	0.5/0.9/0.7 reprimand mystify	0.4/0.9/0.8 work urge
-0.5	2.0/0.9/1.0 interest reform	2.1/1.0/0.9 answer interest	1.7/1.0/0.6 pay esteem	0.8/1.0/0.5 interview reprimand	0.3/1.0/0.5 arrest dissuade	0.1/1.0/0.6 arrest dissuade
-1.5	2.3/1.0/0.9 believe snuggle	2.3/1.1/0.7 snuggle believe	1.8/1.1/0.4 pay remind	0.7/1.0/0.3 psychoanalyze endure	0.0/1.0/0.3 subdue dissuade	-0.1/1.0/0.5 subdue dissuade
-2.5	2.6/1.1/0.8 trust snuggle	2.6/1.2/0.6 trust relieve	1.9/1.2/0.2 remember excuse	0.6/1.1/0.0 psychoanalyze miss	-0.2/1.0/0.1 subdue convict	-0.4/1.0/0.3 restrain sentence

B. Values of $A_e/A_p/A_a$ are 0.0/0.4/1.2

A_e	2.5/0.4/1.2	1.5/0.4/1.2	0.5/0.4/1.2	-0.5/0.4/1.2	-1.5/0.4/1.2	-2.5/0.4/1.2
2.5	0.0/0.4/1.5 kid pinch	-0.2/0.4/1.5 hurry pinch	-0.1/0.4/1.6 hurry flee	0.3/0.5/1.7 astonish titillate	0.7/0.6/1.7 astonish titillate	0.9/0.7/1.6 escape squeeze
1.5	0.3/0.5/1.4 josh pinch	0.1/0.5/1.4 catch kid	0.0/0.5/1.4 catch jostle	0.2/0.6/1.5 catch grasp	0.5/0.6/1.5 astonish titillate	0.6/0.7/1.5 astonish squeeze
0.5	0.6/0.6/1.3 entice hail	0.4/0.6/1.2 query entice	0.2/0.6/1.2 outwit catch	0.1/0.6/1.3 catch outwit	0.2/0.7/1.3 catch outwit	0.4/0.7/1.3 catch outwit
-0.5	0.9/0.6/1.1 hail engage	0.7/0.7/1.1 entice exalt	0.3/0.7/1.0 query clutch	0.0/0.7/1.0 outwit query	0.0/0.7/1.1 outwit catch	0.1/0.7/1.2 outwit catch
-1.5	1.2/0.7/1.0 cue engage	0.9/0.7/0.9 initiate glorify	0.4/0.7/0.8 clutch query	-0.2/0.7/0.8 indoctrinate punish	-0.3/0.7/0.9 punish halt	-0.2/0.8/1.0 halt shake
-2.5	1.5/0.8/0.9 flatter prompt	1.2/0.8/0.7 prompt adorn	0.5/0.8/0.6 mystify reprimand	-0.3/0.8/0.6 punish refuse	-0.5/0.8/0.7 handcuff punish	-0.4/0.8/0.9 punish handcuff

C. Values of $A_e/A_p/A_a$ are -1.5/0.4/1.2

A_e	2.5/0.4/1.2	1.5/0.4/1.2	0.5/0.4/1.2	-0.5/0.4/1.2	-1.5/0.4/1.2	-2.5/0.4/1.2
2.5	-1.2/0.1/1.6 agitate harangue	-1.6/0.1/1.7 hound jerk	-1.5/0.1/2.0 hound claw	-0.5/0.2/2.2 freak-out flee	0.4/0.3/2.3 tickle flee	0.9/0.4/2.2 dazzle tickle

Table 3.2 (*cont.*)

Value of	Values of $O_e/O_p/O_a$					
1.5	−0.9/0.2/1.5 push zap	−1.3/0.2/1.6 hound agitate	−1.3/0.2/1.8 hound agitate	−0.6/0.2/2.0 freak-out chase	0.2/0.3/2.1 flee hurry	0.6/0.4/2.0 tickle astonish
0.5	−0.6/0.3/1.4 bop exhaust	−1.0/0.2/1.4 push zap	−1.2/0.2/1.6 agitate hound	−0.8/0.3/1.8 agitate push	−0.1/0.4/1.9 flee hurry	0.4/0.5/1.9 tickle astonish
−0.5	−0.3/0.3/1.3 jostle bop	−0.8/0.3/1.2 push spook	−1.1/0.3/1.4 shock agitate	−0.9/0.3/1.6 push agitate	−0.3/0.4/1.7 hurry freak-out	0.1/0.5/1.7 hurry flee
−1.5	0.0/0.4/1.2 awake jostle	−0.5/0.4/1.1 exhaust bop	−1.0/0.4/1.2 hustle swat	−1.0/0.4/1.4 push shock	−0.6/0.4/1.5 exhaust push	−0.2/0.5/1.6 hurry jostle
−2.5	0.3/0.5/1.0 query clutch	−0.2/0.5/0.9 rouse joggle	−0.9/0.5/1.0 hustle revile	−1.1/0.4/1.2 swat hustle	−0.8/0.5/1.3 push hustle	−0.4/0.5/1.4 exhaust jostle

potency will be still greater if the actor's transient potency is low. Additionally, the second part of the equation shows that stronger acts are expected from fundamentally good actors, particularly when their transient evaluation is low. Also, potent behaviors are expected from lively actors, more so when they are acting on particularly good or bad objects. (The denominator in the second part of the equation tends to moderate the effects represented in the numerator when evaluation of the object is either very high or very low.) Overall, the formula suggests that the most potent behaviors should come from fundamentally good, powerful, active people who have experienced loss of evaluation and potency in recent events and who are acting on moderately good or moderately bad object persons. Shallow, weak acts are to be expected from fundamentally bad, weak, quiet people whose transient goodness and power have been enhanced by recent events and who are acting on evaluatively neutral others.

The expected activity level of behaviors is mainly determined by the fundamental activity of the actor, as indicated by the first term in equation (54). The fundamental evaluation of the actor also has an impact that depends on the evaluation of the object. That is, when the object is at least quite good (O_e greater than 2.2), then actor goodness causes greater behavior activity; but when the object is anything less than quite good, actor goodness produces less active behaviors. Transient evaluation of the actor also has an impact, nice feelings being associated with more active behaviors. (Again, the denominator quantity in the equation moderates the effects in the numerator for very good or very bad objects.) Overall, the most lively behaviors are theoretically expected from fundamentally active and good people who are in a good mood and acting on very nice others, or else from fundamentally active and bad people who are in a good mood and acting on bad others. Quieter behavior is expected from fundamentally quiet and bad people who are feeling bad and involved with very good others, or else from fundamentally quiet and good people who are feeling devalued and who are engaged with bad others.

Assumptions involved in the solutions

The derivation of the proaction equations has involved more than mathematical manipulations. The affect-control principle that events are constructed to confirm fundamental attitudes was essential in structuring the derivations, and it was necessary to adopt heuristically a number of additional assumptions. Thus, whereas the original reaction formulas can be viewed as succinct descriptions of observed empirical phenomena that are simply accurate or inaccurate in their predictions and their structural forms, the proaction equations actually are extensions of affect-control theory, and their validity depends on the theory's. Moreover, the structures of the proaction equations are subject to change with improvements in their empirical base (the reaction formulas) and with replacement of heuristic assumptions by more refined information from new research.

Most of the assumptions involved in the derivations have been stated explicitly: the key theoretical assumption that new event constructions will minimize deflections, which permits use of mathematical minimization techniques in deriving proaction equations; the assumption that acts are recalled undeflected from memory, which simplifies analyses but precludes possible treatments of imitation and satiation; the assumption that the affect-confirmation principle applies on the potency and activity dimensions as well as on the evaluation dimension, which leads to the derivation of three formulas specifying an *EPA* profile for acts; and the assumptions that actor, act, and object deflections on evaluation sum with weights proportional to those in equation (12) in this chapter and that the same weights apply to potency and activity deflections.

Reidentification

Whereas event constructions are the ordinary means of controlling feelings, reconceptualization is an alternative when a perceived event severely disconfirms fundamental sentiments, generating massive transient deflections, so that the event seems incredible within the current definition of the situation. Interpretations and reinterpretations of acts are viewed as part of the event-perception process, and so reconceptualization arises when reality forces an individual to concede that an extremely disturbing act has occurred, and the identifications of the persons involved are reopened for consideration. For reasons pointed out in Chapter 1, it is the actor's identity rather than the object's that is most likely to be changed in a reidentification operation, and that is all that will be considered for now.

Formal modeling of the reidentification process proceeds as in modeling event constructions. Now, though, the specific act and object in the last event are the givens, and the problem is to make that event maximally plausible and sentiment-confirming by providing a more appropriate actor, answering the question "What kind of person would do that act to that object?" It is assumed heuristically that reidentifications are made using only information in the immediately preceding event; by this assumption, all transients are equal to fundamentals during the reidentification operation.

The derivations given previously are shown here in ordinary algebraic form:

$$A_e = .85B_e + .20B_p - .29B_a + .07O_e + .06O_p + .05O_a + .11B_eO_e + .02$$

$$(55)$$

$$A_p = .14B_e + .58B_p - .15B_a - .13O_e + .02O_p + .01O_a + .15B_eO_e - .11$$

$$(56)$$

$$A_a = -.15B_e + .38B_p + .88B_a + .01O_e + .01O_p - .03B_eO_e - .10 \qquad (57)$$

Equation (55) shows that the predicted evaluation for a reidentified actor is a nonlinear function of the evaluations attached to the act and object; accordingly, Table 3.3 is provided, showing values of A_e for some representative values of B_e and O_e. Examining the equation and the table reveals a number of interesting features in the evaluation dynamics for reidentification. First, characterization of an actor depends most heavily on the person's behavior: Someone who acts unaccountably positively is good, and someone who acts unaccountably negatively is bad, regardless of the object. However, more extreme levels of goodness or badness are attributed to an actor if the object is good rather than bad. Equation (55) shows that evaluation attribution depends also on the potency and activity of behaviors. Overall, the implications are that an actor is especially likely to be viewed as good if he or she has acted on a nice person in a good, deep, and quiet manner.

Equation (55) and Table 3.3 can be interpreted somewhat differently to examine how identifications bringing esteem and contempt are "achieved" in the course of reidentifications. Theoretically, statuses bringing the most admiration are earned by doing kind, potent, and quiet things to good people, whereas the most disesteemed identities are acquired by bad, shallow, fast acts on good people. Acts on bad people have similar consequences, but the potential for either positive or negative achievement is less.

Table 3.3. *Predicted EPA profiles for actors when varying fundamental evaluation of behavior and fundamental evaluation of object (with the two identities that best fit the profile)*

Values of	Values of $O_e/O_p/O_a$					
$B_e/B_p/B_a$	2.5/0.4/1.2	1.5/0.4/1.2	0.5/0.4/1.2	-0.5/0.4/1.2	-1.5/0.4/1.2	-2.5/0.4/1.2
2.5/0.8/0.6	3.1/1.3/0.2 grandmother grandfather	2.7/1.0/0.2 grandmother grandfather	2.4/0.8/0.3 grandmother teacher	2.0/0.5/0.4 dietitian aunt	1.7/0.3/0.5 aunt mailman	1.4/0.0/0.5 cook guest
1.5/0.8/0.6	2.0/0.7/0.4 teacher tutor	1.7/0.6/0.4 aunt mailman	1.5/0.5/0.5 aunt connoisseur	1.3/0.4/0.5 academic connoisseur	1.0/0.3/0.7 relation eyewitness	0.8/0.2/0.6 roommate barkeeper
0.5/0.8/0.6	0.8/0.2/0.6 roommate barkeeper	0.7/0.3/0.6 stepbrother barkeeper	0.6/0.3/0.7 stepbrother critic	0.5/0.4/0.7 stepbrother bohemian	0.3/0.4/0.7 stepbrother bohemian	0.2/0.5/0.7 sleuth bohemian
-0.5/0.8/0.6	-0.3/-0.3/0.9 weirdo freak	-0.3/-0.1/0.9 spy bawd	-0.3/0.1/0.8 spy bawd	-0.3/0.3/0.8 spy sleuth	-0.3/0.5/0.8 spy highwayman	-0.4/0.7/0.8 spy highwayman
-1.5/0.8/0.6	-1.4/-0.8/1.1 tease busybody	-1.3/-0.5/1.1 tease ladykiller	-1.2/-0.1/1.0 adulterer rogue	-1.1/0.2/0.9 adulterer highwayman	-1.0/0.6/0.9 highwayman witch	-0.9/0.9/0.8 witch highwayman
-2.5/0.8/0.6	-2.5/-1.3/1.3 gossip criminal	-2.3/-0.8/1.3 troublemaker vandal	-2.1/-0.3/1.2 crook felon	-1.9/0.2/1.1 housebreaker hood	-1.7/0.7/1.0 tough loan shark	-1.5/1.2/0.9 witch mafioso

Note: Potency and activity values for "join" are used to define the behavior profile; potency and activity values for "adult" are used to define the object profile. Best-fitting identities do not include any having significant sex or conservatism increments or a very small sample of raters.

Equation (56) indicates that potency dynamics in reidentification are similar to evaluation dynamics, except that behavior potency now counts more than behavior evaluation. The $B_e O_e$ term representing evaluative balance between behavior and object is important in potency attributions, just as it was in attributions of goodness (see Table 3.3). Overall, the equation indicates that powerful identities theoretically are attained by unexpectedly strong, quiet, good acts on good people or by unexpectedly strong, quiet, cruel acts on bad people. Identities associated with weakness should result from being discovered in shallow, noisy, nasty acts on good people or shallow, lively, nice acts on evil people.

The nature of activity dynamics in reidentification is indicated in equation (57). A lively identity results mainly from lively, strong behavior, regardless of the object. Bad behavior also contributes somewhat to acquisition of an active identity, but the interaction effect from the $B_e O_e$ term is small. Thus, overall, livelier identities can be acquired through fast, powerful, disvalued actions; quiet identities may be given to those whose acts are unexpectedly slow and weak, but nice.

Over all three dimensions, the formulas indicate that actors are cast into statuses reflecting their recent acts. The potency and activity of object persons does not contribute to the reidentifications predicted by these formulas. Evaluations of object persons do contribute to outcomes, but only by conditioning the meaning of good or bad acts. Thus, theoretically, the character of a person's action is mostly what determines the identities that person achieves.

Mathematics in affect-control theory

This chapter does not exhaust the mathematical analyses that are of interest in affect-control theory. Even at present the derivations could be altered in various ways to address special issues, such as behavior satiation, imitation, self-reflexive acts, and reidentifications that take account of events prior to the last one. A set of equations also could be obtained to specify optimal act–object combinations for an actor in a given transient state in order to study motivated movements between settings.

As research expands beyond actors, behaviors, and objects, entirely new opportunities for analyses will arise. For example, reaction formulas that show the independent effects of actor states (e.g., "the angry judge") can become the basis for supplementary reidentification equations in which reconceptualization of another is achieved by state modification rather than by an identity change; such equations will provide a link between reidentification in affect-control theory and current work in attribution theory (e.g., see Shaver, 1975). Impression-formation equations showing the independent effects of direct and indirect objects will permit deriving proaction equations that can specify a combination of act and instrumentality, so that more of the social construction process is defined by affect-control mechanisms (Osgood and Tanz, 1976, present an important idea that is relevant to this issue). Impression-formation equations for complex, recursively embedded event sentences (e.g., "John hopes that Mary likes Joan") will provide a basis for mathematical analyses extending affect-control theory to communication processes, manding, and conditional events.

   Mathematical analysis is not a "methodological" facet of affect-control theory; it is the means by which the theory is stated precisely, refined, and elaborated. Thus continued development of the theory will always be a joint product of empirical research and mathematical derivations.

4. Analyzing social processes

The formal model of affect-control theory is next elaborated to provide a bridge from abstract affectual processing to qualitative cognitions of situations and events. The first section of this chapter shows how individuals' memory for social identities and interpersonal acts can be represented by catalogs of identity and act words along with associated affective profiles. Then retrieval methods are formulated to simulate cognitive recall of concepts or recall on the basis of affective associations. A detailed example is given to show how the various equations can be used with retrievals from available identity and act catalogs to analyze interaction in a defined social situation. Some additional examples illustrate other kinds of analyses possible in affect-control theory.

Simulating memory

Each person carries a large storehouse of remembered social identities and acts that are used for defining situations and recognizing and constructing events. Every identity or act has an associated denotation, a set of syntactic constraints, and a connotation.

The denotation of an identity encompasses the set of features that a person must display in order to support the identity, along with, perhaps, other features that may be attributed to a person so labeled. The denotation of an act refers to an ordered or partially ordered set of states (including states of motion and transition) that must be perceived before the act is thought to have occurred, along with, perhaps, other conditions – like motives, functions, and effects – that may be presumed to exist with an occurrence. Eventually it should be possible to model the domain of denotative meaning so that elemental information can be processed to determine whether a particular social identity applies to a person or whether a particular action has occurred. Here, however, no detailed representation of denotation will be attempted beyond

91

symbolization by the ordinary English word that signifies a particular identity or act. Thus we will not be attempting to assess whether a particular person is a mother nor whether she caressed someone. The analyst provides such judgments.

Syntactic meaning embraces proscriptive rules denying certain combinations of concepts. Typically, such rules are taxonomically elaborated (Werner and Fenton, 1970) – for example, inanimate objects do not communicate, and therefore my chair cannot talk – so that the syntactic constraints for a vast number of concepts rest in a modest stock of rules defined at the most general levels. Here, too, efforts have been made to elaborate formally the principles involved (e.g., see Schank and Colby, 1973; Beckmann, 1972; Schank and Abelson, 1977).

The fundamental syntactic distinctions between agent, action, and patient (Chafe, 1970) are part of the basic framework of affect-control theory, both in its dependence on *ABO* empirical research and in its construction of events in actor–act–object frames. The distinction between actors and objects on the one hand and acts on the other hand will be implemented here by constituting "memory" in two separate blocks: only concepts from the "noun" block will be entered in actor or object slots; only concepts from the "verb" block will be considered as possible entries for the act position. The focus here is solely on interpersonal behavior, and the only nouns to be considered are social identities for labeling humans engaging in social interaction. Because of this restricted definition of the noun block, its further partitioning into potential actors versus potential objects is unnecessary – all entries serve equally well in either position. Similarly, by limiting verbs just to those that signify ways one person can act on another, we avoid the need for partitioning the verb block into interpersonal behaviors versus other kinds of acts. Thus critically important syntactic rules will be implicit in the selection of elements to be included in the representation of long-term memory.

Following Osgood, Suci, and Tannenbaum (1957), the connotative aspect of meaning will be represented by an evaluation, potency, and activity profile – what here is called the fundamental sentiment associated with a concept. Because this aspect of meaning is central in affect-control theory, an associated profile will be provided for each entry in "memory." Moreover, a formal mechanism for recalling concepts on the basis of these profiles is developed.

Identity and act catalogs

Long-term memory contents are represented here by catalogs of 650 social identities and 600 interpersonal acts. An entry in a catalog consists of the word for an identity or act plus empirical measurements of the evaluation, potency, and activity impressions attached to the concept. The *EPA* measurements are averages computed across the responses of about thirty subjects from a fairly homogeneous population of southern university students, so that in this sense they represent memory content for an average student rather than for any one individual or for an average member of any larger population.

Lists of identities and interpersonal acts were created by examining every entry in *The Doubleday Dictionary* (Landau, 1975), a relatively short dictionary (906 pages) explicitly developed to cover a broad range of general vocabulary, including informal usages, slang, obscenities, and vulgarisms. Slang and argot dictionaries also were examined, but they were found to contain fairly few useful words in relation to their esoteric and out-of-date entries.

The behavior list consists of transitive interpersonal verbs designating acts that people can perform in relation to other people. About twelve hundred such verbs were identified (excluding most multiple-word verbs, like "turn to"). However, by selecting just the words that might define how laymen view social interactions, by excluding odd, esoteric words or references to rare acts, and by deleting entries whose sense is unclear out of context (e.g., "to beat someone"), the list was reduced to six hundred entries.

Thousands of entries in *The Doubleday Dictionary* refer to social identities, but in creating the noun list, names of noncontemporary roles were ignored, and person labels created from verbs plus "-er" (e.g., "corrupter") also were not generally considered. Even these criteria left a vast number of potentially relevant nouns, so attention was focused on particular social domains. Thus the noun set is rich in social identities associated with *courtrooms, hospitals, stores, families, classrooms, entertainments, football, peer groups, sexuality,* and the *underworld*.

The catalogs of words and *EPA* profiles are printed in the Appendix; details on their compilation and various methodological matters are discussed elsewhere (Heise, 1978).

Simulation of recall

One usage of the catalogs is easily operationalized. Verbal definitions of situations are provided by the analyst, and the *EPA* profiles for social identity words can simply be looked up in the alphabetized list to simulate individuals' recall of fundamental profiles associated with cognitive categories. Similarly, once an event has been described by a simple sentence, *EPA* profiles for actor, act, and object can be looked up to represent the cognitively guided retrieval of sentiments entering into affective responses to the event. It is the retrievals in the other direction – from a generated feeling to concrete acts or identities – that are more problematic.

The claim in Chapter 1 was that concepts have affective associations that allow qualitative variations in experience to be translated into the quantitatively continuous domain of affect and that similarly allow affectual solutions to problems to be operationalized by discrete acts on specific people. One way of thinking about this claim is to assume that every social behavior or social identity can be located as a point in an affective "space" with evaluation, potency, and activity axes. Cognitively evoking a concept permits entering the space at the concept's point of location. Likewise, any arbitrarily selected point in the space defines a set of concepts that are located nearest to it, and arriving at a feeling for an optimal act or actor allows leaving the space by addressing the concept nearest the solution point. Thus the translation back and forth from the abstract quantitative domain of affect to the concrete qualitative domain of cognitive experience is possible because, so to speak, constellations of remembered identities and acts exist in affective space, and each serves as a possible entrance to the affectual domain or as an exit back to the conceptual realm.

The distance between a generated profile, *EPA*, and a specific act or identity having profile *epa*, when both are represented as points in the space, is given by the standard formula for distance in three-dimensional Euclidian spaces:

$$d = [(E - e)^2 + (P - p)^2 + (A - a)^2]^{1/2} \tag{1}$$

If this distance is too large, we will presume that no retrieval operation is invoked at all, the point *epa* being beyond the field of recall operations instigated by the ideal point *EPA*. Within the field we assume that concepts are ranked by the size of their ds to specify the order of their retrieval. Thus a concept is first to be retrieved only if its d is less than some maximum value specifying the scope of the retrieval field and, additionally, only if the d is less than the ds associated with other concepts. When multiple concepts are retrieved, their ds all must be less than the limiting value and their order of retrieval is determined by the relative sizes of their ds, the concepts with smallest ds being retrieved first.

Operationally, the indicated procedure involves applying formula (1) repeatedly to each entry in the act catalog or in the identity catalog (depending on which type of concept is being sought). Words are discarded if their ds are greater than a limiting value (1.22 – the square root of 1.5 – is used throughout this monograph). Words with ds less than the limiting value are added to a list ordered by the relative size of their ds, so that those ending up at the top of the list at the end of the process identify the concepts retrieved by the generated feeling. The entire contents of a catalog have to be examined for each retrieval, making the aid of a computer almost imperative in this operation.[1] No doubt brains operate more efficiently than this system, not having to scan all or even major parts of long-term memory for every retrieval; this operational procedure is not offered as a "model" of recall processes, but merely as an operational simulator of them.

Illustrative analyses

Parent-child

The various materials that have been introduced are now assembled to conduct a formal analysis focusing on the example question "Are the role performances of a parent and a child governed by the affect-control principle?" Parent and child both are assumed to be males and moderates on a liberalism-conservatism scale (the catalogs in the Appendix allow profiles to be adjusted for sex and conservatism). It is also assumed that in each other's presence they agree on the definition of the situation: The adult sees himself as parent and the other as child; the youngster sees himself as child and the other as parent.

First, sentiments of male moderates toward parent and child are taken from the Appendix:[2]

	E	P	A
Parent	2.3	2.0	1.2
Child	1.9	-0.5	2.3

The profiles define both fundamentals and the initial transients under the assumption that recent events have not yet deflected the transients.

Next, equations (49), (50), and (51) from Chapter 3 are applied to define the profile for the parent's preferred act toward the child in order optimally to maintain transient feelings near the fundamental values. For example, substituting numerical values in the evaluation equation (49), we get:

$$B_e = [1.9(.41*2.3 + .23*2.0 + .13*1.2 + .03*1.9 + .03*-0.5 + .02*2.3$$

$$- .33*2.3 - .09*2.0 - .04*1.2 + .17*1.9 - .05*-0.5 - .06*2.3)$$

$$+ 1.03*2.3 + .23*2.0 - .17*1.2 + .07*1.9 + .05*-0.5 + .01*2.3$$

$$+ .05*2.3 - .10*2.0 + .20*1.2]/[(.5*1.9)^2 - .10*1.9 + 1.30] = 2.3$$

The complete profile for the parent's act is 2.3, 1.5, and 1.2 for evaluation, potency, and activity, respectively.

A search through the act catalog reveals that this profile is best matched by male moderates' fundamental sentiments toward these behaviors:

	E	P	A
Assist	2.4	1.6	1.3
Congratulate	2.4	1.6	1.3
Hug	2.4	1.6	1.3
Defend	2.2	1.7	1.4
Adopt	2.3	1.6	1.0

That is, the analytic results indicate that a parent maintaining his fundamental sentiments toward the parent and child identities might assist, congratulate, hug, defend, or adopt the child. These are kinds of behaviors that define a parental role, though adopt could apply only in rare circumstances.

Equations (49), (50), and (51) of Chapter 3 also can be applied to define the preferred acts for the child. The ideal profile is 1.6, 0.9, and

2.1, and the best implementations of this profile from the Appendix are:

	E	P	A
Play with	1.5	0.6	2.0
Entertain	1.8	1.0	1.7
Liberalize	1.6	1.3	1.9
Surprise	1.3	1.2	1.9
Sing to	1.8	1.0	1.6

These behaviors might be appropriate for the child role.

Now the analysis can be continued by supposing that one of these acts is implemented: Say, the child plays with the parent. The reaction equations represented in Table 2.1 are applied to determine how this recognized event affects each person's transient feelings toward the self and the other. (Because both persons agree on the definition of the situation and have the same starting sentiments, their new transients also are identical.) The computed values of the new transients are:

	E	P	A
Parent	1.3	0.9	1.2
Child	1.5	0.3	1.8

As these figures indicate, even optimal acts do not always confirm fundamental sentiments, particularly for the object of the event. In this case, the child's act has drawn the parent toward neutrality on evaluation and potency, and from here on the interaction theoretically is molded by efforts to reaffirm fundamental sentiments, rather than merely to confirm them.

The next round of interaction can be predicted by again applying equations (49), (50), and (51) from Chapter 3, remembering that now fundamentals and transients no longer have the same values. If the parent is the actor, then the ideal profile for his behavior is 2.8, 1.8, 1.1, and the best implementations in the catalog are:

	E	P	A
Aid	2.8	1.9	1.1
Praise	2.8	1.8	1.0
Welcome	2.7	1.8	1.2
Rehabilitate	2.7	1.8	0.9
Appreciate	2.6	1.7	1.0

Most of these acts are reasonable components of the parent's role (re-habilitate is odd; it may appear here because of imprecisions in the current formulas or profile measurements). There is some shift toward positive reinforcement, and our understanding of this shift within affect-control theory is that the parent now would act this way to restore his identity after it had been somewhat compromised by his being the object of the child's playful behavior. Note that the qualitative shift in the parent's predicted acts is associated with fairly small shifts in the numerical values of the ideal *EPA* profile for his behavior. This phenomenon – small quantitative variations being associated with interpretable differences in the character of action – appears repeatedly, evidencing considerable orderliness in constellations of fundamental sentiments for identities and acts.

Were the child to act again, the ideal profile for his behavior would be 1.8, 0.9, 1.8, and the cataloged implementations would be entertain, sing to, court, amuse, and play with.

This interaction could be continued through additional cycles, and we could introduce a disturbing event to see how it changes the course of interaction (for example, if we next selected "Parent praises child" and afterwards forced the event "Child disobeys parent," then the predicted responses of the parent would be persuade, miss, confront, shield, and guard). However, the intent in this example has been merely to show the logic of analyses.

Man-girl

The next example illustrates how disturbing events might cause reidentifications. The new situation is set up with two actors, a man and a girl, both ideological moderates. In the imagined setting (say, an after-the-game celebration) the man sees himself as a stranger and sees the girl as a girl. The girl also sees herself as girl, but she identifies the man as an athlete. Thus, according to the values of the affective profiles in the identity catalog, the man's fundamental impression of the self in this setting is near neutral, even a bit powerless. However, the girl sees him as fundamentally good, strong, and lively. Both actors see the girl as nice, lively, and not powerful.

We initiate this interaction with an externally defined event: "The man avoids the girl." We then apply the reaction equations (Table 2.1) to assess how this event affects each person's transients, under the assumption that both the man and the girl recognize that he has avoided her.

From the man's standpoint, avoiding the girl leads to some transient feelings of being a bit nasty (-0.6 on evaluation) but otherwise does not much deflect his self-impression from his basic feeling that he is a stranger in the situation. Avoiding the girl makes her seem less attractive than a girl should be, but the deflection is not so high as to indicate that the behavior is an unlikely one for a stranger, and the man might not reflect on it.

The girl develops a transient impression of the man as being a bit nasty and weak, and her impression of herself after being avoided by the athlete is as less good and less lively than she was before. Although her impression of the man is not very different from his impression of himself, the outcome seems incredible to her because she sees a positively valued athlete – not a stranger – demeaning himself (and her) in this way. Assume that the girl rejects the idea that an athlete would avoid her, leading her to ask "What kind of person would avoid a girl?" Applying equations (55), (56), and (57) of Chapter 3 to derive the optimal profile for such a person yields -0.9, -1.2, -0.5 on evaluation, potency, and activity, respectively. Searching the identity catalog for the twelve profiles closest to this optimum (using the profile values for female moderates), we get the following identities in the order of their fit: a boob, a drudge, a hanger-on, a fuddy-duddy, an egghead, a glutton, a scapegoat, a dolt, a pinhead, a klutz, a dumbbell, and a vagrant. Theoretically, these are identities the girl might consider as she tries to comprehend the man's motivations.

Many of these identities provide an appropriate answer in some conceivable setting to the question of who would avoid a girl. Perhaps in the party situation the girl is likely to conclude that the man is a dolt; therefore, we allow "dolt" to be the girl's reidentification of the man, and we enter its profile as the fundamental sentiment of the girl toward the man. The girl's transient reactions to the reinterpreted last event ("the dolt avoids the girl") are now reevaluated. Now the event deflection is nearer zero, a third less than before, indicating that this event seems likely to her; now she "understands" it. (As Blum and McHugh, 1971, point out, the formulation of a particular kind of person corresponds to attributing motives and thereby understanding events.)

The next event for the girl is constructed in the context that she is a girl who has just been avoided by this dolt, and the predictions are that she in turn might now work him, urge him, disrobe him, outwit him, or outdo him. At least some of these possibilities seem appropriate in the circumstances (disrobe is a touching act that ordinarily would not be acceptable except among intimates).

State trooper–criminal

The next example illustrates how affect-control theory can be applied to the study of subcultures by working with special measurements for a few concepts having subcultural significance, while assuming that the catalog profiles apply for other concepts.[3] The situation consists of a state trooper and a criminal, both males and moderates. An analysis using only the standard catalog values is run first for comparison purposes. It employs male student feelings about a state trooper: approximately neutral on evaluation (edging into negative), somewhat potent, and very slightly active. The students see a criminal as quite bad, quite weak, and somewhat lively. On the first cycle, the predicted behaviors of the criminal toward the trooper are spit on, maim, ridicule, humiliate, and victimize. The trooper's predicted behaviors toward the criminal are handcuff, refuse, punish, deter, and divert. We choose "The criminal ridicules the state trooper" for realization. Then, on the second cycle of event construction, the criminal might wheedle, mock, upstage, spit on, or pester the trooper, whereas the trooper's predicted behaviors are to interrogate, cross-examine, coerce, halt, or punish the criminal. These generated behavior expectations do seem to capture common notions about a trooper–criminal relation as reflected, say, in television crime shows.

The question now is "Do state troopers themselves have such a dramatic view of their interactions with criminals?" To examine this question in the context of affect-control theory, we run a new analysis. For each actor, the profiles assigned to state trooper and criminal are the averaged evaluation–potency–activity ratings of state trooper and criminal obtained from twenty-five North Carolina state troopers. Comparing the troopers' ratings with the average college student ratings reveals that the troopers see themselves as substantially nicer, more powerful, and more lively than students see them; and troopers see a criminal as substantially less bad and less weak than students do.

We generate new sets of predicted behaviors based on the troopers' profiles. On both cycles, the criminal's predicted acts toward a trooper are upstage, evade, fool, mock, and gibe, and theoretically this is how a trooper expects a criminal to behave toward him. These acts are unfriendly and deviant, but they have a tone that is notably less aggressive and provocative than the predicted criminal behaviors generated from student profiles. The trooper's predicted behaviors toward the criminal on the first cycle are captivate, challenge, astound, bed, and amaze. Bed is inappropriate here or in any of a trooper's occupational relationships, and the issue is not one of affective appropriateness but of common sense and taboo – bed is one of those acts that require an object who is immature, incapacitated, or an intimate. Because none of those conditions apply in this case, it is eliminated from the list for syntactic reasons, leaving captivate, challenge, astound, and amaze. On the second cycle (after "The criminal evades the state trooper") the predicted acts for the trooper are overwhelm, oppose, captivate, convince, and astound.

The two lists of trooper acts generated from state troopers' own sentiments have a competitive tone, rather than the conflictual tone characterizing the expectations generated from college student sentiments. Although physical domination becomes an option in the cycle-two acts, it has a nonhostile character, and the presence of "convince" on the list suggests that impulses to use force might alternate with impulses to use psychological control. Thus, overall, the analysis suggests that state troopers might not share the melodramatic laymen's interpretation of the trooper–criminal relationship. Of course, these analytic outcomes really are hypotheses about troopers' viewpoints and behavior, rather than "findings." Their validity would have to be examined empirically through interviews and behavior observations.[4]

North Carolina state troopers were assumed to have the same behavior sentiments as North Carolina college students in order to conduct the analysis just presented.[5] Some justification for this tactic can be derived from the Appendix, which shows that the vast majority of concepts are not associated with major *EPA* variations by sex or conservatism, and the differences that do occur on conservatism apply mainly to identities, not acts. Nevertheless, more determinate analyses of subcultural and cultural variations will require identity and act catalogs for different populations. Then it will be theoretically possible to generate predictions about indigenous norms from sentiment measurements obtained indigenously, and differences in outcomes could be traced back to the original sentiment variations in order to pinpoint the bases of sociocultural differences. Used this way, affect-control theory might provide a method for examining how reality is constructed in different cultures and subcultures, in effect implementing the *verstehen* method of social analysis (Truzzi, 1974) objectively, on the basis of empirical measurements. In principle, it even is possible to work with catalogs from two different cultures simultaneously in order to study intercultural conflicts. Such comparative analyses implicitly involve the assumption that affective-change equations are constant across groups. Some research examining the validity of this assumption already is underway.[6] Regardless of the outcomes, comparative analyses will continue to be feasible as long as some forms of affective-change formulas can be defined in every group. If the formulas are different across groups, it simply means that the mathematical structures have to be shifted, along with the identity and act catalogs, as one moves from analyzing one culture to another.

Status of the predictions

Predictions from affect-control theory have been examined in scores of analyses, using a program that provides computer assistance (Heise, 1978). The results presented in this chapter and the next are typical. The theory, implemented as a mathematical model for simulating social psychological processes, does generate event specifications that seem qualitatively reasonable.

The theory also at times generates event specifications that are absurd, and so the present model is not entirely sufficient for understanding social behavior. A better empirical base would eliminate some errors. Current affective-reaction formulas undoubtedly are missing key interaction terms, and coefficient estimates in the formulas still are subject to substantial improvement. Also, some evidence hints that alternative formulas may be needed for different conditions of action – for example, when an actor is dealing with an impersonal as opposed to a personal object. Weights for summating deflections are subject to improvement, the current values being based on secondary analysis of a study designed for other purposes. Additionally, *EPA* profiles for identities and behaviors have been obtained from minimal numbers of respondents, and large-sample estimates of the profiles would eliminate some errors caused by incorrect numerical inputs.

Beyond this, the affect-control principle is limited in its theoretical scope, operating only within constraints provided by other cognitive principles. Two principles – the requirement of a predefined situation and case-grammar structuring of events – already are incorporated in analyses. However, other principles are barely identified or are just suspected at present. For example, special constraints govern "touching" acts, because event specifications involving such acts often seem bizarre even if affectively appropriate; but no precise hypothesis exists yet for when to include touching acts in event predictions. The acts "marry," "divorce," and "adopt" occur under extra constraints that are undefined in the model, and it is not known whether these are instances from a larger class of behaviors. Commercial acts like "pay" and "hire" also are subject to special constraints. Additional principles clearly are involved when events are respecified through reidentification. Only a small portion of the affectively appropriate identities may be applicable in a given setting. Although an analyst can easily filter out inappropriate choices, no formal rules are available yet to represent this selection process.

Still, the examples in this chapter have shown that concrete hypotheses about social events are readily generated from affect-control theory. In given circumstances, the theory provides a list of acts that theoretically includes the prediction of what one person will do to another when selecting from the 600 acts in the behavior catalog. In the case of reidentification, the theory gives a list of identities that theoretically includes the prediction of how one person will redefine another if selecting from the 650 identities in the identity catalog. Moreover, the theory can be used to derive nonobvious but testable propositions about peculiar perspectives and behaviors in special groups. Thus, with appropriately designed research, it will be possible to see whether the theory does or does not predict people's intentions and expectations and whether it does or does not predict their actual behavior. Affect-control theory generates precise hypotheses that allow the theory to be examined scientifically.

5. Social roles

Though the role concept has been criticized with respect to a variety of issues (e.g., see Komarovsky, 1973), it remains valuable in analyses of social action, drawing attention to various determinants of meaningful behavior. Functionalist role analyses emphasize that actions vary institutionally and across locations where relevant resources and participants are assembled (Spiro, 1961:97). Within settings, varying actions ordinarily are expected from persons in different social positions, a role being the "dynamic aspect of status" (Linton, 1945:77). Persons with a given status act differentially toward others, depending on the others' statuses, a point that Merton (1957:369) emphasized by the concept of "role set" – the array of role relationships centered on a given status. Symbolic interactionist attention to the creativity of role performances (e.g., Turner, 1962) has stressed that behavior varies with circumstances, even when the basic relationship between two persons is a constant.

Affect-control theory can be applied to the study of social roles by focusing on a particular social identity and examining the kinds of events constructed with a person having that identity as actor or object. In the perspective of affect control, a role exists specifically in the process of constructing events confirming fundamental feelings about the identities of the self and others. The approach has roots in interpretive sociology, where it is understood that a role consists of the actions a person generates in confirming an identity (Wilson, 1970), and in Linton's idea that a role arises out of a status, being "what an individual has to do in order to validate his occupation of the status" (1945: 77; the parallel between identity and status has been noted elsewhere – e.g., McCall and Simmons, 1966; Goodenough, 1969). Moreover, pursuing the study of roles in the framework of affect-control theory leads directly to the following understandings. Settings that are interpreted as different situations assemble different identities and therefore different combinations of fundamental affects requiring confirmation, so that, in general, the kinds of actions generated in the service of identity main-

104

tenance differ across settings. Because situations often are defined in terms of an organized set of identities relating to a single institution, situational variations in sentiment-confirming behavior may reflect institutional variations. Within a given situation, persons typically take on different identities and thus different feelings about the self; in general, therefore, their behaviors differ in character. As a person in a given identity deals with different others in the same scene, the constraints on identity-confirming actions shift, depending on the feelings attached to others' identities, so that generally an actor's behavior varies across relationships. Even within relationships, confirming actions have to take account of the transient feelings produced by recent events, and thus behaviors change as disturbing events establish new circumstances.

In a theory of roles obtained by applying the affect-control model, a role is defined by the meaning of the role identity – especially its evaluation, potency, and activity associations. Such a conception was anticipated but not developed in the traditional literature. Nadel said, "Even the simple introduction of a person as a 'priest,' 'elder,' as my 'mother's brother' or as my 'friend,' is a cue or pointer conditioning the expectations of the listener" (1964:30). Goodenough said, "I have found it useful to look upon the cultural content of social relationships as containing (among other things) 'vocabularies' of different kinds of forms and a 'syntax' or set of rules for their composition into (and interpretation as) meaningful sequences of social events" (1969:311). One implication is that role learning involves acquiring only a limited number of meanings for separate identities and acts: their evaluation–potency–activity profiles together with their denotations and syntactic features:

it is possible to view what is learned not as internalized norms but simply as cognitive and evaluative information . . . In this view we think of status-organizing processes (under certain conditions) as making available the cognitive and evaluative information implied by the states of a status characteristic; of this information (under certain conditions) coming to be connected to features of the particular situation; of the whole collection of such connections (under certain conditions) becoming organized into a resultant status structure; of the resultant structure (under certain conditions) coming to be translated into observable behavior [Berger et al., 1977:8].

The relevant meanings can be readily established during socialization from verbal statements concerning regularities in states or behavior. Assertions, such as that a boy is "a male child or youth," or that a prostitute is "a woman who engages in sexual intercourse for money,"[1] establish affective associations – indeed, Fishbein and Ajzen (1975) present a model for the derivation of attitudes from salient beliefs about states. Such statements also establish denotative and syntactic features: Knowing already that a child is human, we are told by the definition that a boy is also; knowing that sexual intercourse is an intimate act, we are told by the definition that a prostitute will be involved generally in intimate behaviors. Thus a small number of "exemplar" beliefs or statements (Imershein, 1976) can establish the meaning of an identity, which then can be employed generatively to establish almost unlimited additional expectations.[2] In the generative approach, role learning might even be largely auxiliary to language learning – an idea encouraged by a variety of existing studies (Cressey, 1962; Donahoe, 1961; Friendly and Glucksberg, 1970; Goldfried and Kissel, 1963; Kulik, Sarbin, and Stein, 1971; Kutner and Brogan, 1974; Lerman, 1967; Schwartz and Merten, 1967; Szalay and Brent, 1967).

Role analyses

The applicability of affect-control theory to role research is demonstrated best by showing that a variety of analyses conducted in the framework of the theory yield sensible results. That is the central task of this chapter. Illustrative analyses are provided here to show that affect-control theory allows generation of role expectations that are appropriate to institutional context, vary appropriately with an actor's status, vary appropriately with an object's status, and vary appropriately with the circumstances created by recent events.

Identities in a variety of institutional areas have been selected from the catalog in the Appendix and entered pairwise in analyses using Program INTERACT (Heise, 1978), which gives computer assistance in studies involving affect-control theory. In each case, a dyad was set up with actors agreeing on their respective identities. All actors were specified as males and moderates on a liberalism–conservatism scale; in effect, therefore, the predicted behaviors theoretically are the expectations of male moderate southern college students. The first round of event construction was conducted with transients set equal to fundamentals; the second round of event construction was conducted with transients deflected by one of the events specified on the first round. The behavior producing maximum deflection reduction on round one was always used to move the analysis to round two, even when other acts in the behavior lists appeared more suitable.

The tables in this chapter list acts in the order of their appearance on round one (that is, by their goodness of fit to the round-one optimal profiles), and then by their order of appearance on round two, with repetitions deleted. Certain acts involving physical contact are inappropriate in many kinds of relationships. Because such acts are distracting when they appear in behavior lists for other kinds of relationships, analyses were run with a modified behavior catalog in which all "touch" acts were deleted.

Institutions

Courthouse roles. Generated role relationships among judges, prosecuting attorneys, attorneys, defendants, and thieves are shown in Table 5.1. Each identity has a core of behaviors that appear in the generated lists for three or more role partners. For a judge the core acts are mothering, remembering, excusing, counseling, and enduring (paying is an obvious error). The prosecuting attorney has the core acts exalting, glorifying, relishing, lauding, enthralling, influencing, and urging. An attorney's core acts involve facing, leading, esteeming, training, and guiding others. A defendant is generally disposed to indulge, examine, watch, observe, favor, or penalize others. A thief is predicted in general to antagonize, badger, or taunt role partners.

Aside from the core behaviors, Table 5.1 indicates that a judge would be particularly disposed to remind, honor, or accommodate another judge; to consider, release, or soothe a prosecuting attorney; to remind, caution, and accommodate an attorney; and to consider, quiet, and contemplate a defendant. Nearly all of the predicted acts toward a thief are unique, and some are appropriate to the judge's sociolegal function: miss, psychoanalyze, hush, subdue, sentence, convict, and dissuade.

A prosecuting attorney acts mainly in his core manner toward a judge, according to the analysis. However, a prosecutor is predicted to have unique dispositions toward the others in his role set: awing, confronting, and enthralling another prosecutor; disciplining an attorney; awing, enticing, persuading, and confronting a defendant. The unique acts toward a thief are working, outwitting, outdoing, arresting, and dissuading - some of which are appropriate.

Besides the core behaviors, an attorney is predicted to advise, interest, instruct, and adore a judge and to exonerate and advise a prosecuting attorney (overall, this may be too dominant and positive a representation

Table 5.1. *Specimens of male college student behavior expectations for legal roles, generated analytically from the affective profiles for actor and object identities*

Object	Actor				
	Judge	Prosecuting attorney	Attorney	Defendant	Thief
Judge	mother, remember, pay, remind, excuse, counsel, honor, accommodate	exalt, glorify, relish, laud, enthrall	face, advise, lead, esteem, interest, instruct, train, guide, adore	indulge, examine, watch, observe, favor, idealize	aggravate, antagonize, browbeat, disobey, offend, laugh at, heckle, badger
Prosecuting attorney	mother, endure, consider, pay, release, counsel, excuse, soothe, remember	exalt, glorify, influence, relish, urge, awe, confront, enthrall, laud	lead, face, esteem, guide, exonerate, train, advise	indulge, examine, watch, exhort, idealize, penalize	heckle, taunt, badger, bully, antagonize, cuss, interrupt, pester
Attorney	mother, pay, remind, remember, caution, honor, counsel, accommodate, excuse	relish, exalt, laud, glorify, enthrall, discipline	face, befriend, interest, reform, charm, adore, instruct, train	indulge, examine, favor, idealize, observe, watch	bias, disobey, browbeat, dog, aggravate, taunt, cuss, bully, badger, pester
Defendant	mother, endure, consider, quiet, contemplate, counsel, excuse, remember	influence, urge, awe, glorify, entice, urge, persuade, confront	exonerate, lead, face, esteem, guide, gratify, guard	indulge, watch, examine, exhort, penalize	heckle, taunt, badger, annoy, insult, laugh at, haze, antagonize
Thief	miss, psychoanalyze, hush, endure, subdue, sentence, convict, dissuade	work, urge, outwit, outdo, influence, arrest, dissuade	awe, influence, persuade, urge, miss, shield, supervise, consider, confront	indulge, examine, idealize, favor, observe, penalize, scrutinize, watch, humble, beckon	tease, startle, jest, dare, mimic, banter, haze, harangue

of the attorney's role). The attorney is predicted to befriend, interest, reform, charm, adore, or instruct another attorney; and to exonerate, gratify, and guard a defendant. The predicted acts toward a thief are simultaneously aggressive and protective.

According to the analyses, a defendant's behaviors are highly stereotyped, usually involving just the core role. Theoretically, however, a defendant would be particularly disposed to exhort a prosecuting attorney or another defendant, and to scrutinize, humble, or beckon a thief.

A thief might aggravate, browbeat, disobey, offend, or laugh at a judge; bully, antagonize, cuss, interrupt, or pester a prosecuting attorney; bias, disobey, browbeat, dog, aggravate, cuss, or bully an attorney; insult, laugh at, haze, and antagonize a defendant; and tease, startle, jest, dare, mimic, banter, haze, or harangue another thief.

Medical roles. Generated behavior expectations for surgeon, doctor, nurse, psychoanalyst, and patient are presented in Table 5.2.

The surgeon-to-surgeon prescriptions include interesting, advising, and believing, which are instrumental and appropriate. Serenading is inappropriate here and throughout Table 5.2. The surgeon's relationships to doctor, nurse, and psychoanalyst all are very similar in the table and similar to the surgeon–surgeon predictions. With a patient, however, the surgeon takes on a comforting and educative role.

Overall, the generated behavior prescriptions for a doctor toward other healing professionals define a role that is extremely supportive, educative, and occasionally instrumental (the appearance of adore seems excessive and probably is due to an imprecise *EPA* profile). With a patient, the doctor is comforting and engages in appropriate instrumental behavior (medicate). The appearance of hire in the doctor–patient relationship (as elsewhere in the table) clearly is erroneous.

The nurse's predicted behaviors toward a surgeon, doctor, or other nurse are socioemotional in character. The nurse's predicted actions toward a psychoanalyst are heavily educative. Her acts toward a patient are supportive.

The predicted acts of a psychoanalyst toward a surgeon, doctor, or nurse are similar and difficult to characterize. With a patient or another psychoanalyst the predicted pattern is observant and analytic.

Religious roles. Generated behaviors in the religious sphere are listed in Table 5.3.[3] The predictions are that God inspires, saves, rescues,

Table 5.2. *Specimens of male college student behavior expectations for medical roles, generated analytically from the affective profiles for actor and object identities*

Object	Actor[a]			
	Surgeon	Doctor	Nurse	Psychoanalyst
Surgeon	interest, reform, serenade, advise, charm, believe	satisfy, adopt, instruct, adore, assist, congratulate, please	invite, serenade, greet, befriend, charm, visit, adore, instruct	evaluate, signal, cover, extol, call
Doctor	interest, reform, charm, acclaim, treat, serenade, advise, visit	adore, instruct, serenade, visit, greet, assist, congratulate, satisfy, adopt, please	charm, seduce, invite, greet, befriend	evaluate, signal, brief, extol, call, address, cover
Nurse	interest, reform, serenade, advise, answer, believe	satisfy, adopt, assist, congratulate, instruct, please	serenade, invite, greet, befriend, charm, visit, adore, interest	evaluate, signal, call, cover, extol
Psychoanalyst	advise, oblige, believe, answer, hire, relieve	uplift, adopt, please, bless, educate, appreciate, rehabilitate, compliment	advise, face, instruct, interest, reform, believe, hire, adore	address, admonish, cover analyze, study, regard
Patient	accommodate, honor, advise, esteem, oblige, gratify, counsel, guide	gratify, hire, bless, medicate, value, respect, reassure, console, comfort	lead, face, guide, advise, esteem, gratify, exonerate, honor	admonish, analyze, study, test, address

[a] A patient's predicted acts are similar for all others, being drawn from the set indulge, watch, follow, sweet-talk, mollify, shush, pamper.

Table 5.3. *Specimens of male college student behavior expectations for religious roles, generated analytically from the affective profiles for actor and object identities*

Object	Actor			
	God	Minister	Christian	The Devil
God		greet, invite, befriend, charm, seduce, satisfy, visit, assist, congratulate, serenade	alert, invite, liberalize, marry, greet, defend, back, assist	pursue, radicalize, hurry, invite, outdo, scare, threaten, outrage, attack, seize
Minister	inspire, save, rescue, cure, delight, love	serenade, visit, adore, greet, instruct, satisfy, adopt, assist, congratulate, please	invite, greet, alert, defend, serenade, assist, congratulate, back	radicalize, incite, chase, shake, stun, scare, threaten, attack, outrage, seize
Christian	save, rescue, inspire, cure, delight, love	serenade, visit, adore, instruct, satisfy, please, assist, congratulate, back, alert	invite, defend, greet, alert, serenade, assist, congratulate, back, teach, support	incite, assail, chase, radicalize, stun, scare, threaten, attack, outrage, ostracize
The Devil	enrapture, convince, confront, captivate, appoint, forgive, protect, guard, respect	confront, shield, awe, supervise, persuade, exonerate, guard, consider, mother	confront, captivate, persuade, influence, enthrall, appoint, discipline, guard, supervise	

cures, delights, and loves ministers and Christians. God's predicted acts toward the Devil are enrapture, convince, confront, captivate, appoint, forgive, protect, guard, and respect.

A minister's core role consists of satisfying, visiting, assisting, congratulating, and serenading. Special predicted acts toward God are greet, invite, befriend, charm, and seduce (the latter probably appears because of an unreliable male increment for seduce). A minister is predicted to adore, instruct, and please both other ministers and Christians, and in particular to greet and adopt another minister and to back and alert a Christian. A Christian's core role consists of alerting, inviting, defending, backing, and assisting. Specific acts generated for Christian to God are liberalizing, marrying, and greeting. The Christian might serenade and congratulate both ministers and other Christians and teach and support other Christians. The predicted acts of both a minister and a Christian toward the Devil seem mostly too supportive, except for confronting, awing, and disciplining. However, the lists would appear more appropriate if the Devil is thought of as personalized in a "sinner."

The Devil has a core role of radicalizing, inciting, scaring, threatening, outraging, and attacking. Additionally, the predictions are that he might try to pursue, hurry, outdo, or seize God; he might chase, shake, stun, or seize a minister; and he might assail, chase, stun, or ostracize a Christian.

University roles.   Table 5.4 presents results for a professor interacting with different kinds of students. The behaviors for an undergraduate suggest enthusiastic efforts to impress and coopt the professor (if the

Table 5.4. *Specimens of male college student behavior expectations for university roles, generated analytically from the affective profiles for actor and object identities*

Student	Professor as object	Professor as actor
Undergraduate	surprise, escape, rally, play with, liberalize, amaze, coach	dream of, extol, patronize, ask, brief, obey
Coed	coach, acclaim, charm, inform, seduce, direct	dream of, extol, patronize, ask, brief, obey
Graduate student	brief, revere, patronize, call, cover	dream of, patronize, extol, revere, cover, obey, release

professor cannot be escaped). The expectations for the professor suggest a rather submissive person doing his duties. Analytic results suggest that a coed should relate to a professor in an assertive, seductive manner. The professor in turn treats her in his standard, submissive way. According to the results, graduate students act attentive and respectful toward professors, who act in essentially their usual way in return. Perhaps it is particularly necessary here to remember that these definitions are constructed from the sentiments of male college undergraduates in the South. They may not correspond to the definitions of most professors or to the definitions of undergraduates in the North.

Another side of university life can be considered by analyzing behavior expectations for a football quarterback and some members of his role set. A situation with an enemy tackle was defined from the quarterback's viewpoint by averaging the profiles for quarterback and rival and the profiles for tackle and villain (enemy is not in the catalog). The viewpoint of the tackle was defined as tackle combined with rival for himself and quarterback combined with villain for the other. Under these definitions, the predicted acts for the quarterback are opposing, overwhelming, outdoing, grasping, tackling, and captivating ("touch" acts are included here, because football is a contact sport). The predicted behaviors of the tackle toward the quarterback are outdoing, grasping, opposing, catching, pursuing, overwhelming, radicalizing, and tackling. A coach and a quarterback are predicted to thrill, applaud, and alert each other (also marry – an obvious error). Additionally, the coach might back, inspire, or rescue the quarterback; the quarterback might excite the coach (also desire, which seems an error). Overall, these anlytic results do capture the spirit of the different relationships, despite the errors, including the misspecification of a quarterback tackling a tackle.

Service establishment roles. An analysis of the waiter–diner relationship indicates that a waiter should brief, ask, humor, patronize, and correct a diner (dream of was generated but seems incorrect). Acts for the diner toward the waiter are call, brief, idealize, approach, evaluate, revere, and address. The simulation seems to be near the mark, though not entirely right. A waiter–chef analysis leaves the waiter's predicted acts unchanged, except for substituting prompt for dream of. The chef's predicted acts toward the waiter are prompt, cue, engage, humor, flatter, and ask.

An analysis indicates that a barkeeper might mystify, upbraid, query, contradict, approach, test, eye, and question a drunk, and he can expect the drunk to deflate, befuddle, embarrass, pooh-pooh, rook, wheedle, mock, distress, or trick him. On the other hand, the barkeeper might humor, engage, cue, initiate, and prompt a gentleman, and he could expect the gentleman to advise, oblige, answer, accommodate, and believe him in return. The predicted actions of a barkeeper toward his barmaid are to approach, initiate, evaluate, signal, and call her; and she is predicted to astonish, titillate, entice, hail, josh, catch, or outwit him.

These generated interactions in the service realm are sensible enough to indicate that role processes in this area may be governed by affect control. However, the routinized nature of these roles might justify an alternative analysis in terms of scripts (Schank and Abelson, 1977).

Family roles. All nuclear family roles are rated as good and lively in this population of college students, major differences being associated instead with potency: the father is most potent, the mother and son are on the next plane, and the daughter is least. Consequently, the tenor of generated acts is positive for all family members: all are more or less enthusiastically attentive to one another (see Table 5.5).

According to the simulations, a man in a southern middle-class family might expect to be alerted, embraced, backed, and applauded by his wife; "marry" also appears, but here and elsewhere in the table has to be counted as inappropriate. The man also can expect to be alerted, backed, and applauded by his son, as well as thrilled and enjoyed. His daughter might hail, acclaim, flatter, amaze, coach, cue, or escape him. A woman might expect to be assisted, backed, defended, alerted, encouraged, embraced, caressed, and enjoyed by her husband; thrilled, applauded, backed, alerted, and enjoyed by her son; engaged, hailed, flattered, coached, cued, and escaped by her daughter.

A father's core role includes welcoming, encouraging, helping, and curing. For the father, a son is additionally the object of defending, supporting, assisting, inspiring, and congratulating; a daughter is aided, praised, understood, saved, and healed. A mother's core role involves assisting, satisfying, and congratulating. For the mother, a son is additionally the object of inviting, visiting, greeting, adoring, defending, and serenading; the mother pleases the daughter (and might want to adopt one). A brother's core role consists of applauding, backing, alerting, thrilling, liberalizing, and liking his siblings. A sister's core role is the

Table 5:5. *Specimens of male college student behavior expectations for nuclear family roles, generated analytically from the affective profiles for actor and object identities*

Object	Actor			
	Husband or father	Wife or mother	Son or brother	Daughter or sister
Husband or father		alert, embrace,[a] back, marry, applaud	thrill, applaud, back, alert, marry, enjoy	hail, excape, coach, cue, amaze, flatter, acclaim
Wife or mother	back, defend, embrace,[a] alert, assist, encourage, caress,[a] enjoy		thrill, applaud, back, alert, marry, enjoy	hail, excape, coach, cue, engage, flatter
Son or brother	defend, support, assist, congratulate, encourage, cure, inspire, help, welcome	serenade, visit, invite, greet, adore, assist, congratulate, satisfy, defend	applaud, back, alert, thrill, liberalize, like	applaud, alert, back, liberalize, marry, like
Daughter or sister	welcome, aid, encourage, praise, help, heal, cure, save, understand	satisfy, assist, congratulate, please, adopt	applaud, back, alert, thrill, liberalize, like	applaud, alert, back, liberalize, marry, like, enjoy

Note: The results are based on analyses of the following dyads: Husband–Wife, Father–Son, Father–Daughter, Mother–Son, Mother–Daughter, Brother–Sister, Brother–Brother, and Sister–Sister.

[a] "Touch" acts are included in the Husband–Wife analysis because the relationship permits physical contact.

same, with "thrill" deleted; "enjoy" is added for a sister–sister relationship.

According to these analyses, the adult roles are the most differentiated, the children's roles the least. Both adults are drawn into teaching relationships with the children, and both (but particularly the father) provide unconditional support and regard for the children. The children contribute excitement to family life. Such a statement of normative patterns is plausible, and it encompasses some social science research findings about parent–child interactions (Maccoby and Jacklin, 1974: chap. 9).

The generated behaviors for some extended family relationships are shown in Table 5.6. The predictions are that a grandfather would remind, caution, counsel, remember, admire, and excuse all of his role partners. A grandmother's predicted acts are the same, except that "notice" and "need" are substituted for "counsel" and "excuse," and a disposition to join the grandfather is predicted for her. A grandson's core role consists of liberalizing, surprising, entertaining, and singing to; playing with is added for grandparents, and desiring and courting are added (perhaps erroneously) in the interaction with a granddaughter. The granddaughter's core role is entertaining, singing to, courting, coaching, playing with, and acclaiming ("seduce" is added erroneously in the interaction with the grandson).

These various specifications do seem to define some aspects of grandparent–grandchild relations. Additionally, these specifications for extended family roles show significant and meaningful contrasts with the specifications for nuclear family roles.

Summary.   Overall, these descriptions do seem to capture lay understandings of social relationships in various institutional settings. Most of the generated behaviors are reasonably appropriate for the given actors, and sometimes the nature of the action changes appropriately as the object persons change.

Though affect-control theory is derived without reference to the structure of larger society or to the interdependence of roles, the prescriptions often reflect functions of each status. Evidently, fundamental feelings about identities and acts evolve in such a way that the functional demands of roles are met as people go about the personal business of confirming the meanings of self and others in a social situation.

Table 5.6. Specimens of male college student behavior expectations for extended family roles, generated analytically from the affective profiles for actor and object identities

Object	Actor			
	Grandfather	Grandmother	Grandson	Granddaughter
Grandfather		admire, remind, notice, caution, join, remember, need	liberalize, surprise, entertain, sing to, play with	entertain, sing to, court, coach, play with, acclaim
Grandmother	remind, remember, caution, admire, excuse, counsel		liberalize, surprise, entertain, play with, sing to, court	coach, entertain, sing to, court, play with, acclaim
Grandson	remember, caution, remind, excuse, admire, counsel	admire, remind, caution, need, notice, remember		entertain, sing to, coach, court, play with, seduce, acclaim
Granddaughter	remember, caution, remind, excuse, admire, counsel	admire, remind, caution, notice, need, remember	liberalize, surprise, entertain, desire, sing to, court	

Role relations with deviants

Parsons (1951:250) defined deviance as interaction disturbances arising when an actor purposively behaves "in contravention of one or more institutionalized normative patterns." In the legal literature, crimes are understood as events that are formally prohibited, demoralizing, and controllable through punishments. Influential treatises view delinquency as alienation from normative patterns (e.g., Cloward and Ohlin, 1960), and efforts have been made to assess delinquency by the extent of actions in a prohibited domain (e.g., Scott, 1954; Heise, 1968). In a dominant sociological perspective (e.g., Merton, 1957: chap. 4; Parsons, 1951), the causes of deviance are seen as failures in socialization that allow a person to be insufficiently attracted to permissible behaviors or insufficiently inhibited about engaging in prohibited alternatives.

Nadel argued for this approach to roles, deviance, and social control, but he also identified a problem with the interpretation: "certain forms of deviant behavior are also positively expressed, suggestive of roles proper, though disapproved ones, whether they refer summarily to individual conduct (a 'criminal,' a 'sceptic') or to specific actions and even occupations considered undesirable ('rebel,' 'prostitute,' 'deserter')" (Nadel, 1964:49). Nadel went on to regard such "deviant roles" as being defined not by their own rights and obligations but rather by the rights and obligations of others in sanctioning positions. However, as Nadel here recognized, deviance sometimes *is* normative and organized by the same sociocultural system that defines normal roles – a point emphasized by labeling theorists, with their concept of secondary deviance (Hawkins and Tiedeman, 1975, and Gove, 1975, offer recent reviews of labeling theory). People acting in deviant roles do not just commit random behaviors from the proscribed domain. Their actions accord with prescriptions that are defined culturally and that are understood by typical members of society. If this is the case, deviant role interactions may be predictable in the framework of affect-control-theory.

Underworld roles.   The predicted behaviors of four underworld characters with three noncriminals are shown in Table 5.7. According to the analyses, the behavior of the noncriminals is fairly stereotyped in dealing with all the criminals. In every case, the generated acts for a state trooper include arrest, indoctrinate, and upbraid. A victim's acts include

Table 5.7. Specimens of male college student behavior expectations for crime roles, generated analytically from the affective profiles for actor and object identities

Criminal	State trooper	Victim	Hostage
Gangster			
As actor	outrage, scare, enrage, threaten, hound, con	threaten, enrage, scare, outrage, con, capture, hound, assail	threaten, enrage, scare, ostracize, outrage, capture, hound
As object	work, indoctrinate, mystify, arrest, upbraid	emulate, parody, entreat, favor, sweet-talk, beseech, criticize	indulge, sweet-talk, beseech, emulate, follow, beseech, mollify
Crook			
As actor	hassle, damn, swindle, impede, infuriate, harass, fight, con, torment	hassle, infuriate, fight, harass, con, bawl out, hound, harangue, rile	hassle, harass, infuriate, fight, swindle, bawl out, hound, rile, harangue
As object	arrest, indoctrinate, work, upbraid, mystify	emulate, parody, entreat, sweet-talk, favor, parody, beseech, criticize	indulge, sweet-talk, beseech, follow, watch, mollify,
Mugger			
As actor	torment, swindle, con, assault, harass, shoot, infuriate	torment, con, harass, infuriate, fight, hound, bawl out, hassle	torment, con, harass, infuriate, swindle, fight, hound, bawl out, hassle
As object	work, arrest, indoctrinate, mystify, upbraid	emulate, parody, entreat, favor, sweet-talk, criticize, beseech	indulge, sweet-talk, watch, beseech, emulate, follow, mollify
Pickpocket			
As actor	needle, fluster, dog, ride, berate, haze, antagonize, aggravate, bawl out	ride, fluster, needle, dog, rile, dare, haze, rattle	ride, needle, dog, fluster, aggravate, dare, rattle
As object	arrest, indoctrinate, upbraid, mystify, contradict, question	parody, sweet-talk, beseech, emulate, criticize, imitate, overrate	sweet-talk, follow, beseech, mollify, indulge

entreat, sweet-talk, and beseech for all four types of criminals. A hostage should indulge, mollify, sweet-talk, and beseech the captor, regardless of the captor's specific identity, according to these results.

The predicted behaviors of the criminals are somewhat more differentiated, though uniformly negative in spirit. According to analyses, a gangster has a core role of threatening, enraging, scaring, outraging, and hounding. Additionally, he might try to con a state trooper or a victim; he might capture and assault a victim; and he might capture and ostracize a hostage. A crook's core role consists of hassling, infuriating, harassing, and fighting. Damning, swindling, and impeding are among the additions for a state trooper; conning and hounding for a victim; bawling out, riling, and haranguing for a hostage. Core acts for a mugger are tormenting, harassing, infuriating, and conning. Additionally, he might assault and shoot a state trooper and bawl out, hassle, and fight either a victim or a hostage. A pickpocket is predicted to fluster, needle, ride, and dog all three role partners. Also, he might berate and antagonize a trooper; dare, rattle, haze, and rile a victim; and aggravate a hostage.

A second question is addressed by results reported in Table 5.8: Can a set of role relations be identified within the underworld itself? Examination of the table shows that each criminal type has a core of behaviors that tend to be used with all or most other underworld associates. The gangster is generally given to chasing, inciting, and assailing. The crook startles, harangues, and agitates associates. The mugger hounds, harangues, agitates, and fights others. The pickpocket startles, rattles, and jests associates. Thus the analysis suggests that the various figures have somewhat different styles of interaction with their cohorts. None of the interactions is really friendly, but it is notable that some are less violent than the interactions of the criminals with noncriminals.

Some differentiation within dyads also appears in Table 5.8: The predicted behavior of the characters varies somewhat, depending on who the object of action is. However, the variations do not involve instrumental actions so much as expressive aspects of behavior. Thus the underworld as a structured system of coercion or as an economy dealing in illegal goods and services does not show clearly in these results. This could be because the catalogs do not include relevant acts and identities or because we are trying to reconstruct the underworld social structure from affective measurements of college undergraduates, rather than from the measured affects of criminals who know how the system operates.

Table 5.8. *Specimens of male college student behavior expectations for underworld roles, generated analytically from the affective profiles for actor and object identities*

	Actor			
Object	Gangster	Crook	Mugger	Pickpocket
Gangster	chase, hurry, incite, pursue, freak-out, assail, agitate, capture, hound	freak-out, flee, hurry, jest, startle, hound, harangue, agitate, bawl out, fight	freak-out, flee, hurry, startle, chase, hound, fight, infuriate, harangue, agitate	jest, kid, tantalize, pass, chatter to, startle, dare, rattle, harangue
Crook	chase, hurry, incite, pursue, freak-out, assail, scare, agitate	freak-out, flee, hurry, jest, startle, harangue, agitate, hound, bawl out	freak-out, flee, hurry, startle, chase, hound, fight, agitate, bawl out, harangue	jest, kid, pass, tantalize, pass, chatter to, startle, dare, jest, rattle, harangue
Mugger	pursue, chase, hurry, incite, freak-out, assail	flee, freak-out, hurry, jest, kid, startle, harangue, agitate	freak-out, flee, hurry, jest, chase, hound, agitate, harangue, bawl out, fight, startle	kid, jest, pass, tantalize, chatter to, startle, cajole, dare, rattle
Pickpocket	chase, assail, scare, incite, agitate, hound	harangue, agitate, startle, rattle, hound, bawl out	hound, harangue, agitate, bawl out, fight	startle, cajole, jest, dare, elude, harangue, rattle, zap, mimic

Deviant political roles.   Table 5.9 shows the generated expectations for a fanatic, traitor, and assassin interacting with an authority and a G-man. It seems somewhat appropriate that a fanatic should incite, shake, and freak-out an authority; that a traitor should degrade, desert, and doublecross an authority; that an assassin should assault, shoot, and injure an authority. The predicted actions of these deviants toward a G-man overlap the predicted acts toward an authority, but some of the differences are of interest. The fanatic might flee a G-man; the traitor might mug or murder a G-man; the assassin might damn the G-man and confuse or harm him.

Both the authority and the G-man were assigned many standard acts for an agent of social control dealing with a deviant: arrest, upbraid, reprimand, and discipline. Additionally, the results suggest that a G-man has a protective role as well as a sanctioning role, whereas the authority is more punitive. However, the G-man's role also moves in a more punitive direction once deviants act on him; for example, the G-man's acts

Table 5.9. *Specimens of male college student behavior expectations for political deviants and control agents, generated analytically from the affective profiles for actor and object identities*

Deviant	Authority	G-Man
Fanatic		
As actor	hurry, incite, chase, exhaust, shake, freak-out	hurry, pursue, flee, catch, incite, chase, freak-out, exhaust
As object	reprimand, interview, mystify, address, upbraid, shield, extol, evaluate	glorify, initiate, shield, interview, supervise, consider, laud, discipline
Traitor		
As actor	cheat, humiliate, degrade, blackmail, desert, ridicule, abuse, mug, doublecross	desert, belittle, exclude, distress, degrade, ridicule, humiliate, abuse, mug, murder
As object	question, upbraid, mystify, hush, arrest, dissuade	awe, influence, urge, dissuade, arrest, miss, reprimand, shield
Assassin		
As actor	despise, injure, assault, wrong, swindle, shoot, torment, harass, con	damn, pervert, confuse, despise, irritate, shoot, torment, assault, harass, harm
As object	mystify, upbraid, question, reprimand, arrest, hush, dissuade	awe, influence, urge, work, dissuade, shield, miss, reprimand

toward an assassin are merely confrontational until, say, the assassin irritates him: then the G-man dissuades, subdues, arrests, or interrogates (and also, erroneously, sentences).

Deviant neighborhood roles. Generated behaviors for a gossip, spinster, half-wit, and hobo relating to a neighbor, child, and handyman are presented in Table 5.10. According to analyses, a neighbor shows

Table 5.10. *Specimens of male college student behavior expectations for neighborhood deviants and normals, generated analytically from the affective profiles for actor and object identities*

Deviant	Neighbor	Child	Handyman
Gossip			
As actor	needle, bias, dog, fluster, ride, cuss, taunt, harass, interrupt, badger	dare, needle, rib, mimic, ape, haze, bawl out, harass, ride, rile	dare, needle, rib, ape, fluster, cuss, taunt, harass, interrupt, badger
As object	reprimand, address, approach, call, evaluate, cover, signal, interview	amaze, escape, titillate, astonish, astound, outdo, catch, outwit, oppose, work	awe, influence, glorify, initiate, interview, consider, supervise, shield, laud, release
Spinster			
As actor	watch, indulge, shush, monitor, mollify	watch, indulge, shush, follow, mollify, monitor	watch, indulge, shush, follow, mollify, monitor
As object	extol, ask, dream of, correct, obey, release	coach, entertain, sing to, court, surprise, acclaim, charm, inform, seduce	pay, esteem, inform, release, join, exonerate, lead, guide, honor
Half-wit			
As actor	pamper, appease, beg, overhear, classify, hide from, avoid	pamper, overhear, mollify, follow, beg, classify, hide from	pamper, overhear, mollify, follow, appease, beg, classify
As object	evaluate, extol, signal, cover, interview, dream of	coach, escape, amaze, surprise, astound, entice, urge, outwit, catch	consider, laud, supervise, release, obey, miss, shield, awe, endure, influence
Hobo			
As actor	follow, mollify, beseech, overhear, shush, gibe, pamper, hide from	follow, mollify, beseech, sweet-talk, shush, overhear	follow, mollify, beseech, sweet-talk, shush, overhear
As object	extol, evaluate, signal, interview, cover, dream of, ask, patronize, obey	coach, escape, surprise, amaze, sing to, relish, astound, challenge, exalt	release, consider, laud, pay, obey, shield, supervise, endure, miss

ambivalence toward a gossip, reflected on the one side by acts of approaching, calling, and interviewing and on the other by reprimanding. Predicted acts by a neighbor toward a spinster suggest a solicitous orientation – extolling, asking, and obeying. In interaction with the half-wit, the neighbor's acts lack a clear focus. The specifications for a neighbor to a hobo are patronizing.

A child is predicted to take a somewhat competitive orientation toward a gossip; a rather friendly orientation toward a spinster; a dominant but supportive orientation toward a half-wit; and a friendly, admiring orientation toward a hobo.

The generated acts for a handyman toward a gossip seem to suggest a person trying to take an integrative stance beyond pettiness. The handyman's relation to the spinster is supportive, and he acts somewhat as a giver of care to both a half-wit and a hobo.

The predicted acts for the neighborhood deviants can be grouped partly into core roles that tend to differ from one another. According to analyses, a gossip needles, harasses, and rides people; a spinster watches, indulges, shushes, and mollifies; a half-wit pampers, begs, and overhears; a hobo follows, mollifies, beseeches, overhears, and shushes. Additionally, each deviant is predicted to act somewhat less positively toward a neighbor than toward a child or a handyman.

Summary.   Behavior by and toward persons with stigmatized identities can be defined by using the same affect-control model that applies to "normal" actors and objects. Thus deviant behavior is recognizable as culturally defined in the same sense as normal behavior. In the analyses, sanctions frequently appear as acts confirming the identities of sanctioner and deviant. Thus sanctions sometimes are natural responses to certain kinds of culturally defined people.

Role creativity

Symbolic interactionists and interpretive sociologists repeatedly have criticized the static nature of traditional approaches to roles, emphasizing that roles are formulated in the process of their enactment and that role performances are creatively responsive to changing circumstances: "the actual role performance . . . is *improvised* to deal in some variable fashion with the broad demands of one's social position and one's character" (McCall and Simmons, 1966:67; see also Wrong, 1961;

Wilson, 1970). Ralph Turner's (1962) detailed critique presents the case in terms most relevant to the present discussion:

> The idea of role-taking shifts emphasis away from the simple process of enacting a prescribed role to devising a performance on the basis of an imputed other-role. The actor is not the occupant of a position for which there is a neat set of rules – a culture or set of norms – but a person who must act in the perspective supplied in part by his relationship to others whose actions reflect roles he must identify [p. 23, italics removed].
>
> ... The parent who on one occasion treats his child with gentleness and on another spanks him is unlikely to be adjudged inconsistent because both types of behavior, under appropriate circumstances, are supposed to be reasonable manifestations of the same parental role [p. 24].

As seen in previous sections, affect-control theory defines core role expectations. It also specifies adaptive reactions to unusual events. An unusual event causes peculiar transient feelings, which then act as special constraints for the construction of subsequent events confirming fundamental sentiments. Typically, the predicted reactions following disturbing events are different from the core actions. Thus affect-control theory can escape the artificiality involved in viewing roles as rote responses and offer a model of creativity in role performances, predicting what kind of special behaviors should arise in different circumstances.

For example, a parent's ordinary behavior toward a child is predicted (in Chapter 4) to be assisting, congratulating, hugging, defending, adopting, aiding, praising, welcoming, rehabilitating, and appreciating. Suppose, however, that the child disobeys the parent. Then, according to an analysis, the parent is disposed to guard, shield, appoint, supervise, or confront the child. These new predicted behaviors are completely different from those obtained in ordinary circumstances, and although not all of the predictions are equally plausible, some are appropriate and constitute just the kind of creative role playing we might expect in such a situation. Furthermore, these acts reflect the special character of the parent–child relationship and are not simply standard responses to disobedience. For example, if a patient disobeys a doctor, then the doctor's predicted acts would be mostly different: to miss, persuade, awe, shield, or dissuade the patient (whereas a doctor ordinarily is disposed to gratify, medicate, value, respect, reassure, console, and comfort a patient, according to Table 5.2).

In these examples, less positive responses followed the unusual event, and one interpretation of the outcomes would be that a child or patient is subjected to control for disobedience. In the other direction, affect-control theory predicts that positive responses sometimes will follow unusual behaviors. Returning to the doctor and patient, imagine that the patient reminds the doctor of something. This time the analysis predicts that the doctor will be inclined to appreciate, educate, rehabilitate, please, or compliment the patient. These predictions are different from any of those obtained previously for the doctor–patient relation; again, at least some of them would provide an appropriate response in the particular circumstance; and if, say, the doctor complimented the patient, this could be interpreted as a bit of reward for a desirable behavior.

With the available formulas and sentiment measurements, simulations of role creativity are far from perfectly accurate, as indicated by errors in the examples given and also in other, unreported analyses. Nevertheless, affect-control theory is capable in principle of explaining role creativity, and improved parameterization of the model may permit accurate predictions.

Though affect-control theory does embrace the notion of improvisation in role performances, the understanding of this process is notably different from that provided by traditional symbolic interactionist analyses, which stress that role creativity may be personalized and a-cultural (Turner, 1962:23; McCall and Simmons, 1966:67). Our analyses suggest that exactly the same processes and cultural materials are involved in devising a special performance in unusual circumstances as are involved in generating routine norms: Culture in the form of fundamental feelings and projection rules is no less at work in role creativity than it is in role conformity. Indeed, it is the impact of culture that provides the sense of correctness in specially devised performances. The difference between the two kinds of role enactment relates only to whether recent events have caused unusual deflections in transient feelings.

Various examples in this section and the last have indicated that punishments and rewards (in the sense of negatively and positively valued acts) are delivered generally to persons who have attained stigmatized or esteemed identities (like a thief or a doctor) and conditionally to persons with more moderate identities (like patient) who get involved in events deflecting observers' transient impressions in unusual ways. Thus, in affect-control theory, the same model that underlies ordinary role behavior also accounts for sanctioning behavior and, moreover, for generalized sanctioning and for conditional sanctions, for punishments and for rewards. Indeed, in the perspective of affect-control theory, there is no intrinsic difference between sanctions and other kinds of behavior: both are attempts by some actor to confirm fundamentals optimally, given the constraints of current transient feelings. Interpreting some acts as sanctions amounts to functional analysis of behavior under the assumption that punishments and rewards have socialization and rehabilitative impacts, and such a distinction is not necessary in studying the production of ordinary interaction, though it probably would be significant were affect-control theory expanded to include a model of learning.

Reidentification

As symbolic interactionists, sociological labeling theorists, and ethnomethodologists have emphasized, role creativity lies not only in organizing adaptive performances for special circumstances, but also in reorganizing definitions of the situation so that conceptions of people remain congruent with what they are doing:

The perceived purpose and meaning in the other's action are always provisional and subject to revision in the light of subsequent events in the course of interaction. Thus, what was initially seen as one role may later be seen in retrospect as having actually been a very different role, resulting in thoroughgoing reinterpretation of the actions the other was performing all along . . .
. . . It is apparent that in the interpretive view of social interaction . . . definitions of situations and actions are not explicitly or implicitly assumed to be settled once and for all by literal application of a preexisting culturally established system of symbols. Rather, the meanings of situations and actions are interpretations formulated on particular occasions by the participants in the interaction and subject to reformulation on subsequent occasions [Wilson, 1970:700-1].

These ideas fit with Orcutt's (1973) review of some classic studies on reactions to deviants in small groups, in which he distinguished between inclusive and exclusive interpersonal responses. A person's transitory deviance, if it seems limited in scope in an area of peripheral importance, ordinarily is met with interactional hostility, while others maintain a fundamentally positive orientation toward the actor – that is, sanctions are applied while the definition of the situation evidently remains stable. On the other hand, persistent, pervasive, and extreme deviance in areas of central importance to a group is met with negative shifting of fundamental attitudes toward the deviant actor and ostracism, suggesting that such a deviant is reassigned a stigmatized status.

Affect-control theory's procedure for reidentification provides a formal model for part of this reinterpretive process. When an event is recognized that lacks credibility, given the current identification of the actor, a new identity for the actor is selected – an identity that the disturbing event would confirm and that thus accounts for the disturbing event by suggesting the kind of motivation that produced it (McCall and Simmons, 1966:132; Blum and McHugh, 1971). Thereafter, expectations involving that actor are constructed using the new identity, and the actor's subsequent behavior is interpreted from the standpoint of the new identity, as posited in sociological labeling theory (Hawkins and Tiedeman, 1975). One example of the procedure already was presented in Chapter 4. In the scenario, a girl at an after-the-game party identifies a man as an athlete until his avoiding her leads her to reconsider her definition of him, asking what kind of a man would ignore a girl. The analysis suggested the following possibilities: boob, drudge, hanger-on, fuddy-duddy, egghead, glutton, scapegoat, dolt, pinhead, klutz, dumbbell, vagrant. Once the girl reidentifies the man as, say, a dolt, the character of her future action toward him shifts, becoming more negative and aggressive than it would be toward an athlete.

Affect-control theory allows one to generate concrete lists of identities that are affectively appropriate for interpreting an unexpected act. The selection of a single final identity for reidentification involves processes that go beyond the affect-control principle. For example, public reidentification of a person normally requires negotiations with the person and others in the scene to determine whether the new identification of the person will be held in common[4] (e.g., see Lofland, 1969; Emerson, 1970). Moreover, the new identity typically must fit the same social "devices" (Sacks, 1972) as the original; for example, in the girl–athlete case, the new identity must be appropriate for a male and it must refer to a character who might be found at an after-the-game party.

The cognitive constraints associated with social devices are particularly crucial in dealing with the lists of identities produced by reidentification analyses. For example, suppose that, at the same after-the-game party, the host or hostess confronts the girl and says, "You smell; why don't you go outside and let the rest of us get some air?" In this relationship, the girl might see herself as guest and, stunned by the remark, ask, "What kind of person would insult a guest?" The answers generated by analyses are jerk, fink, jackass, thief, ass, faultfinder, firebug, hypocrite, sneak, bigot, criminal, quack. Given the middle-class party setting, the underworld and deviant characters in the list (thief, firebug, criminal, quack) are eliminated. Thus we are left with reasonable answers to the reidentification question.

Or suppose that, at the same party, the girl sees a well-known prude lewdly caressed and propositioned by someone who is a stranger to the girl. The girl tries to comprehend this behavior by asking, "What kind of person would shock a prude?" The analytic answers are big-shot, ladykiller, bitch, madman, gigolo, bookie, vamp, busybody, bigamist, tease, gunman, and adulterer. Again, because of the setting, the girl can eliminate deviant and criminal characterizations – gigolo, bookie, bigamist, gunman. If the person is female, the characterizations that are mainly of male gender also can be eliminated: big-shot, ladykiller, madman, and adulterer. This leaves the reasonably plausible possibilities of bitch, vamp, and tease (plus busybody, which may be an analytic error).

In another setting, suppose events lead someone to the question "What kind of person would convince a skeptic?" Analytic answers are star, bachelor, maverick, reporter, referee, salesman, halfback, jock, whiz kid, lineman, celebrity, fan. The sports and entertainment identities can be eliminated, as they invoke a different social device than that implied by skeptic. This elimination leaves bachelor, maverick, reporter, salesman, and whiz kid, and one of these might provide a sensible answer in some circumstances. Or suppose we have the question "What kind of person would visit a call girl?" Analytic answers are practical nurse, technician, handyman, gent, heterosexual, host, housewife, wage earner, cousin, lady, brother-in-law, darling. Housewife and lady are the wrong gender for such an actor. Nurse, technician, handyman, and wage earner involve normal work-world devices that are not shared by the call girl, and so they can be eliminated. Host involves a place-anchored device that precludes visiting a call girl (unless she is at the place). Cousin and brother-in-law require a family device of extreme specificity – very few persons can be assigned these identities by a particular observer – so that these options generally might be deleted. At this point we are left with gent and heterosexual, which seem reasonable, possible answers to the reidentification question, and darling, which seems to be an error.

These examples reveal that affect-control theory provides a capability for simulating social labeling processes, once auxiliary cognitive analyses are added, which indicates that affect control is important in societal reaction to deviance. This presumption leads to observations like the following. First, labeling occurs when observers give up on the construction of new events to restore their fundamental feelings about an actor; that is, redefinitions are a last resort, and that is why people seem so reticent about indulging in them (McHugh, 1968; Emerson, 1970). Second, the character of the stimulating event – what act on which object – defines the new label to be assigned, and this is probably why negotiations about labeling (as in courts of law) so often focus on an examination and careful definition of the instigating event itself. Third, unexpected behavior, rather than negative, immoral behavior, is the condition for labeling, and so instances of "improper" behavior that are expected (e.g., a cop harming a criminal) do not typically lead to redefinitions of the actor's identity. Fourth, recovery from deviant labeling requires relabeling with a positive identity, which would require engaging in behavior thoroughly unexpected for a deviant (e.g., protecting a lawman). However, such extreme acts will not typically lead to reidentification with ordinary identities: in social reaction, the escape from deviance has to be to the opposite extreme of unusual virtue and character.

Positive labeling.   Sociological labeling theory has focused on the acquisition of negative statuses through deviant actions, but affect-control theory provides a more general model of status assignment. For example, the question "Who would silence a bully?" leads to predicted status assignments that specify sanctioner roles: disciplinarian, warden, plainclothesman, sleuth, and nark (the specifications also include henchman, he-man, and dike, which seem possible in some situations; and landlord, stepfather, flagellant, and probationer, which may involve the wrong social devices or else may be misspecifications). The question "What kind of person would help a beginner?" yields positive identities: pal, buddy, companion, mate; mother, my mother, my father; minister, Christian; medic, nurse, surgeon (answers here are grouped roughly by underlying social devices). So, too, does the question "What kind of person would save a child?": friend, lover, husband, parent, doctor, God (the only identities close to the ideal profile).

These specifications suggest that a pal, buddy, chum, or companion might help a beginner, and thus such an event might mark the beginning of a companionate relationship. Friend and lover are among the generated identities for someone who would save a child, and so this event, or a similar one, might initiate an intimate attachment of the observer to the actor. Kemper (1972) provided a detailed development of the idea that intimate relationships form from assignments of status to another. Affect-control theory adds the idea that such an attribution of positive status might occur as a reidentification process. This idea in turn leads to the hypothesis that the initiating event in a romance must be one that is originally unexpected.

In the framework of affect-control theory, the labeling process is a general mechanism by which individuals informally achieve new identities, good or bad, when they perform in unexpected ways. Affect-control theory provides a model defining the general character of the new identity – its *EPA* profile – in terms of the character of the performance leading to the reidentification, and the same model applies to both stigmatization and achievement.[5]

Adequacy of the model. Because identities have to be dropped subjectively from lists when they involve the wrong social device, an element of arbitrariness enters analyses of reidentification; therefore, it is sometimes difficult to tell exactly how reasonable the simulations of labeling processes are.

In all, twenty reidentification analyses were run in preparation for this monograph; probably between 50 and 80 percent of these can be counted as minimally successful in providing some plausible reidentification options. The analyses that have not been discussed up to now in this chapter are presented below in summary form, so that readers can judge for themselves (generated options are listed by their fit to the ideal profile, without grouping by social devices).

> *Harass newcomer:* blabbermouth, vandal, gossip, shoplifter, troublemaker, criminal, pest, psychopath, adulteress, thief, crook, liar
>
> *Bully subordinate:* firebug, jackass, bigot, fink, thief, jerk, criminal, liar, gossip, scoundrel, lunatic, sorehead
>
> *Eye sexpot:* floorwalker, sleuth, hillbilly, nark, sophisticate, courtesan, stepmother, stepfather, roomer, stepsister, look-out, stepbrother
>
> *Seduce virgin:* handyman, practical nurse, heterosexual, technician, gent, host, cousin, housewife, lady, wage-earner, worker, I (myself as I really am)

Overdose patient: shyster, felon, culprit, secondstory man, pimp, paranoid, evildoer, bigot, gun moll, pusher, sorehead, bigamist

Abandon buddy: sponger, phony, acid head, copycat, traitor, addict, drunk, stool pigeon, snoop, degenerate, drug addict, quack

Release captive: academic, virgin, connoisseur, uncle, relation, client, accountant, genius, nursemaid, eyewitness, guest, bailsman

Silence bigot: he-man, dike, henchman, nark, sleuth, plainclothesman, warden, landlord, disciplinarian, stepfather, flagellant, highwayman

Attack homosexual: outlaw, devil, roughneck, gunman, desperado, gangster (all other identities have very poor fit to the ideal profile)

Defy authority: fanatic, satyr, gold digger, vixen, ruffian, sharpie, rival, bookie, stripper, playboy, daredevil, desperado

Visit prostitute: half-brother, cashier, co-worker, bellboy, headwaiter, brother-in-law, sister-in-law, cousin, prodigy, lad, waitress, bartender

Ignore girl: stool pigeon, drug addict, spoilsport, lout, snoop, turncoat, degenerate, louse, souse, ass, heel, hypocrite

Granting the limitations, it nevertheless has been demonstrated that affect-control theory provides a framework for understanding underlying affective dynamics in reinterpretation processes, that it correctly selects identities that might be assigned following various deviant acts, and that it provides a model for status achievement as well as stigmatization.

Relations to other role research

Dimensional systems

Dimensional systems for classifying social acts and social relationships from behavior observations or questionnaire data have been developed repeatedly (see reviews by Borgatta and Crowther, 1965; Kemper, 1972 and 1978; Benjamin, 1974; Triandis, 1977). While the empirical work is largely descriptive, aimed at reducing the complexity of social interaction to comprehensible proportions, some of the work has been linked to dynamic hypotheses, providing theoretical models that can be used in role research.

Benjamin (1974) classified a range of parent and child behaviors in two dimensions – affiliation and interdependence – each on two planes, one representing an active concern-with-the-other domain (parentlike behavior) and the other representing the domain of reactive concern with the self (childlike behavior). The behaviors typically are concrete (like "greet warmly," "criticize," "imitate," "temper tantrum"), and various empirical studies are described, indicating that the theoretical positioning of the behaviors on circles in each two-dimensional plane relates to the behaviors' judged similarities and their frequencies of cooccurrence. Benjamin's theoretical additions to this descriptive system focus on issues in socialization, child development, and the origins of neurotic behavior. The most intriguing hypotheses from the standpoint of role analysis are the principles of complements and antidotes. According to the principle of complementarity, if a person commits behavior at a point on one plane, an interaction partner should be inclined to produce behaviors at the corresponding point on the other plane. The principle of antidotes is an extension of the same idea: to eliminate an unwanted behavior (e.g., "defy, suspect"), find its complement ("bluff, illogic"), and engage in acts that are spatially opposite to that point ("reasoned persuasion"), theoretically evoking the complementary behavior ("comply willingly") that is the opposite of the original unwanted behavior.

Bales (1970) presented a classification of individual character types based on factor analyses of data from questionnaires, observations of interaction, and peer ratings. The system has an underlying three-dimensional structure, which, as Bales notes (p. 57), can be rotated to correspond to evaluation, potency, and activity. Bales's dynamic principles seem to include the following ideas. A person has a fairly stable character that disposes him or her to engage in characteristic behaviors and therefore to drift into relationships that encourage such behavior. When a group of people come together, the composition of the group in terms of their varying characters is crucial in determining how they will relate to one another and therefore what kind of informal role structure will emerge.

Triandis (1964 and 1971:51– 4) developed a "behavioral differential" to study dimensions of variation in relationships. In this technique, events involving a specific actor, act, and object are presented as stimuli to obtain likelihood ratings for multivariate analysis. Factor analyses have revealed several clusters of acts: respect (admire ideas of, ask for opinions of), marital (marry, fall in love with, make love to), friendship (be partners in athletic game with, eat with, gossip with), social distance (exclude from my neighborhood, prohibit from voting), and super-ordination (treat as a subordinate, command, criticize work of); and cross-cultural studies suggest that these or similar clusters may not be entirely culture-specific (see Triandis, 1972). His "role differential" is essentially the same device but focuses on actors and objects with explicit role identities and asks for normative judgments ("should or should not") rather than likelihood judgments ("would or would not"); factor analyses of the role-differential data yield roughly the same clusters.[6] Triandis combined his findings about behaviors and roles with ideas from cognitive-consistency theory to arrive at the following hypotheses: "Any role pair can be defined by a set of coordinates on behavior factors"; "Any interpersonal behavior can be defined by a set of coordinates on behavior factors"; and "The distance between a role pair, defined as a point in the behavior factor space, and any behavior, defined also as a point in the behavior factor space, is inversely propor-tional to the judged appropriateness of the behavior taking place between persons occupying that role" (Triandis, 1972:267, italics removed). The first two propositions are essentially empirically induced, and some empirical support is reported for the third proposition.

Affect-control theory employs ideas in common with these other dimensional systems. Sentiment restoration relates in some ways to Benjamin's notion of antidotes. The discussion of structures emerging from individual processes is not too unlike Bales's approach to group structure. Acts are selected according to distances in *EPA* space, employing the principle specified by Triandis. Moreover, Benjamin, Bales, and Triandis all have commented on possible relationships be-tween their dimensions and the *EPA* dimensions that are the framework of the theory presented here. At the same time, affect-control theory goes significantly beyond earlier formulations. It shows that the *EPA* dimensions apply not just to attitudes and sentiments but also to be-havior expectations, to interaction processes, and to the behavioral structure of roles. It shows that the relationships between these dif-ferent domains can be specified mathematically, by equations with estimated parameters. It shows that the principle of affect control is the unifying condition allowing results in one domain to be translated into theoretical principles specifying process in another. And affect-control theory permits concrete simulations of innumerable role relationships under diverse circumstances.

Inventorial systems

Affect-control theory and some of the other dimensional systems for analyzing interaction just mentioned are generative in their presumption that complex, but general, psychological processes determine behaviors at a given time. Thus roles theoretically can be defined by their dimensional profiles, as such information theoretically is sufficient to unfold characteristic behaviors in any circumstances of interest. In contrast, a great deal of the literature on normative behavior has developed within an inventorial framework, in which a role is defined as the set of behavior expectations associated with a status, and a particular role would be specified by cataloging the expected behaviors in various conditions. This conception is a key element in the statement of major theories of social organization by sociologists (Parsons, 1951) and social anthropologists (Nadel, 1964; Harris, 1964; Goodenough, 1969); the perspective dominates scholarly reviews of the status-role literature (Gross, Mason, and McEachern, 1958; Biddle and Thomas, 1966; Sarbin and Allen, 1968); and the orientation has been influential in research on interaction stress (Gross, Mason, and McEachern, 1958), socialization (Heise and Roberts, 1970), sex identification (e.g., Hartley, 1966), marriage (e.g., Herbst, 1952; Blood and Wolfe, 1960), delinquency (Cloward and Ohlin, 1960), and other substantive topics.

Attempts to operationalize roles literally as sets of expected behaviors reveal problems with the approach as it was conceived in some quarters. For example, Biddle and Thomas (1966:chap. 2) explored the sets approach using person–behavior matrices – tables in which each person in a community is assigned a row and each conceivable act is represented by a column. If the cells of such a table were filled with data on the likelihood of a given act by a particular person, then collecting rows for persons with a given status presumably would reveal the communalities in their actions, thereby providing an operational definition of the set of behaviors corresponding to the status. However, a social act is a specific behavior directed at a particular object in defined circumstances; so the number of columns in the matrix is roughly the number of possible behaviors times the number of possible objects times the number of distinct circumstances. Even in a small, homogeneous community, this unfolding would lead to a monumental catalog of social acts. Cancian (1975:41) reports that the lexicon of one traditional community in Mexico consists of about 16,000 words.

Supposing that 10,000 of these refer to kinds of persons or things, 5,000 refer to acts, and 1,000 refer to place-time settings, then the product just suggested yields an estimate of 2.5×10^{14} distinctive acts. There are well over 450,000 words in English (Gove, 1971), and any realistic partitioning of this number into parts corresponding to labels for behaviors, objects, and circumstances yields figures whose product is immense. Some research operationalized the "sets" notion of role by sampling social actions. For example, Gross, Mason, and McEachern (1958) used their good judgment to define a sample of behaviors that would be relevant to the school superintendent role. Heise and Roberts (1970) conceptualized blocks of family-related behaviors, sampled blocks randomly, and constructed a specific behavior to represent each selected block. Whatever the benefits obtained from these studies, judgmentally selecting a few acts to represent an immense number of possibilities does not represent an operational procedure solving the definitional problem inherent in the "sets" approach to roles – that is, that the universe of actor-behavior-object combinations is essentially unbounded, and sets within the universe are hardly specifiable.

If a role were the set of behavioral prescriptions associated with a status, then learning the role would require learning the contents of this set. This view of role learning has sometimes been quite explicit, as in this statement by Hartley (1966:354): "The function of these [learning] processes would be to specify the appropriate behaviors out of a matrix of all possible behaviors, to stabilize the appearance of these behaviors, and to inhibit the appearance of inappropriate behaviors." Indeed, Hartley's statement implies that role learning requires learning all of the cell contents in one row of a "status-behavior matrix," as one must know not only the prescribed behaviors but also which acts are inappropriate. However, even if persons learned one cell of a culture's status-behavior matrix each second of their lives, from birth to seventy-five years of age, then each person would learn only about 2.33 billion (American billion) associations. Large as that figure seems, it is small compared to the size of a behavior matrix and it would not even be enough to master the complete contents of one role. Generalization processes, as posited in Learning Theory, might increase the speed and efficiency of social learning, but one empirical study that explicitly tested for generalization processes in role learning found none. Heise and Roberts (1970) partitioned sixteen common roles into similarity groupings, using nonmetric scaling procedures (the major dimensions distinguishing the roles were sex and authority). They then found that children's knowledge scores for similar roles correlated no more than their scores for dissimilar roles, which is contrary to what one would expect if generalization processes were operative.

Moreover, studies of behavior norms reveal that much of the variance in behavior acceptability depends on interactions among the components of action. Price and Bouffard (1974) obtained appropriateness ratings of fifteen behaviors in fifty-one different situations. Interactions between behaviors and situations accounted for 45.7 percent of the variance in ratings. Raush, Farbman, and Llewellyn (1960) observed children's behavior in a variety of situations: The likelihood of a behavior could not be predicted solely from identification of the behavior, the situation, or the child but depended also on interactions among the three. The existence of such interactions means that knowledge about characteristic behavior for an actor and a situation cannot simply be generalized to predict accurately the suitability of a behavior for a given actor-situation combination (Endler and Magnusson, 1976). Accordingly, ordinary generalization is not sufficient to explain how persons might learn the acceptability of specific behaviors with nearly endless combinations of actors, objects, and situations.

Research involving the original sets-of-expectations approach to roles peaked before the 1970s. However, an inventorial orientation for analyzing normative behavior recognizably continues in the ideas of fixed action patterns in ethology (e.g., McGrew, 1972; Hinde, 1972; von Cranach and Vine, 1973) and the frames or scripts employed in work on artificial intelligence (e.g., Minsky, 1975; Goldstein and Papert, 1977; Schank and Abelson, 1977). These current inventorial approaches avoid some of the problems of the "sets" approach by proposing, in essence, that social events (and knowledge about them) are so highly structured that the vast majority of actor-act-object combinations are intrinsically meaningless, irrelevant, and never even considered. Behavior occurs within "frameworks" (Goffman, 1974; Minsky, 1975) – settings, scenes, situations – and particular types of actors, objects, and behaviors are sensible only within certain frameworks. For example, it would be culturally bizarre for a judge to be in a surgical operating room (except transformed into a patient) or for suturing to happen in a courtroom; thus one need never bother with the question whether a judge should suture a patient. By recognizing that many roles are confined to certain settings, and many behaviors are confined to certain roles, the combinatorial possibilities for specifying prescribed and proscribed events are reduced to the point that inventorial definitions of roles seem feasible in principle; for example, "What it means specifically to be a waitress would be given in detail in the Conceptual Dependency representation of the RESTAURANT script by collecting all the conceptualizations in which the waitress had a part" (Schank and Abelson, 1977:153). Also, if socialization is simply a matter of learning scripted behavior within a series of specific settings, then one can imagine that a child could acquire the detailed information about norms needed to operate as a socialized adult (Schank and Abelson, 1977:68).

The new inventorial approaches, like the traditional ones, are compatible with functionalist explanations of how individual behavior comes to serve social requirements: Through conscious design or evolutionary process, specific role activities become organized instrumentally to achieve certain effects and are then included in role repertories. Moreover, the contemporary work in artificial intelligence provides a compelling explanation of how people are able to comprehend events even when they discern only scattered clues about what is happening: The formulations (e.g., Minsky, 1975; Schank and Abelson, 1977) propose that the clues recall a remembered knowledge frame that provides default assumptions about unexplicit conditions and further happenings, so that one can operate as if much more had been discerned.

Contemporary inventorial approaches to the analysis of interaction and affect-control theory's generative approach are complementary rather than competitive. Human behavior is structured and interpretable from two different perspectives: the naturalistic domain of space, motion, cause, and effect; and the subjective domain of motives, purposes, and reasons.

Guided doings appear, then, to allow for two kinds of understanding. One, more or less common to all doings, pertains to the patent manipulation of the natural world in accordance with the special constraints that natural occurrings impose; the other understanding pertains to the special worlds in which the actor can become involved [Goffman, 1974:23].

It seems fairly clear that we have two groups or families of concepts with which to explain human action. On the one hand, there is a family whose principal concept is *cause;* and on the other is the family of reason, purpose, intention, and, to some extent, motive. This demarcation of the two families of concepts correlates with that between human actions and mere behavior [Wilks, 1977:237].

Contemporary inventorial approaches provide detailed analyses of the natural constraints on and requirements for social action and demonstrate how people's knowledge of physical conditions and cause-effect relations are used to disambiguate and interpret discerned events. The focus is on "behavioral physics" and people's lay knowledge of that topic. Affect-control theory, on the other hand, merely alludes to logical-physical constraints on action and focuses on how social interpretations of situations lead to intentions for new events, expectations for others, and motivational interpretations of completed events – on subjectivity in actions. A complete model of behavior would link these two perspectives together, and indeed Schank and Abelson (1977) began to work in this direction, recognizing that "an action is often not completely described solely by its Conceptual Dependency representation" (p. 130). Their exploratory work on the subjective aspect used a three-dimensional scheme similar to *EPA* for characterizing relationships (p. 142) and used "expectancy rules" (rather than the formulas in affect-control theory) for specifying roughly how affective conditions influence behavior (pp. 122, 144).

Contemporary inventorial approaches, with their focus on behavioral physics, apply most naturally to habitual social interactions (including complex forms like having dinner at a restaurant – see Schank and Abelson, 1977), whereas affect-control theory applies mainly to non-habitual interactions requiring a measure of creativity. This division of focus is clear in the context of Triandis's (1977) theory of behavior, which posits that the likelihood of a behavior is a function of an intention component plus a habit component, the sum multiplied by a factor representing facilitating conditions. Triandis pointed out that institutionalized, routinized acts have a significant habit component, so that an analysis of intentions may be largely irrelevant in explaining such acts (pp. 205-6). Thus, taking the habit for granted, the facilitating conditions are all that is available to explain why the acts do or do not occur, and these are exactly the matters that are the focus of the behavioral physics, inventorial approach. On the other hand, Triandis suggested that "when a behavior is new, untried, and unlearned, the behavioral-intention component will be solely responsible for the behavior" (p. 205). Then understanding the behavior requires explaining the formation of the intention – the central focus of affect-control theory. Of course, facilitating conditions are a factor in new, untried behaviors, too, but knowledge of the subjective factors involved in forming intentions is the relevant and useful information when account-ing for nonhabitual human acts (Wilks, 1977).

Actually, affect-control theory does generate specifications of even some routinized role behaviors (such as judges sentencing thieves or doctors medicating patients), which seems curious if only habits and facilitating conditions are supposed to contribute to the prediction of routine acts. However, there is a possible explanation. By design or evolution, in order to achieve certain definite consequences regularly, particular interaction sequences are routinized in a role relationship, becoming standard events that characterize the relationship. As salient beliefs about the roles (Fishbein and Ajzen, 1975), they cause adjust-ments in the fundamental sentiments for role identities and for special-ized behaviors, so that these sentiments conform to the standard events. The standard events cause the formation of sentiments that could gen-erate those events. Thereafter, persons might learn the sentiments alone (rather than specific prescriptions for behavior) and still generate the standard events. Moreover, analyses in affect-control theory also should be able to generate the standard events, to the extent that the theory simulates the subjective operations of people who have learned the sentiments.

This idea – that standard events cause the formation of sentiments that regenerate these events – helps in understanding how *EPA* profiles code so much sociological information: the standard events are the orig-inal sources of the sentiments that regenerate those events. Of course, once the sentiments have been set, they also serve to generate nonstan-dard events in special circumstances: people construct novel events in new circumstances to confirm the meanings of identities and acts that are given by standardized exemplar sequences. This idea is an elaboration of Imershein's (1976:32–3) proposals for expanding the theory of paradigms to social knowledge in general: "The ordering of what partic-ipants are to do in a given setting (the patterning of their concerted ac-tivity) is provided by their joint reliance upon common examples of such activity . . . Participants . . . rely on central examples from their past experience to guide their present conduct" (see also Albert, 1977).

Role functions

Affect-control theory has both strengths and weaknesses in studying the social functionality of behavior. At the individual level the theory has the benefit of reinforcing the arguments of Spiro (1961) and Wallace (1970) that people act from personal motivations, and rarely is knowledge of the social significance of their acts a significant consideration in action. Of course, people do plan and then act on those plans, and so some of their behavior is functional at the individual level in the sense of being instrumental in the realization of other intended events. However, broad social needs are fulfilled mainly because the meanings that people maintain seem to have developed culturally in just such a way that their maintenance does create socially functional events. A mother constructing events to maintain the meanings of her identity, of her baby's identity, and of the acts that are chosen behaves nurturingly because the meanings are culturally organized exactly so that their confirmation produces nurturance events; a judge constructing events that confirm the meanings of judge and thief identities behaves as a sanctioning agent because these meanings are culturally organized in such a way that confirming them creates sanctioning events. Thus people naturally do perform socially functional actions as they go about confirming meanings, but the social functions are essentially unrelated to the construction process itself, arising instead out of the cultural organization of the meanings. The simulations that have been presented demonstrated the adequacy of this perspective. By assuming that events are constructed to confirm meanings, it has been possible to specify the concrete instrumental actions serving role functions – the acts that are required for a doctor to help patients cope with illness, for a minister to proselytize, for a waiter to facilitate dining, for judges and police to control crime.

On the other hand, the nature of the code that achieves these results is enigmatic within the confines of affect-control theory. For example, one might suppose that identities and acts serving different functions are located in different regions of the *EPA* three-dimensional space. Table 5.11 shows the identities that are highest and lowest in evaluation in regions defined by different combinations of potency and activity (*EPA* values are based on assumed-interval metric, whereas the Appendix values are based on a derived metric described in Heise, 1978). Among the positive identities, there are some clusters that perhaps can be interpreted in terms of the functionalist system proposed by Parsons, Bales, and Shils (1953).[7] Some of the identities listed at the top right of the table might be viewed as relating mainly to pattern maintenance; some of those at the top middle perhaps are related to adaptation; and

Table 5.11. *Potency–activity classification of social identities*

Potency	Activity			
	Very quiet	Quiet	Lively	Very lively

A. Identities evaluated positively, or identities in a given classification with highest evaluations

Potency	Very quiet	Quiet	Lively	Very lively
Very powerful		grandfather, father-in-law, judge, juror, alumnus, professor	doctor, surgeon, gentleman, specialist, teacher, practical nurse, tutor, counselor, instructor, lady, handyman	lover, friend, truelove, mother, buddy, sweetheart, father, parent, husband, brother, mate, son
Powerful		grandmother, grandparent, night watchman, auntie	technician, dietitian, scholar, mailman, wage earner, aunt	sister, playmate, baby sitter, housewife, hostess, youth, darling, clown, grandson, granddaughter
Powerless	oldtimer, granny, bookworm	old maid, underdog, cripple, widower, janitor, widow, lodger, saleslady, doorkeeper, doorman, straight	doll, maid, innocent, newcomer, moppet,[b] sidekick, typist, chambermaid, bellman, servant, consumer, applicant, niece	girl, grandchild, child, kid, lass, nymph,[a] salesgirl, girl scout, daughter, boy,[a] youngster
Very powerless	invalid	homebody, slave,[b] patient, mark	gamin, orphan, yokel, waif	baby, libertine,[a] tot, infant

B. Identities evaluated negatively, or identities in a given classification with lowest evaluations

Potency	Very quiet	Quiet	Lively	Very lively
Very powerful		sodomite,[b] warden, disciplinarian	mafioso, vampire, witch, henchman, slavedriver	mobster, gangster, rival, brute, vigilante
Powerful	ogre,[a] ghoul	killjoy, convict	tough, loan shark, thief,[b] housebreaker, fiend, burglar, culprit	bully,[a] villian, cutthroat, hood, devil, bandit,[a] roughneck, racketeer, outlaw, vixen,[b] pimp[a]
Powerless	miser,[b] grouch,[b] wretch,[b] scrooge, sorehead,[b] boor, stuffed shirt, zombie	snot, snob, sodomite,[a] safecracker, thug, goon, clod, crab, inmate, crank, grind, tightwad, prig	pusher, evildoer, assassin, sorehead,[a] psychopath, paranoid,[a] guttersnipe, rat, bigamist, rogue, gun moll	mugger, crook, hoodlum,[b] hothead, busybody, fugitive, bully,[b] pest, troublemaker, brat, vandal, maniac, bandit[b]

Table 5.11 (*cont.*)

	Activity			
Potency	Very quiet	Quiet	Lively	Very lively
Very powerless	junkie,[a] acidhead, lecher, do-nothing, hag, sluggard, slob	junkie,[b] snoop, hypocrite, ass, spoilsport, quack, drug addict, degenerate, drunkard, copycat, sponger, addict, drunk, phony	liar, thief,[a] crim-inal, gossip, fink, shoplifter, scoun-drel, faultfinder, sneak, slut, jackass, cad, lunatic, braggart, paranoid[b]	smart aleck, peep-ing tom, blabber-mouth, gambler, imp, runaway, rascal,[a] scatterbrain

Note: Most identities are located on the basis of *EPA* profiles that represent the mean ratings of both males and females who are moderates on a liberalism–conservatism scale. However, male (*a*) and female (*b*) locations are assigned separately when their profiles are significantly different, $p < .01$.

some of the positive roles on the right side of the table might be asso-ciated with goal attainment and integration. However, not all of the roles in a given region are particularly related to the function served by other roles in the region; for example, it is not clear how the roles of gentleman and lady relate functionally to other roles in their region, like doctor, specialist, teacher, and handyman. Additionally, only a limited number of the positive regions of the space can be identified with specific functions – at least when using just the Parsons, Bales, and Shils (1953) scheme. Roles in the "powerless" regions, in particular, seem resistant to functional classification – for example, oldtimer, granny, and bookworm in one region; gamin, orphan, yokel, and waif in another region. Moreover, classifying all of the roles in even a rela-tively limited region of the space as similar in function does not explain why roles in the same region involve different actions. Small variations in spatial location carry important information about role performances, and functional classification of whole regions is too crude to capture this variation.

Turning to the negatively evaluated roles (part B of Table 5.11), one can see some correspondence between region and dysfunction.[8] For example, using the system derived by Merton (1957: chap. 4), it is pos-sible to characterize some of the roles at the upper left as ritualist and some roles in the lower left corner as retreatist; some roles at the upper right are innovative in Merton's sense; and some at the lower right might be viewed as rebellious. The classification of negatively evaluated roles by dysfunction seems more satisfactory than the functional classification of positive roles, in that it more adequately covers all regions. However, here, too, we have the problems of roles relating to different dysfunctions occurring in the same region, and of a classification system too crude to capture all the information that actually exists in the *EPA* measurements.

Perhaps roles have to be separated by institutional areas before the functional significance of their locations in the *EPA* space becomes evident. Figure 1 presents some materials that allow this idea to be examined, showing plots on potency and activity axes for the following groups of identities:

> *Law and courtroom:* accused, attorney, bailiff, bailsman, defendant, district attorney, felon, judge, lawyer, prosecuting attorney
>
> *Medicine and hospital:* anesthetist, doctor, intern, medic, nurse, outpatient, patient, physician, practical nurse, psychiatrist, surgeon
>
> *Nuclear family:* brother, daughter, father, husband, mother, parent, sibling, sister, son, spouse, wife
>
> *Service establishments:* barkeeper, barmaid, bartender, busboy, cashier, chef, cook, customer, diner, doorman, headwaiter, saloon-keeper, waiter, waitress

The roles in a cluster are connected by lines simply to aid visual interpretation. Dotted lines have been used to suggest the relative location of the clusters on the evaluation dimension: The family roles are most positive, the medicine and service roles are next, and the law roles are least positive.

The horizontal ordering of sets again seems related to the distinction between adaptive and pattern-maintenance functions on the left and goal-attainment and integrative functions on the right,[9] and, moreover, an examination of separate identities reveals that this same distinction tends to hold within sets, as suggested in Parsons's theory (e.g., judge and juror are on the left of the law set, whereas attorney is on the right). Within institutions, the potency dimension relates to the relative power of roles. The same thing seems true in the comparison of occupational sets: Law and medicine roles overall are more powerful than service roles, though it might strike some as odd that roles in the family are as "powerful" as those in law and medicine, which is what the graph shows.

Here again traditional functional interpretations are somewhat applicable, but they do not seem specific enough to add much to our understanding of how *EPA* location codes social information (though functional analyses might yet be important in understanding how roles come to a given *EPA* location). What is most important in Figure 1 is that it indicates that institutions – at least the ones graphed – are rather clearly defined and separated from one another in the *EPA* space. This fact no doubt is crucial in the acceptability of our analyses, which are carried out with coherent sets of identities from institutional sets.

The functional appropriateness of events generated using affect-control theory derives from the *EPA* profiles for both identities and acts. Perhaps more understanding of the underlying code can be obtained by examining the distributions of acts in *EPA* space. Table 5.12 shows acts that are highest and lowest in evaluation, again in sectors of the *EPA* space defined by a joint partitioning on potency and activity (mea-

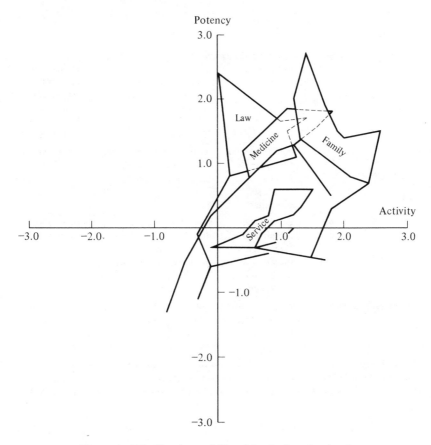

Figure 1. Distributions of identities in four institutions.

Table 5.12. *Potency-activity classification of interpersonal acts*

Potency	Activity			
	Very quite	Quiet	Lively	Very lively

A. Acts evaluated positively, or acts in a given classification with highest evaluations

Potency	Very quite	Quiet	Lively	Very lively
Very powerful		calm, miss	forgive, heal, understand, thank, console, rehabilitate, appreciate, comfort, compliment, please, trust	love, rescue, save, cure, delight, laugh with, enjoy, aid, praise, welcome, caress
Powerful	lull[a]	contemplate, quiet, psychoanalyze, placate,[b] pacify, suckle, coddle	feed, join, bathe, undress,[a] remind, need, notice, stroke, admire, dress	toast, amuse, seduce,[a] acclaim, treat, pet
Powerless			emulate, indulge, criticize	
Very powerless				

B. Acts evaluated negatively, or acts in a given classification with lowest evaluations

Potency	Very quite	Quiet	Lively	Very lively
Very powerful		oppress, sentence, lure	murder,[b] slay, manipulate,[a] entrap, repulse,[a] dominate, vanquish, enslave	club, annihilate,[b] stab,[a] attack, sock, punch, seize, hit, force, ram, flagellate
Powerful	fetter	constrain, confine, placate,[a] stymie, flunk, overdose,[a] disenchant	mutilate, rob,[a] strangle, kill, corrupt, disable,[a] kick, injure, destroy	choke, endanger, flog, threaten, ostracize, belt, con, strike
Powerless	poison,[a] execute[a]	deceive, demoralize, use,[a] forget, ignore, loathe, mislead, hinder, undermine, deprave	mug, harm, abuse, doublecross, blackmail, hurt, assault, mace, terrorize, poison[b]	rape, stab,[b] torment, shoot
Very powerless	idolize[a]	use,[b] overdose,[b] betray, disgrace, torture	spit on, disable,[b] maim, murder,[a] humiliate, rob[b]	pester, bully

Note: Most acts are located on the basis of *EPA* profiles that represent the mean ratings of both males and females who are moderates on a liberalism–conservatism scale. However, locations for males (*a*) and females (*b*) are assigned separately when their profiles are significantly different, $p < .01$.

surements being on assumed-interval metric, rather than the Appendix values). The table makes it strikingly evident that most good acts are highly concentrated on potency and activity: There are practically no good acts that can be characterized as powerless or as very slow and quiet. The reasons for this are not clear, but at least two immediate implications can be noted. First, good, powerless roles are constricted in the interpersonal acts available to them; perhaps this is why they have eluded functional analysis. Second, functional distinctions among good, powerful roles must be represented by fine differences on the *EPA* dimensions, reducing hopes that classification by general regions might capture the information stored in the *EPA* measurements.

In fact, the spatial locations of acts seem poorly related to the societal functions they might serve. For example, tension management acts that might be related to the integrative function occur in perhaps six different cells (e.g., calm, comfort, praise, amuse, admire, pacify). Similarly, on the negative side, acts related to general dysfunctions seem to be widespread. For example, acts that might be used in rebellion – perhaps vanquish, con, humiliate, betray, demoralize, doublecross, corrupt, stymie – are scattered throughout the negative regions. Violence also is widespread: torture, maim, shoot, flog, club, slay, mutilate, and mug occur in as many different regions. Thus localization in the *EPA* space by general function is less evident in the case of acts than it was in the case of identities.[10]

Could it be that acts effecting a particular consequence are scattered throughout the *EPA* space so that they are available to any role whatsoever, albeit with a different label and a different connotation? Examining this issue requires classifying acts in terms of their consequences – a problem with a literature of its own (e.g., Harris, 1964; Schank, 1973). To simplify matters, we will deal with just three types of instrumental behaviors that can be defined relatively easily in terms of interpersonal consequences: acts that induce a joint interpersonal setting; acts that actually establish a joint interpersonal setting; and acts that terminate a joint interpersonal setting. The acts from the catalog that roughly fit these classifications are shown in Figure 2. The behaviors included in each classification are as follows:

> *Enabling behaviors:* approach, entrap, follow, invite, lure, summon
> *Establishing behaviors:* capture, catch, engage, face, halt, join, nab, rescue, seize, visit, welcome
> *Terminating behaviors:* abandon, desert, escape, flee, forsake, leave

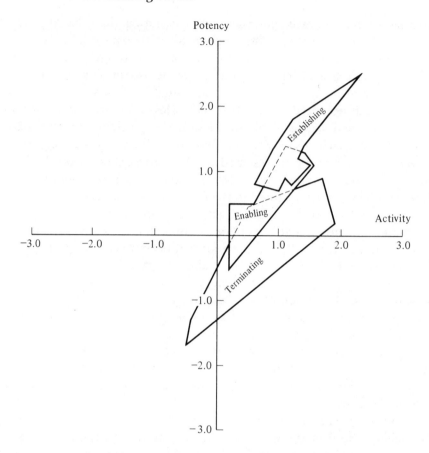

Figure 2. Distributions of behaviors that enable an interaction, establish an interaction, and terminate an interaction.

Although the acts serving each specific function have a considerable spread in the *EPA* space, it is notable that these three functional groups have practically no overlap, at least when the evaluation dimension also is taken into account. Acts establishing a joint setting are seen as stronger than acts terminating a joint setting, and acts establishing a joint setting also tend to be seen as more positive in evaluation. Acts by which a person attempts to create a joint setting tend to fall in between. Thus it is not the case that behaviors serving a specific function are distributed throughout the *EPA* space – the *EPA* coordinates of an act do provide some definite information concerning its function.

In summary, affect-control theory generates functionally appropriate events because institutions and acts effecting specific consequences are regionalized in the *EPA* space. However, the basis of such regionalization can be only loosely interpreted in traditional functionalist terms, and a more illuminating perspective is not yet evident.

Role structures

Persons in a particular status have a characteristic pattern of relationships with others. In the structuralist perspective (e.g., see Levi-Strauss, 1963; Nadel, 1964; Boorman and White, 1976), such patterns of relationships become the criteria for defining statuses. For example, position in a group might be specified according to members' patterns of association, the patterns by which they distribute esteem and dislike, and their patterns of subordination and superordination. This specification is almost opposite to the affect-control theory approach, where statuses (i.e., identities) are taken as elemental units generating interpersonal events, including those that can be characterized as indications of sentiment ("*A* likes *B*"; "*B* dislikes *A*") or of another relationship ("*A* dominates *B*"). That is, if we know persons' identities, then affect-control theory should allow us to compile the distribution of relational acts across all dyads in a group, thus theoretically generating the network containing the patterns of interest to structuralists.

The principles of such an analysis can be illustrated by considering the sentiment behaviors "like" and "dislike" applied among the courtroom characters judge, attorney, prosecutor (the composite of district attorney and prosecuting attorney), defendant, and thief. Each dyad, *A–B*, is set up as a separate situation, forcing the events "*A* likes *B*," "*B* likes *A*," "*A* dislikes *B*," "*B* dislikes *B*," in order to record the total deflection produced by each (transients are set equal to fundamentals before each event). Then each total deflection is converted into a likelihood estimate for the corresponding event, using a variation of equation (12) from Chapter 3: $L = .864 - .131D$. Likelihood estimates less than zero indicate events that theoretically would cause reidentifications; here such negative values are set equal to zero. The results of these procedures are presented in Table 5.13.

The figures in Table 5.13 represent theoretical estimates of the average likelihood that would be attributed to the various events by informants. For example, if we asked informants, "How likely is it that one

Table 5.13. *Generated likelihoods of courtroom characters liking (L) and disliking (D) one another*

"Respondent"	Object of sentiment									
	Judge		Attorney		Prosecutor		Defendant		Thief	
	L	D	L	D	L	D	L	D	L	D
Judge	.51	.43	.55	.38	.59	.44	.38	.41	0^a	.32
Attorney	.73	.45	.74	.37	.76	.42	.61	.45	0^a	.37
Prosecutor	.69	.57	.68	.49	.72	.54	.60	.58	0^a	.47
Defendant	.19	.67	.24	.65	.30	.70	.24	.78	0^a	.72
Thief	0^a	.48	0^a	.46	0^a	.49	0^a	.62	0^a	.52

^{a}Computed likelihood is negative.

judge likes another?" we theoretically expect[11] to get the average likelihood rating of .51. If we ask a different set of informants, "How likely is it that one judge dislikes another?" we expect to get the mean rating, .43. The two numbers do not add to 1.0, presumably because we have not explicitly or implicitly imposed the logical constraint that liking implies not disliking and vice versa. Actually, informants asked who likes whom usually are presented with explicit constraints, and they probably understand that still other constraints are implicit. For instance, a typical kind of data-gathering question would be "Which one kind of person do judges like?" The question implies directly that the respondent is to make a comparison across object persons, and perhaps it implies indirectly that consideration is to be given to the preponderance of tendencies to like over tendencies to dislike. Thus the theoretical prediction of the choice might be based on the relative ranks of the differences, likelihood of liking minus likelihood of disliking, yielding attorney as the object person with the largest positive value.

Using this kind of logic and supposing that the specific directives are "Name up to two people that an *A* most likes" and "Name up to two people that an *A* most dislikes," we come up with the following as the predicted "sociometric matrix" for the five courtroom characters:

	A	P	J	D	T
A	1	1	0	0	-1
P	1	1	0	0	-1
J	1	1	0	-1	-1
D	0	0	0	-1	-1
T	0	0	0	-1	-1

Viewed from a structuralist perspective, this matrix suggests a partitioning into three sets: attorneys (defense and prosecuting attorneys being grouped together), the judge, and the outsiders (with the defendant more integrated than a convicted thief).

Current structuralist analyses do not focus on relations among institutional characters using data from informants, as suggested above, but rather attempt to define informal structures using personal-report data from individuals in groups. A parallel analysis using affect-control theory would require obtaining *EPA* profiles for all the persons in a group, each person rating every other (and the self) by name. Then analyses would be run to obtain the likelihoods that one person likes another, dislikes another, dominates another, and so on.

If such a procedure does predict sociometric choices, there would be several implications. Methodologically, it would be preferable to have individuals provide *EPA* ratings rather than personal responses to relation questions, because a relatively small number of *EPA* measurements would serve to generate a large number of theoretical relation matrices. If sociometric data are in fact generated within the affect-control system, then whatever information they contain also is contained in purer form in the original affective measurements. Thus, at the theoretic level, it might be more productive and less distracting to conduct structural analyses on the more basic data consisting of distributions of individuals and behaviors in *EPA* space. (Of course, analyses of data matrices could not be bypassed in this way if the data derive from something more than the direct choices of individual actors, as in studies of large populations, corporate interlocks, urban migrations, and so on.) In the other direction, structuralist formulations may ultimately provide key insights concerning how identities and acts come to be so precisely and delicately defined in terms of *EPA* profiles.

6. Current status of affect-control theory

The preceding pages have demonstrated a theoretical procedure for specifying acts that seem appropriate in a given social relationship. The behaviors that are selected vary essentially as they should by the institutional setting of the relationship, by the identity of the actor, by the identity of the object person, and as a function of prior events. The selection procedure is generative in the sense that it depends only on measurements of the goodness, strongness, and liveliness of identities and acts, without using stored information concerning the likelihoods of actor–act combinations. It might be thought that the technical procedures are only a semantic method for restoring combinations of actors, behaviors, and objects that were in mind when raters provided the evaluation–potency–activity ratings (e.g., raters might have thought "doctors medicate patients" while rating the word "medicates"). Although that itself would be an accomplishment, the procedure is more than a semantic method, as it appropriately combines words that would not ordinarily be associated during the rating task; for example, "A doctor reassures a patient" is generated and is culturally appropriate, but it is doubtful that a rater would have thought of this sentence when asked to rate "reassure." Alternatively, it might be thought that the procedure is only an elaborate way of selecting acts whose *EPA* profiles match the profile for an actor's identity. Though the generated profiles for acts do tend to correspond roughly to the profile for the actor, their exact numerical values involve subtleties beyond this correspondence that lead to predicting appropriate variations in an actor's behavior, depending on the identity of the object person and on the circumstances created by recent events.

Besides providing a procedure that generates culturally sensible actor–act–object combinations, this work permits the following major conclusions: (1) Subjective psychological processes can be analyzed rigorously in a quantitative empirical framework; (2) sentiments, dispositions, expectations, and attributions have an underlying unity;

152

(3) viewing behavior as the control of subjective states leads to concrete, sensible analyses of human action and social interaction; and (4) constellations of affective associations, including social attitudes, store enormous amounts of information about culture and social organization.

Affect-control theory now needs more empirical studies of impression formation: large-scale replications of past work to improve estimates of equation parameters; cross-cultural studies to assess generalizability of the processes; and studies of more complex structures (like sentences with modifiers, negations, passive voice, locative clauses, and recursive constructions), so that more complex cognitive structures can be represented in the affect-control model. Experiments are needed to test the numerous hypotheses suggested here, in order to validate affect-control theory's predictions of intentions, expectations, and behaviors and to confirm its ability to generate accurate representations of culture and social relationships. Available knowledge about attitude formation and general learning needs to be subsumed theoretically in order to model humans' capacity to change fundamental sentiments in response to events. Individual differences in psychological processes and in patterns of sentiments deserve examination, so that the model may be applied idiographically. Research focused on how people define situations and on the cognitive constraints (apart from affect control) that shape thinking is needed in order to increase the objectivity of the model as a method of analyzing ongoing social process.

A finished theory of social behavior has not been presented here – merely an approach to developing such a theory and tentative results from exploratory work.

Appendix: Catalogs of social identities and interpersonal acts

Semantic differential ratings of 1,250 words specifying 650 social identities and 600 social behaviors were collected from more than 300 University of North Carolina undergraduates in the spring of 1975, using scales described in the Current Formulas section of Chapter 2. The methodology of the project is discussed elsewhere (Heise, 1978). This Appendix gives the evaluation, potency, and activity profiles for the words, in terms of metrics defined by successive-intervals scaling. Identities are listed first and behaviors follow, all in alphabetical order. The numbers after a word have the following meanings.

Column 1. Average evaluation of the concept by moderate females, ranging from about - 4 (bad, unhelpful, awful, sour) to about +4 (good, helpful, nice, sweet).

Column 2. Average potency rating by moderate females, ranging from about - 4 (weak, powerless, little, shallow) to about +4 (strong, powerful, big, deep).

Column 3. Average activity rating by moderate females, ranging from about - 4 (slow, dead, quiet, stiff, old) to about +4 (hurried, alive, noisy, fiery, young).

Column 4. Increment that has to be added to figure in column one to get average evaluation of concept by moderate males. All nonzero values are significant, $p < .10$, in a two-tailed test; an asterisk indicates significance with $p < .01$.

Column 5. Increment to add to figure in column two to get average potency rating by moderate males.

Column 6. Increment to add to figure in column three to get average activity rating by moderate males.

Column 7. Increment to add to figure in column one to get average evaluation rating by conservative females (subtract to get average evaluation rating by liberals). Conservatism was measured using a thirty-item ideological checklist similar to those presented in Wilson (1973).

Column 8. Increment to add to figure in column two to get average potency rating by conservative females (subtract to get average potency rating by liberals).

Column 9. Increment to add to figure in column three to get average activity rating by conservative females (subtract to get average activity rating by liberals).

Column 10. Minimum number of observations involved in evaluation, potency, or activity calculations.

Column 11. Number of respondents who indicated that they did not know the word's meaning.

A few additional identities and behaviors were rated in the formula study described in Chapter 2 in the Current Formulas section: myself as I really am, myself as others see me, my mother, my father, Christian, the Devil, God, minister, peek at, and chatter to. The profiles for these concepts are given in Heise (1978).

	1	2	3	4	5	6	7	8	9	10	11
ACADEMIC	0.6	0.6	-0.1	0.9	0.0	1.0	0.5	0.4	0.9*	26	1
ACCOMPLICE	0.3	0.0	1.0	0.0	0.0	0.0	0.0	0.0	0.0	28	1
ACCOUNTANT	1.0	0.2	0.3	0.0	0.0	0.0	0.0	0.5	0.0	29	0
ACCUSED	-0.1	-1.1	-0.3	0.0	0.0	0.0	0.0	0.0	0.0	31	0
ACID HEAD	-2.2	-2.4	-0.8	0.0	0.0	0.0	0.0	0.0	-0.5	29	0
ADDICT	-1.6	-2.2	-0.2	0.0	0.0	0.0	0.0	0.0	0.8*	30	1
ADOLESCENT	0.6	-0.1	2.2	0.0	0.0	0.0	0.0	0.0	0.0	31	0
ADONIS	0.2	-0.5	0.6	0.0	0.0	0.0	0.0	0.0	-0.7	14	19
ADULT	1.1	0.4	1.2	-0.9	0.0	0.0	0.0	0.0	0.0	30	0
ADULTERER	-1.3	0.1	0.8	0.0	0.0	0.0	-0.5	0.5	0.0	30	0
ADULTERESS	-1.6	-1.4	1.1	0.0	0.0	0.0	-0.8*	-0.8*	-0.6	29	1
ADVISOR	1.4	0.9	0.4	0.0	0.0	0.0	0.0	0.0	0.0	29	0
ALCOHOLIC	-1.3	-2.2	-0.9	0.0	0.0	0.0	-1.1*	0.0	0.0	28	0
ALUMNUS	1.1	1.0	-0.1	0.0	0.0	0.0	0.0	0.0	0.0	28	1
AMATEUR	0.4	-0.3	0.9	0.0	0.0	0.0	0.0	0.0	0.0	29	2
ANESTHETIST	1.2	0.2	-0.1	0.0	0.0	0.0	0.0	0.0	0.0	29	3
APPLICANT	1.1	0.1	0.8	0.0	-1.0	0.0	0.0	0.0	0.0	29	1
APPRENTICE	1.2	-0.2	1.0	0.0	0.0	0.0	0.0	0.0	0.0	29	0
ASS	-1.9	-1.0	0.1	0.0	-0.7	0.0	0.0	0.0	-0.5	32	0
ASSAILANT	-2.5	0.7	0.9	0.0	0.0	0.0	0.0	0.0	0.0	25	2
ASSASSIN	-3.1	-0.3	0.9	0.0	0.0	0.0	0.0	0.0	0.0	31	0
ASSISTANT	1.3	0.1	1.3	0.0	0.0	-0.8	0.0	0.0	0.0	31	1
ATHLETE	1.5	1.9	2.3	0.0	0.0	0.0	0.0	0.0	0.0	31	0
ATTORNEY	1.6	2.1	1.0	0.0	-0.9	0.0	0.0	0.0	0.0	33	0
AUDITOR	0.9	0.4	-0.2	-1.0	0.0	0.0	0.0	0.0	0.0	29	3
AUNT	1.6	0.4	0.5	0.0	0.0	0.0	0.0	0.6	0.0	29	0
AUNTIE	1.8	0.3	-0.1	-0.7	-0.8	0.0	0.4	0.4	0.4	34	0
AUTHORITY	0.8	1.3	0.5	0.0	0.0	0.0	0.0	0.0	0.0	30	0
BABE	0.7	-0.7	1.2	0.0	0.0	0.0	0.0	0.5	0.0	28	3
BABY	1.6	-2.2	2.5	0.0	0.0	0.0	0.6	0.0	0.0	27	0
BABY SITTER	2.0	0.3	1.8	0.0	0.0	0.0	0.0	0.0	0.0	30	0
BACHELOR	0.8	0.7	1.7	0.0	0.0	0.0	0.0	0.5	0.0	34	0
BACKER	1.3	1.3	1.2	0.0	0.0	0.0	0.0	0.0	0.0	25	7
BAILIFF	0.5	-0.1	-0.3	0.0	0.0	0.0	0.0	0.0	0.0	27	3
BAILSMAN	1.0	0.8	0.2	0.0	0.0	0.0	0.0	0.0	0.0	26	6
BANDIT	-2.7	-0.6	1.5	1.1	1.0	0.0	0.0	-0.8	0.0	29	0
BARKEEPER	0.8	0.2	0.8	0.0	0.0	0.0	0.0	0.0	0.0	32	0
BARMAID	0.5	-0.5	1.7	0.0	0.0	0.0	-0.4	0.0	0.0	33	0
BARTENDER	0.9	0.3	1.3	0.0	0.0	0.0	0.0	0.0	0.0	28	0
BAWD	-0.4	-0.2	1.3	0.0	0.0	0.0	0.0	0.0	0.0	8	23
BEAUTY	1.1	-0.3	1.7	0.0	0.0	0.0	0.0	0.0	0.0	33	0
BEGGAR	-1.1	-2.0	-1.4	0.8	0.0	0.0	0.0	0.0	0.0	33	0
BEGINNER	0.5	-0.9	0.6	0.0	0.0	0.0	0.0	0.0	0.0	33	0
BELLBOY	1.4	0.1	1.3	0.0	0.0	0.0	0.0	0.0	0.0	32	0
BELLMAN	1.1	-1.0	0.4	0.0	0.9	0.0	0.0	0.0	0.0	25	5
BIG SHOT	-1.4	-0.7	1.6	0.0	1.0	0.0	-0.4	0.0	0.6	30	0
BIGAMIST	-1.7	-0.4	0.5	0.0	0.0	1.0	0.0	0.0	0.0	33	1
BIGOT	-2.1	-1.0	0.6	0.0	0.0	0.0	0.5	0.0	0.0	29	0
BISEXUAL	-0.9	-1.4	0.2	1.2*	1.2	0.0	-0.9*	0.0	-0.5	30	0
BITCH	-1.7	0.3	1.5	0.0	-1.2	0.0	0.0	0.0	0.0	32	0
BLABBERMOUTH	-1.9	-1.1	1.5	0.0	0.0	0.0	-0.5	0.0	0.0	34	0
BLEEDER	-0.3	-1.1	0.1	0.0	0.0	0.0	0.0	0.0	0.0	26	3
BLIND DATE	0.0	-0.7	-0.1	0.0	0.0	0.0	0.0	0.0	0.0	30	1
BLOCKHEAD	-0.5	-1.3	-0.6	0.0	0.0	0.0	0.0	0.0	0.0	30	2
BOARDER	0.4	-0.3	-0.1	0.0	0.0	0.0	0.0	0.0	0.0	30	0
BODYGUARD	1.5	1.6	1.2	0.0	0.0	0.0	0.0	0.0	0.0	28	1

	1	2	3	4	5	6	7	8	9	10	11
BOHEMIAN	0.6	0.6	0.8	0.0	0.0	0.0	0.0	0.0	0.0	20	14
BONEHEAD	-0.8	-1.7	-0.9	0.0	0.0	0.0	0.0	0.0	0.0	26	7
BOOB	-0.2	-1.2	-0.5	-1.0	0.0	0.0	0.0	0.0	0.0	21	6
BOOKIE	-1.4	0.1	1.5	0.8	0.0	0.0	-0.6*	0.5	0.4	29	1
BOOKWORM	0.7	-0.4	-1.3	0.0	0.0	0.0	0.0	0.0	0.0	34	0
BOOR	-0.9	-0.9	-0.9	0.0	0.0	0.0	0.0	0.0	0.0	26	4
BOOTBLACK	0.1	-1.0	0.4	0.0	0.0	0.0	0.0	0.0	0.0	16	15
BOSS	0.9	1.7	0.4	0.0	0.0	0.0	0.0	0.0	0.0	32	0
BOUNCER	0.0	1.7	1.6	0.0	0.0	-1.1	0.0	0.0	0.0	27	5
BOXER	0.4	2.0	1.6	0.0	0.0	1.1	0.0	0.0	0.0	31	0
BOY	1.4	1.0	2.3	0.0	-1.4*	0.0	0.0	0.0	-0.7	29	0
BOY FRIEND	1.8	1.4	1.8	0.0	0.0	0.0	0.0	0.0	0.0	29	0
BOY SCOUT	1.9	1.0	2.0	0.0	0.0	0.0	0.0	0.0	0.0	29	0
BRAGGART	-1.6	-1.8	0.4	0.0	0.0	0.8	0.0	0.0	0.0	33	0
BRAIN	1.5	1.8	1.5	0.0	0.0	0.0	0.8	0.0	0.0	29	0
BRAT	-1.5	-0.7	2.3	0.0	0.0	0.0	0.0	0.0	0.0	33	1
BROAD	0.4	-0.4	0.6	0.0	0.0	0.0	-0.9	-0.8	-1.2*	26	3
BROTHER	2.3	2.3	2.9	0.0	-1.6*	-1.0	0.0	0.0	0.0	30	0
BROTHER-IN-LAW	1.3	0.7	1.0	0.0	0.0	0.0	0.4	0.5	0.0	31	1
BRUTE	-2.2	1.0	1.2	0.0	0.0	0.0	0.0	0.0	0.0	31	0
BUDDY	2.5	1.4	1.8	0.0	0.0	0.0	0.0	0.0	0.0	29	0
BUFFOON	0.1	-1.0	1.5	0.0	0.0	-1.1	0.0	0.0	0.0	22	9
BULLY	-2.2	0.0	1.3	0.0	0.0	0.0	-0.5	-1.0	-0.7	28	1
BUM	-1.1	-1.6	-1.0	0.0	0.0	0.0	-0.5	-0.6	0.0	29	0
BUMPKIN	0.3	-0.9	-0.1	0.0	0.0	0.0	0.0	0.0	0.0	24	5
BURGLAR	-2.6	0.0	0.6	0.0	0.0	0.0	-0.4	-0.5	0.0	31	0
BUS BOY	0.8	-0.2	1.0	0.0	0.0	0.0	0.0	0.0	0.0	30	1
BUSYBODY	-1.6	-0.6	1.3	0.0	0.0	0.0	0.0	0.5	0.0	32	0
BUTTERFINGERS	-0.4	-0.9	1.0	0.0	0.0	0.0	0.0	0.0	0.0	30	3
BYSTANDER	0.0	-1.2	-0.6	0.0	0.0	0.0	0.0	0.0	0.0	32	1
CAD	-1.8	-1.2	0.5	0.8	0.0	0.0	0.0	0.0	0.0	22	7
CALL GIRL	-0.7	-0.4	1.6	1.0	0.0	0.0	-0.9*	0.0	0.0	29	0
CAPTIVE	0.0	-1.4	-0.6	0.0	0.0	0.0	-0.5	0.0	0.0	27	0
CARD	0.7	0.0	2.2	0.0	0.0	0.0	0.0	0.0	0.0	29	2
CASHIER	1.1	0.2	1.2	0.0	0.0	0.0	0.0	0.0	0.0	32	0
CELEBRITY	1.0	1.2	2.2	0.0	0.0	0.0	-0.4	0.0	0.0	30	0
CENTER	1.0	1.8	2.0	0.0	0.0	0.0	0.0	0.0	0.0	30	1
CHAMBERMAID	1.3	0.0	0.5	0.0	-1.0	0.0	0.0	0.0	0.0	26	3
CHAMPION	1.3	2.3	2.4	0.0	0.0	0.0	0.0	0.0	0.0	32	0
CHAP	0.9	0.1	0.8	0.0	0.0	0.0	0.0	0.0	0.7	29	3
CHAPERON	0.1	0.3	-0.4	0.8	0.0	0.0	0.0	0.0	0.0	30	1
CHARWOMAN	0.8	0.1	0.4	0.0	0.0	0.0	0.0	0.0	0.0	15	19
CHATTERBOX	-0.5	-0.8	1.8	0.0	0.0	0.0	0.0	0.0	0.5	31	0
CHEF	1.1	0.6	0.9	0.0	0.0	0.0	0.0	0.0	0.0	27	0
CHICK	0.3	-0.3	1.5	0.8	0.0	0.0	0.0	0.0	0.0	32	1
CHILD	1.9	-0.5	2.8	0.0	0.0	-1.1	0.0	0.6	0.0	29	0
CHUM	1.9	1.2	1.7	0.0	0.0	0.0	0.0	0.0	0.0	34	0
CIVIL SERVANT	1.0	0.0	0.2	0.0	0.0	0.0	0.0	0.0	0.0	29	0
CLASSMATE	0.9	-0.1	1.0	0.0	0.0	0.0	0.0	0.0	0.0	32	0
CLERK	1.1	-0.3	0.8	0.0	0.0	0.0	0.0	0.0	0.0	29	0
CLIENT	0.8	0.5	0.5	0.0	0.0	0.0	0.0	0.0	0.0	30	0
CLOD	-0.4	-1.0	-0.3	0.0	0.0	0.0	0.0	0.0	0.0	29	0
CLOWN	1.7	0.3	2.4	0.0	0.0	0.0	0.0	-0.6	0.0	29	0
CO-WORKER	1.2	0.6	1.0	0.0	0.0	0.0	0.0	0.0	0.0	27	0
COACH	1.6	2.3	2.7	0.0	0.0	0.0	0.4	0.0	0.0	28	2
COED	1.2	0.5	1.7	0.0	0.0	0.0	0.0	0.0	0.0	34	0

	1	2	3	4	5	6	7	8	9	10	11
COLLEAGUE	1.3	0.9	0.8	0.0	0.0	0.0	0.0	0.0	0.0	29	1
COMPANION	2.1	1.5	1.2	0.0	0.0	0.0	0.0	0.0	0.0	28	1
CONCUBINE	-0.7	-1.1	0.7	0.0	0.0	0.0	-0.4	0.0	0.0	24	8
CONFIDANT	2.3	1.9	1.6	0.0	0.0	-1.1	0.0	0.0	0.0	27	3
CONFORMIST	-0.2	-0.6	-0.5	0.0	0.0	0.0	0.8*	0.0	0.0	28	1
CONNOISSEUR	1.3	0.6	0.3	0.0	0.0	0.0	0.0	0.0	0.0	30	2
CONSUMER	0.6	-0.5	0.6	0.7	0.0	0.0	0.0	0.0	0.0	30	1
CONVICT	-1.2	-0.1	0.0	0.0	0.0	0.0	0.0	0.0	0.0	27	0
COOK	1.2	0.1	0.6	0.0	0.0	0.0	0.0	0.0	0.0	30	0
COP	1.3	1.1	0.7	-0.7	0.0	0.0	0.0	0.0	0.0	30	0
COPPER	1.0	0.9	0.8	0.0	0.0	0.0	0.0	0.0	0.0	25	5
COPYCAT	-2.2	-2.5	-0.6	0.6	0.9	0.0	0.0	0.0	0.0	29	0
CORONER	1.1	0.0	-0.5	0.0	0.0	0.0	0.4	0.0	0.0	30	2
COUNSELOR	1.7	1.3	0.6	0.0	0.0	0.0	0.0	0.0	0.0	30	0
COURTESAN	0.4	0.0	0.8	0.0	0.0	0.0	0.0	0.0	0.0	16	14
COUSIN	1.4	0.8	1.3	0.0	0.0	0.0	0.0	0.0	0.0	32	0
COWARD	-1.4	-2.5	-1.0	0.0	0.0	0.0	0.0	0.0	0.0	29	0
CRAB	-1.0	-0.8	0.0	0.8	0.0	0.0	0.0	0.0	0.0	31	1
CRACKPOT	-0.9	-1.0	0.5	0.0	0.0	0.0	0.0	0.0	0.0	28	2
CRANK	-1.1	-0.8	-0.1	0.0	0.0	0.0	0.0	0.0	-0.5	29	1
CRIMINAL	-2.4	-1.4	1.0	0.9	0.0	0.0	0.0	0.0	0.0	33	0
CRIPPLE	0.7	-0.7	-0.4	0.0	0.0	0.0	0.0	0.0	0.0	32	0
CRITIC	0.8	0.8	0.8	0.0	-1.1	0.0	0.0	0.0	0.0	33	0
CRONE	0.2	-0.5	-0.6	0.0	0.0	0.0	0.0	0.0	0.0	21	10
CROOK	-2.5	-0.4	1.2	0.0	0.0	0.0	0.0	0.0	0.0	34	0
CRYBABY	-1.1	-1.6	0.1	0.0	0.0	1.1	0.0	0.0	0.0	29	0
CUCKOLD	-1.0	-1.2	-0.1	0.0	0.0	0.0	0.0	0.0	0.0	11	17
CULPRIT	-1.7	0.2	0.5	0.0	-0.8	0.0	0.0	0.0	0.0	32	2
CUSTOMER	0.8	0.1	0.9	0.0	0.0	0.0	0.0	0.0	0.0	30	0
CUTTHROAT	-2.2	0.2	1.3	-0.6	0.0	0.0	0.0	0.0	0.0	30	1
CYNIC	-0.7	-0.4	0.3	0.0	0.0	0.0	0.0	0.0	0.0	28	4
DAME	0.7	0.2	1.3	0.0	0.0	0.0	0.0	0.0	0.0	30	0
DANDY	0.7	0.1	1.4	0.0	0.0	0.0	0.5	0.0	0.0	26	8
DAREDEVIL	0.0	0.8	2.7	0.0	0.0	0.0	-0.4	0.0	0.0	31	0
DARLING	1.7	0.2	1.3	0.0	0.0	0.0	0.0	0.0	0.0	31	1
DAUGHTER	1.3	-0.4	1.5	0.0	0.0	0.0	0.0	0.0	0.0	31	0
DAUGHTER-IN-LA	1.2	-0.2	1.3	0.0	0.0	0.0	0.0	0.0	0.0	32	0
DEADBEAT	-1.3	-1.8	-1.4	0.0	0.0	0.0	-0.3	0.0	0.0	34	0
DEADHEAD	-0.9	-1.9	-1.5	0.0	0.0	0.0	0.0	0.0	0.0	31	1
DEFENDANT	0.3	-0.6	-0.1	0.0	0.0	0.0	0.0	0.0	0.0	31	0
DEGENERATE	-1.6	-1.8	-0.7	0.0	0.0	0.0	0.0	0.0	0.0	30	1
DELINQUENT	-1.0	-0.8	1.4	0.0	0.0	0.0	0.0	0.0	0.0	27	1
DEPUTY	1.1	1.0	0.9	0.0	0.0	0.0	0.5	0.0	0.0	32	0
DESPERADO	-1.3	0.2	2.1	0.0	0.0	0.0	0.0	0.0	0.0	30	3
DETECTIVE	1.4	1.4	1.2	0.0	0.0	0.0	0.0	0.0	0.7	29	0
DEVIL	-2.3	0.7	1.4	0.0	0.0	0.9	0.0	0.0	0.0	34	0
DIETITIAN	1.7	0.4	0.1	0.0	0.0	0.0	0.0	0.0	0.0	31	0
DIKE	0.3	0.3	0.1	-0.9	0.0	0.0	0.0	0.0	-0.7	21	9
DIMWIT	-0.3	-1.3	-1.1	0.0	0.0	0.0	0.0	0.0	0.0	29	2
DINER	0.7	-0.1	0.4	0.0	0.0	0.0	0.5	0.0	0.0	29	1
DISCIPLINARIAN	0.2	1.1	-0.4	0.0	0.0	0.9	0.7	0.0	0.5	28	1
DISTRICT ATTOR	1.5	1.7	1.4	0.0	0.0	0.0	0.0	0.0	0.0	32	0
DIVORCEE	0.3	-0.7	0.4	0.0	0.0	0.8	-0.5	0.0	0.0	30	0
DO-NOTHING	-1.6	-2.3	-1.6	-1.0	0.0	0.0	-0.4	0.0	0.0	25	1
DOCTOR	2.4	2.3	1.1	0.0	-0.9	0.0	0.0	0.0	0.0	30	0
DOLL	2.0	-0.2	1.0	0.0	0.0	0.0	0.0	0.4	0.0	34	0

	1	2	3	4	5	6	7	8	9	10	11
DOLT	-0.8	-1.1	-0.8	0.0	0.0	0.0	0.0	0.0	0.0	17	14
DOORKEEPER	1.1	-0.4	-0.6	0.0	0.0	0.0	0.0	0.0	0.0	30	1
DOORMAN	1.1	-0.3	-0.1	0.0	0.0	0.0	0.0	0.0	0.0	30	0
DOPE	-0.7	-1.6	-0.9	0.0	0.0	0.0	0.0	0.0	0.0	31	0
DRIP	-0.6	-1.4	-1.1	0.0	0.0	0.0	0.0	0.0	0.0	29	2
DROPOUT	-0.9	-1.8	0.1	0.0	0.0	0.0	-0.4	0.0	0.0	32	0
DRUDGE	-0.7	-1.1	-0.6	0.0	0.0	0.0	0.0	0.0	0.0	17	14
DRUG ADDICT	-1.7	-1.6	-0.7	0.0	0.0	0.0	-0.5	-0.4	-0.4	32	0
DRUNK	-1.6	-2.1	-0.2	0.0	0.0	0.0	0.0	0.0	-0.7	31	0
DRUNKARD	-1.4	-1.8	-0.8	0.0	0.0	0.0	0.0	0.0	0.0	30	0
DULLARD	-0.6	-1.6	-1.4	-1.4*	0.0	0.0	0.0	0.0	0.0	20	8
DUMBBELL	-0.7	-1.5	-0.7	0.0	0.0	0.0	0.0	0.0	0.0	31	0
DUMMY	-0.5	-1.3	-1.1	0.0	0.0	0.0	0.0	0.0	0.0	33	0
DUNCE	-0.2	-1.4	-0.5	0.0	0.0	0.0	0.0	0.0	0.0	29	0
EASY MARK	-0.1	-1.8	-0.5	0.0	0.0	0.0	0.0	0.0	0.0	28	3
EGGHEAD	-0.6	-1.2	-1.2	0.0	0.0	1.3	-0.4	-0.5	-0.4	31	1
EMPLOYEE	1.4	0.6	1.2	0.0	-0.8	-0.9	0.0	0.0	0.0	29	0
EMPLOYER	1.0	1.4	0.5	0.0	0.0	0.0	0.0	0.5	0.4	31	1
END	0.9	1.8	2.2	0.0	-1.1	0.0	0.0	0.0	0.0	25	2
EVILDOER	-2.5	-0.1	1.2	0.0	-0.8	-1.1	0.0	0.0	0.0	31	0
EXECUTIVE	0.7	1.4	1.1	0.0	0.0	0.0	0.0	0.0	0.0	31	0
EXPERT	1.7	1.6	1.6	0.0	0.0	0.0	0.0	0.0	0.0	26	0
EXTROVERT	0.7	1.1	2.8	0.0	0.0	0.0	0.0	0.0	0.0	32	1
EYEWITNESS	1.0	0.4	1.2	0.0	0.0	-0.9	0.4	0.0	0.0	32	1
FAG	-1.0	-1.1	0.7	0.0	0.0	0.0	-0.8*	0.0	0.0	30	0
FAIRY	0.6	-0.2	0.9	-1.5*	-1.6*	0.0	0.0	0.0	-0.7	26	3
FALL GUY	0.5	-0.4	0.7	-1.2	-1.3	-1.5	0.0	0.0	0.0	14	14
FAN	0.6	0.6	1.9	0.0	-1.0	0.0	0.0	0.0	0.0	29	1
FANATIC	-0.8	0.5	1.9	0.0	-0.9	0.0	0.0	0.0	0.0	31	0
FATHER	2.4	2.7	1.4	0.0	0.0	0.0	0.4	0.0	0.0	30	0
FATHER-IN-LAW	1.5	0.9	-0.1	0.0	0.0	0.0	0.5	0.0	0.0	29	1
FAULTFINDER	-1.7	-1.5	0.3	0.0	0.0	0.0	0.0	0.0	0.0	27	1
FELLOW	0.8	0.1	0.9	0.0	0.0	0.0	0.0	0.0	0.0	30	2
FELON	-2.2	-0.3	1.2	0.0	0.0	-0.8	0.0	0.0	0.0	29	4
FEMALE	1.8	0.9	1.7	0.0	0.0	0.0	0.6*	0.0	0.4	34	0
FIEND	-1.8	0.0	0.2	-0.9	0.0	0.0	0.0	0.0	0.0	32	0
FINK	-1.9	-1.3	0.6	0.0	0.0	0.0	0.0	0.0	0.0	34	0
FIREBUG	-2.0	-0.4	0.6	0.0	-1.3	0.0	0.0	0.0	0.0	27	3
FIRSTBORN	0.8	0.6	1.3	0.0	0.0	-0.9	0.0	0.0	0.0	33	0
FLAGELLANT	-1.0	0.8	1.0	0.0	0.0	0.0	0.0	0.0	0.0	9	22
FLATFOOT	0.0	-0.5	-0.3	0.0	0.0	0.0	0.0	0.0	0.0	20	7
FLIRT	-0.1	-0.5	2.2	0.0	0.0	0.0	0.0	0.0	0.0	30	0
FLOORWALKER	0.3	-0.1	0.5	0.0	0.0	0.0	0.0	0.0	0.0	23	6
FLUNKY	-1.4	-1.9	-0.8	0.0	0.0	0.0	0.0	0.0	0.0	28	2
FOOL	-1.3	-1.5	0.2	0.0	0.0	0.0	0.0	0.0	0.0	34	0
FREAK	-0.2	-0.7	0.9	0.0	0.0	0.0	-0.5	0.0	0.0	32	0
FRESHMAN	1.0	-0.5	1.7	0.0	0.0	0.0	0.4	0.0	0.0	34	0
FRIEND	2.9	2.2	2.2	0.0	0.0	-1.5*	0.0	0.6	0.0	32	0
FRUIT	0.4	-1.2	0.0	-0.8	0.0	0.0	-0.5	0.0	0.0	24	7
FRUMP	-0.3	-1.0	-0.5	0.0	0.0	0.0	0.0	0.0	0.0	11	21
FUDDY-DUDDY	-0.7	-1.1	-0.7	0.0	0.0	0.0	0.0	0.0	0.0	24	4
FUGITIVE	-1.7	-0.6	1.5	0.0	0.0	1.0	-0.5	0.0	0.0	29	0
FULLBACK	0.5	1.7	2.3	0.0	0.0	-0.7	0.5	0.5	0.0	32	1
G-MAN	-0.2	0.5	0.9	1.5*	1.5	0.0	0.0	0.0	0.5	25	7
GAL	1.3	0.4	1.5	0.0	-0.9	0.0	0.0	0.0	0.0	29	1
GAMBLER	-0.7	-1.7	1.2	0.0	1.0	0.0	0.0	0.0	0.0	29	0

	1	2	3	4	5	6	7	8	9	10	11
GAMIN	0.6	-1.1	0.7	0.0	0.0	0.0	0.0	0.0	0.0	2	33
GANGSTER	-2.4	1.0	1.8	0.0	0.0	0.0	0.0	-0.8*	0.0	29	0
GEEZER	0.2	-0.6	-0.7	0.0	0.0	0.0	0.0	0.0	0.0	22	7
GENIUS	1.0	0.2	0.0	0.0	1.1	1.1	0.0	0.0	0.0	30	0
GENT	1.5	0.8	1.1	0.0	0.0	0.0	0.0	0.0	0.0	30	2
GENTLEMAN	2.0	1.2	0.8	0.0	0.0	0.0	0.5	0.5	0.7	31	0
GHOUL	-0.5	-0.6	-0.7	-1.6*	1.2	0.0	-0.4	0.0	0.0	20	7
GIGOLO	-0.5	-0.3	1.3	-0.9	0.0	0.0	0.0	0.0	0.0	25	6
GIRL	1.7	-0.2	2.0	0.0	0.0	0.0	0.0	0.0	0.0	33	0
GIRL SCOUT	1.3	-0.1	1.3	0.0	0.0	0.0	0.0	0.5	0.0	29	0
GLUTTON	-1.1	-1.1	-0.3	0.0	0.0	0.0	0.0	0.0	0.0	28	1
GOLD DIGGER	-0.4	-0.1	2.0	0.0	0.0	0.0	0.0	-0.6	0.0	24	10
GOODY	0.2	-1.0	0.1	0.0	0.0	0.0	0.0	0.0	0.0	28	2
GOON	-0.5	-1.0	-0.6	0.0	0.0	0.0	0.0	0.0	0.0	26	5
GOSSIP	-2.0	-2.1	1.1	0.0	1.3	0.0	0.0	0.0	0.0	29	0
GOURMET	0.7	-0.2	0.3	0.0	0.0	0.0	0.0	0.0	0.0	27	0
GRADUATE STUDE	0.9	0.0	0.3	0.0	0.0	0.0	0.0	0.0	0.0	32	0
GRANDCHILD	1.8	-0.2	2.2	0.0	0.0	0.0	0.5	0.0	0.0	34	0
GRANDDAUGHTER	1.6	-0.1	1.8	0.0	0.0	0.0	0.0	0.0	0.0	34	0
GRANDFATHER	2.2	1.3	0.4	0.0	0.0	-1.4	0.0	0.8	0.0	31	1
GRANDMOTHER	2.3	0.7	0.0	0.0	0.0	0.0	0.0	0.5	0.5	32	0
GRANDPARENT	2.0	0.4	-0.5	0.0	0.0	0.0	0.0	0.0	0.0	33	0
GRANDSON	1.5	0.2	2.3	0.0	0.0	0.0	0.4	0.0	0.0	34	0
GRANNY	1.8	-0.4	-0.9	0.0	0.0	0.0	0.4	0.0	0.0	34	0
GRIND	-0.9	-0.7	-0.6	0.0	0.0	0.0	0.0	0.0	0.0	21	10
GROUCH	-1.7	-0.7	-1.0	0.0	0.0	0.0	0.0	0.0	0.0	27	0
GROWN-UP	1.2	1.4	0.5	0.0	0.0	0.0	0.0	0.0	0.0	34	0
GUARD	0.5	1.7	2.1	0.0	0.0	0.0	0.3	0.0	0.0	29	1
GUEST	1.2	0.1	0.5	0.0	0.0	0.0	0.0	0.0	0.0	30	0
GUN MOLL	-1.5	-0.5	0.7	0.0	0.0	0.0	0.0	0.0	0.0	16	15
GUNMAN	-1.7	0.2	1.9	0.0	0.0	0.0	0.0	0.0	0.6	30	0
GUTTERSNIPE	-1.2	-0.7	0.5	0.0	0.0	0.0	0.0	0.0	0.0	7	25
GUY	0.8	0.4	0.9	0.0	0.0	0.0	0.0	-0.6	-0.5	29	1
HAG	-1.8	-1.6	-1.8	0.0	0.9	0.9	0.0	0.0	0.0	29	1
HALF-BROTHER	1.1	0.4	1.1	0.0	0.0	0.0	0.0	0.0	0.0	26	2
HALF-SISTER	0.8	-0.1	0.8	0.0	0.0	0.0	0.0	0.0	0.0	31	1
HALF-WIT	-0.6	-1.5	-0.7	0.0	0.0	0.0	0.0	0.0	0.0	30	1
HALFBACK	0.5	1.3	1.9	0.0	0.0	0.0	0.0	0.6	0.0	28	1
HANDYMAN	1.8	0.9	1.1	0.0	0.0	0.0	0.0	0.0	0.0	32	0
HANGER-ON	-0.8	-1.3	-0.3	0.0	0.0	0.0	0.8*	0.8*	0.0	26	4
HARLOT	-1.3	-1.2	1.3	0.0	0.0	-1.1	-0.7*	0.0	0.0	27	5
HAS-BEEN	-0.2	-1.6	-1.3	0.0	0.0	0.0	0.0	0.0	0.0	32	1
HE-MAN	-0.1	0.9	1.9	0.0	0.0	-1.7*	0.0	0.0	0.0	30	0
HEADWAITER	1.2	0.6	1.5	0.0	0.0	0.0	0.0	0.0	0.0	30	0
HEEL	-2.1	-1.8	-0.4	0.0	1.2	0.0	0.0	0.0	0.0	28	1
HENCHMAN	-0.5	0.8	0.3	-1.3	0.0	0.0	-0.7	0.0	0.0	18	9
HERMIT	0.2	-0.5	-0.9	0.0	0.0	0.0	0.0	0.0	0.5	32	0
HERO	2.1	2.1	1.8	0.0	0.0	0.0	0.0	0.0	0.0	34	0
HEROINE	2.0	1.7	2.3	0.0	0.0	0.0	0.0	0.0	0.0	32	0
HETEROSEXUAL	0.8	0.3	1.3	1.2*	1.0	0.0	0.7*	0.6	0.8*	31	0
HICK	0.0	-0.7	-0.4	0.0	0.0	0.0	0.0	0.0	0.0	27	1
HIGHWAYMAN	-0.8	0.5	1.1	0.0	0.0	0.0	0.0	0.0	0.7	26	2
HILLBILLY	0.4	-0.1	0.3	0.0	0.0	0.0	0.0	0.0	0.0	30	0
HIPPIE	-0.4	-1.0	0.2	0.0	0.0	0.0	-0.5*	-0.4	-0.5	32	0
HIPSTER	-0.1	-0.7	1.1	0.0	0.0	0.0	0.0	0.0	0.0	25	5
HOBO	-0.3	-1.3	-0.4	0.0	0.0	0.0	0.0	0.0	0.0	29	0

	1	2	3	4	5	6	7	8	9	10	11
HOMEBODY	0.8	-1.0	-1.0	0.0	0.0	0.0	0.0	0.0	0.0	31	3
HOMO	-0.1	-0.7	0.7	-1.0	0.0	0.0	-0.4	0.0	0.0	29	2
HOMOSEXUAL	-0.8	-1.7	0.1	0.0	0.9	0.0	-1.1*	-0.6	0.0	29	0
HOOD	-2.1	0.5	1.4	0.0	0.0	0.0	-0.4	0.0	0.0	34	0
HOODLUM	-2.3	-0.4	1.6	0.0	0.0	-2.0*	0.0	0.0	0.0	32	0
HOOKER	-1.0	-0.4	1.0	1.2*	0.0	0.0	-0.6*	-0.7	-0.5	32	0
HOOLIGAN	-0.7	-0.4	1.3	0.0	0.0	0.0	0.0	0.0	-0.9	20	11
HOST	1.5	0.8	1.7	0.0	0.0	-1.2	0.0	0.0	0.0	33	0
HOSTAGE	-0.2	-1.6	-0.6	0.0	0.0	0.0	-0.6	0.0	0.0	28	1
HOSTESS	1.9	0.3	1.7	0.0	0.0	0.0	0.0	0.0	0.0	27	0
HOTHEAD	-1.7	-0.4	2.1	0.0	0.0	0.0	0.0	-0.3	-0.6	32	0
HOTSHOT	-0.9	-1.1	1.5	0.0	0.9	0.0	0.0	0.0	0.0	30	0
HOUSE GUEST	0.9	-0.4	0.4	0.0	0.0	0.0	0.0	0.0	0.0	33	0
HOUSEBREAKER	-2.2	0.2	1.0	0.0	0.0	0.0	0.0	0.0	0.0	31	3
HOUSEKEEPER	1.2	0.1	0.3	0.0	0.0	0.0	0.0	0.0	0.0	27	1
HOUSEMAID	1.4	-0.3	0.5	0.0	0.0	0.0	0.5	0.0	0.0	32	0
HOUSEWIFE	1.9	0.4	1.0	0.0	0.0	0.0	0.4	0.7*	0.9*	32	0
HUNCHBACK	0.2	-0.9	-1.1	0.0	0.0	0.0	0.0	0.0	0.0	29	0
HUSBAND	2.4	1.9	1.7	0.0	0.0	0.0	0.0	0.0	0.5	29	1
HUSSY	-1.1	-0.6	0.5	0.0	0.0	0.0	0.0	0.0	0.0	27	0
HYPOCHONDRIAC	-0.9	-1.7	-0.6	0.0	0.0	0.0	0.0	0.0	0.0	34	0
HYPOCRITE	-1.9	-1.3	0.1	0.0	0.0	0.0	0.0	-0.4	0.0	34	0
IDIOT	-0.7	-1.6	-1.0	0.0	0.0	0.0	-0.8*	-0.8	0.0	28	1
IGNORAMUS	-0.9	-1.6	-1.0	0.0	0.0	0.0	0.0	0.0	0.0	32	0
IMBECILE	-1.2	-2.1	-1.1	0.0	0.0	0.0	0.0	0.0	0.4	29	0
IMP	-0.8	-1.2	1.5	0.0	0.0	0.0	0.0	0.0	-0.7	24	7
IN-LAW	0.9	0.4	0.5	0.0	0.0	-1.2	0.0	0.0	0.0	27	0
INFANT	1.4	-2.0	1.6	0.0	0.0	0.0	0.6	0.0	0.0	32	0
INFORMANT	-0.4	-0.3	0.5	0.0	0.0	0.0	0.4	0.8*	0.4	28	1
INFORMER	-0.6	-0.9	1.2	0.0	0.0	-1.2	0.6*	0.5	-0.6	32	0
INMATE	-0.2	-0.8	0.0	0.0	0.0	0.0	0.0	-0.4	0.0	30	0
INNOCENT	1.1	-1.0	0.1	0.0	0.0	0.0	0.0	0.0	0.5	34	0
INSIDER	0.5	0.0	0.0	0.0	0.0	0.0	0.0	0.0	0.0	24	5
INSPECTOR	0.9	1.2	0.3	0.0	0.0	0.0	0.5	0.0	0.0	32	0
INSTRUCTOR	1.7	1.3	0.9	0.0	0.0	0.0	0.0	0.0	0.0	32	0
INTERN	1.4	0.5	1.8	0.0	0.0	0.0	0.0	0.0	0.0	29	0
INTIMATE	1.6	1.4	2.1	0.0	0.0	-1.5*	0.0	0.0	0.0	27	4
INTROVERT	-0.3	-1.1	-1.2	0.0	0.0	0.0	-0.7*	0.0	0.0	30	0
INVALID	0.5	-1.7	-1.3	0.0	0.0	0.0	0.0	-0.4	0.0	29	1
JACKASS	-0.9	-1.2	0.4	-1.3*	0.0	0.0	0.0	0.0	0.0	27	0
JANITOR	1.4	-0.5	-0.7	-0.9	0.0	0.0	0.0	0.0	0.0	31	1
JERK	-1.9	-1.5	0.5	0.0	0.0	0.0	-0.5	0.0	0.0	28	1
JOCK	0.5	1.3	1.6	0.0	0.0	0.0	0.5	0.0	0.6	31	0
JUDGE	1.2	2.4	0.0	0.0	0.0	0.0	0.5	0.0	0.6	32	0
JUNKIE	-2.6	-1.3	0.2	0.0	0.0	-1.5	-0.4	0.5	0.0	31	0
JUROR	0.9	1.3	-0.1	0.0	0.0	0.0	0.0	0.0	0.0	32	0
JUVENILE	0.1	-0.8	1.9	0.0	0.0	0.0	0.0	0.0	0.0	31	0
KID	1.6	0.2	2.6	0.0	-1.0	0.0	0.0	0.0	0.0	29	0
KILLJOY	-1.5	0.0	0.0	0.0	0.0	0.0	-0.3	0.4	0.0	30	0
KLUTZ	-0.2	-1.3	-0.1	-0.7	0.0	-1.1	0.0	0.0	0.0	25	2
KOOK	-0.4	-1.0	0.6	0.0	0.0	0.0	0.0	0.0	-0.6	31	1
LAD	1.3	0.2	1.6	0.0	0.0	0.0	0.0	0.0	0.0	28	1
LADY	1.7	0.9	0.8	0.0	0.0	0.0	0.6*	0.5	0.6	34	0
LADYKILLER	-1.4	-0.4	1.3	0.0	0.0	0.0	-0.5	-0.4	0.0	31	0
LANDLADY	0.6	0.2	0.0	0.0	0.0	0.0	0.0	0.4	0.0	32	0
LANDLORD	0.2	0.5	0.0	0.0	0.0	0.0	0.6	0.0	0.0	29	0

	1	2	3	4	5	6	7	8	9	10	11
LASS	1.7	-0.5	1.8	0.0	0.0	0.0	0.0	0.0	-0.5	28	2
LAW-BREAKER	-1.4	-0.5	0.7	0.0	0.0	0.0	-0.5	0.0	0.0	29	0
LAWYER	1.4	1.1	0.8	0.0	0.0	0.9	0.0	0.0	0.0	30	0
LECHER	-1.9	-1.2	-0.8	0.0	0.0	0.0	0.0	0.0	0.0	20	7
LESBIAN	-0.9	-0.9	0.2	0.0	0.0	0.0	-0.6*	-0.7*	-0.5	31	0
LIAR	-2.2	-1.3	0.6	-0.8	0.0	0.0	-0.6*	0.0	0.0	30	0
LIBERTINE	0.6	1.4	2.1	0.0	-2.5*	0.0	0.0	0.0	0.0	12	20
LIFER	-0.4	-0.4	-0.7	0.0	0.0	0.0	0.0	0.0	0.0	19	14
LINEBACKER	1.0	1.7	2.2	0.0	0.0	0.0	0.5	0.7	0.5	31	1
LINEMAN	0.9	0.9	2.1	-0.7	1.0	0.0	0.3	0.0	0.0	29	1
LOAFER	-2.1	-2.3	-1.6	0.9	0.0	0.0	-0.4	0.0	0.0	30	0
LOAN SHARK	-1.8	0.4	0.6	0.0	0.0	0.0	0.0	0.0	0.0	31	3
LODGER	0.6	-0.4	-0.1	0.0	0.0	0.0	0.0	0.0	0.0	23	8
LONER	0.1	-0.5	-0.8	0.0	0.0	0.0	0.0	0.0	0.0	31	0
LOOK-OUT	1.1	0.4	1.0	-1.1	0.0	-1.3	0.0	0.0	0.0	27	5
LOUSE	-1.6	-1.2	-0.1	0.0	0.0	0.0	0.0	0.0	0.0	28	1
LOUT	-1.5	-1.3	-0.2	0.0	0.0	0.0	0.0	0.0	0.0	18	12
LOVER	2.6	2.8	2.2	0.0	-1.1	0.0	0.0	0.0	0.0	29	0
LUMMOX	0.0	-0.8	-1.2	0.0	0.0	0.0	0.0	0.0	0.0	11	21
LUNATIC	-1.0	-1.2	0.6	-1.1	0.0	0.0	0.0	0.0	0.0	26	1
LUSH	-1.1	-1.6	-0.4	0.0	0.0	0.0	0.0	0.0	0.0	23	11
MADMAN	-1.4	0.2	1.6	0.0	0.0	0.0	-0.7*	0.0	0.0	29	0
MAFIOSO	-1.6	1.5	1.1	0.0	0.0	0.0	-0.8	0.0	0.9	17	13
MAID	1.7	-0.2	0.9	0.0	0.0	0.0	-0.4	0.0	-1.0*	29	0
MAIDEN	1.4	-0.8	0.6	0.0	0.0	0.0	0.0	0.0	0.0	32	0
MAILMAN	1.7	0.5	0.7	0.0	0.0	0.0	0.0	0.0	0.0	31	1
MAN	1.1	0.7	0.9	0.0	0.0	0.0	0.0	0.0	0.0	31	0
MANAGER	1.3	1.0	0.9	0.0	0.0	0.0	0.0	0.0	0.0	30	0
MANIAC	-1.8	-0.4	2.3	0.0	-0.9	0.0	0.0	0.0	0.0	30	0
MARK	0.4	-1.4	-0.7	0.0	0.0	0.0	0.0	0.0	0.0	10	21
MASTERMIND	0.9	1.5	1.1	0.0	0.0	0.0	0.0	0.0	-0.5	33	0
MATE	2.3	1.5	1.4	0.0	0.0	0.0	0.0	0.0	0.0	28	1
MAVERICK	0.3	1.1	2.1	0.0	0.0	0.0	0.0	0.0	0.0	22	12
MEDIC	2.2	1.6	1.6	0.0	0.0	0.0	0.5	0.0	0.0	29	0
MENTOR	0.8	1.4	0.8	0.0	0.0	0.0	0.0	0.0	0.0	12	20
MIDGET	0.6	-0.3	0.7	0.0	0.0	0.0	0.0	0.0	0.0	32	0
MILQUETOAST	0.0	-1.4	-0.9	0.0	0.0	0.0	0.0	0.0	0.0	10	21
MINOR	0.4	-0.5	1.7	0.0	0.0	0.0	0.0	0.0	0.0	31	0
MINX	-0.7	-0.8	0.9	0.0	0.0	0.0	0.0	0.0	0.0	9	22
MISER	-1.4	-0.2	-1.3	0.0	-1.6*	0.0	0.0	0.0	0.0	26	0
MISS	0.8	-0.4	0.9	0.0	0.0	0.0	0.0	0.0	0.0	30	3
MISTRESS	-0.3	-0.7	0.8	1.0	0.0	0.0	-0.5	0.0	-0.6	28	0
MOBSTER	-2.3	1.7	1.9	0.0	0.0	0.0	-0.5	0.0	0.0	34	0
MOPPET	1.1	-0.9	0.8	-2.1*	0.0	0.0	0.0	0.0	0.0	11	19
MORON	-0.4	-1.7	-0.6	0.0	0.0	0.0	0.0	0.0	0.0	27	0
MOTHER	2.4	1.4	1.3	0.0	0.0	0.0	0.4	0.5	0.0	31	0
MOUTHPIECE	0.3	-0.1	1.1	0.0	0.0	0.0	0.0	0.0	0.0	28	4
MUGGER	-3.0	-0.2	0.7	0.0	0.0	1.2	0.0	0.0	0.0	31	0
NARK	-0.1	0.3	1.1	0.0	0.0	-1.1	1.0*	0.5	-0.5	32	1
NEIGHBOR	1.4	0.3	0.7	0.0	0.0	0.0	0.0	0.0	0.0	27	0
NEPHEW	0.9	-0.2	1.0	0.0	0.0	0.0	0.0	0.0	0.0	33	0
NEUROTIC	-1.1	-2.1	1.0	0.0	0.0	-1.1	0.0	0.0	0.0	29	0
NEWCOMER	0.9	-0.8	0.8	0.0	0.0	0.0	0.0	0.0	0.0	27	0
NIECE	1.1	-0.4	1.0	0.0	0.0	0.0	0.0	0.0	0.0	30	1
NIGHT WATCHMAN	1.4	0.3	-0.7	0.0	0.0	0.0	0.0	0.0	0.0	32	0
NINNY	-0.3	-1.3	-0.6	0.0	0.0	0.0	0.0	0.0	0.0	25	6

	1	2	3	4	5	6	7	8	9	10	11
NITWIT	-0.6	-1.7	0.1	0.0	0.0	0.0	0.0	0.0	0.0	33	0
NOBODY	-0.3	-1.6	-1.2	0.0	0.0	0.0	0.0	0.0	0.0	32	0
NONCONFORMIST	0.5	1.5	1.5	0.0	0.0	0.0	-0.4	0.0	0.0	30	0
NOVICE	0.7	-0.3	0.8	0.0	0.0	0.0	0.0	0.0	0.0	25	2
NUMSKULL	-1.0	-1.8	-0.5	0.0	0.0	0.0	0.0	0.0	0.0	34	0
NURSE	2.0	1.3	1.2	0.0	0.0	0.0	0.0	0.0	0.0	30	0
NURSEMAID	1.1	0.4	0.1	0.0	0.0	0.0	0.5	0.0	0.0	31	0
NUT	-0.2	-0.9	1.6	0.0	0.0	0.0	-0.3	-0.4	-0.4	31	0
NYMPH	0.2	-0.5	1.7	1.6*	0.0	0.0	0.0	0.0	0.0	20	12
ODDBALL	0.0	-0.7	0.3	0.0	0.0	0.0	0.0	0.0	0.0	34	0
OGRE	-1.2	0.6	0.2	0.0	0.0	-1.5	0.0	0.0	0.0	23	4
OLD FOGY	-0.4	-0.9	-1.4	0.0	0.0	0.0	0.0	0.0	0.0	31	0
OLD MAID	0.6	-0.9	-0.7	0.0	0.0	0.0	0.0	0.0	0.0	34	0
OLDTIMER	1.5	-0.2	-0.8	0.0	0.0	0.0	0.0	-0.4	0.0	32	0
ONLOOKER	-0.1	-1.2	-0.7	0.0	0.0	0.0	0.0	0.0	0.0	30	1
ORPHAN	0.9	-1.2	0.2	0.0	0.0	0.0	0.0	0.0	0.0	32	0
OUTLAW	-2.0	0.7	1.9	0.0	-0.8	0.0	-0.4	0.0	0.0	30	0
OUTPATIENT	0.3	-0.5	-0.5	0.0	0.0	0.0	0.0	0.0	0.0	33	1
OUTSIDER	0.1	-0.6	0.0	0.0	0.0	0.0	0.0	0.0	0.0	32	0
PAL	2.3	1.5	1.6	0.0	0.0	0.0	0.0	0.0	0.0	30	0
PANSY	-0.8	-2.0	-0.6	0.0	0.0	0.0	0.0	0.0	0.0	34	0
PARANOID	-1.6	-2.3	0.1	0.0	1.6*	1.2	0.0	0.0	0.0	30	0
PARENT	2.3	2.0	1.2	0.0	0.0	0.0	0.6*	0.7*	0.7*	34	0
PATIENT	0.2	-1.3	-0.8	0.0	0.0	0.0	0.0	0.0	0.0	27	0
PATROLMAN	1.1	1.1	1.1	0.0	0.0	0.0	0.0	0.7	0.5	27	0
PAWNBROKER	0.1	-0.5	-0.2	0.0	0.0	0.0	0.0	0.0	0.0	31	0
PEDERAST	0.4	-0.1	0.0	0.0	0.0	0.0	0.0	0.0	0.0	5	28
PEEPING TOM	-2.4	-2.2	1.9	1.1	0.0	-1.4*	0.0	0.0	-0.7*	32	0
PEST	-1.9	-0.8	1.4	0.0	0.0	0.0	0.0	0.0	0.0	32	0
PHONY	-2.0	-2.5	-0.2	0.0	0.0	0.0	-0.7	0.0	-0.6	29	0
PHYSICIAN	2.2	1.8	1.8	0.0	0.0	0.0	0.5	0.5	0.0	34	0
PICKPOCKET	-1.6	-1.0	0.8	0.0	0.0	0.0	0.0	0.0	0.0	30	0
PICKUP	-0.5	-0.9	1.0	0.7	0.0	0.0	0.0	0.0	0.0	29	2
PIMP	-1.9	-1.5	-0.1	0.0	1.5*	1.4	0.0	0.0	0.0	27	2
PINHEAD	-0.7	-1.5	-0.6	0.0	0.0	0.0	0.0	0.0	0.0	19	8
PIPSQUEAK	-0.5	-1.6	0.7	0.0	0.0	0.0	0.0	0.0	0.6	29	3
PLAINCLOTHESMA	0.2	0.8	0.2	0.0	0.0	0.0	0.9*	0.0	0.0	32	0
PLAYBOY	0.0	-0.2	1.7	0.0	0.0	0.0	0.0	0.0	0.0	31	0
PLAYMATE	2.2	0.6	2.5	0.0	0.0	0.0	0.0	0.0	0.0	32	0
POLICEMAN	1.0	1.1	1.4	0.0	0.0	0.0	1.0*	0.6	0.0	32	1
PORNO STAR	-0.7	-0.7	1.6	0.9	0.0	1.0	-0.6	-0.8	0.0	31	0
POTHEAD	-1.2	-1.8	0.1	0.0	0.0	0.0	-1.2*	-0.8*	-0.6	30	2
PRACTICAL NURS	1.8	0.8	0.5	0.0	0.0	0.9	0.0	0.0	0.0	30	1
PREY	-0.4	-1.2	0.2	0.0	0.0	0.0	0.0	0.5	0.5	27	0
PRIG	-0.9	-0.6	-0.3	0.0	0.0	0.0	0.0	0.0	0.0	14	20
PRINCIPAL	0.8	1.2	0.2	0.0	0.0	0.0	0.0	0.0	0.0	29	0
PRISONER	-0.5	-1.0	-0.5	0.0	0.0	0.0	0.0	0.0	0.0	31	0
PROBATION OFFI	1.2	1.2	0.3	0.0	0.0	0.0	0.0	0.0	0.5	32	0
PROBATIONER	0.4	0.5	0.1	0.0	0.0	0.0	-0.4	-0.7	0.0	27	4
PROCTOR	1.0	0.4	0.0	0.0	0.0	0.0	0.0	0.0	0.0	18	13
PRODIGY	1.4	0.7	1.5	0.0	0.0	0.0	0.6	0.0	0.0	27	2
PROFESSOR	1.0	0.9	0.1	0.0	0.0	0.0	0.4	0.4	0.0	32	0
PROSECUTING AT	0.4	1.5	1.1	0.0	0.0	0.0	0.0	0.0	0.0	31	0
PROSTITUTE	-1.3	-1.2	0.6	0.0	0.0	0.0	-0.7*	0.0	0.0	32	0
PRUDE	0.0	-1.2	-1.1	-1.2	0.0	0.0	0.0	0.0	0.0	31	2
PSYCHIATRIST	1.6	1.2	0.4	0.0	0.0	0.0	0.0	0.0	0.0	32	0

	1	2	3	4	5	6	7	8	9	10	11
PSYCHOANALYST	1.7	1.2	0.2	-1.2*	-0.9	0.0	-0.4	0.0	0.0	33	0
PSYCHOLOGIST	1.8	1.6	0.5	-1.0	-1.1	0.0	-0.4	0.0	0.0	33	0
PSYCHOPATH	-1.8	-1.5	1.0	0.0	1.3	0.0	0.0	0.0	0.0	31	1
PSYCHOTIC	-1.3	-1.5	0.4	0.0	0.8	0.0	-0.4	0.0	0.0	30	0
PUNK	-1.1	-1.8	0.3	0.0	0.0	0.0	0.0	0.0	0.0	34	0
PUPIL	0.7	-0.5	1.2	0.0	0.0	0.0	0.0	0.0	0.0	29	0
PURITAN	0.4	0.2	-0.6	0.0	0.0	0.0	0.5	0.7	0.0	30	1
PUSHER	-2.5	-0.1	0.8	0.0	-1.2	-1.0	-0.4	0.0	0.0	26	0
QUACK	-2.6	-1.6	-0.2	0.0	0.0	0.9	0.0	0.0	0.0	28	2
QUARTERBACK	1.0	2.0	2.8	0.0	0.0	0.0	0.0	0.6	0.6	31	0
QUEER	-0.9	-0.9	0.3	0.0	-0.9	0.0	-0.5	-0.6	0.0	32	0
RACKETEER	-1.9	0.4	1.4	0.0	0.0	0.0	0.0	-0.7*	0.0	27	3
RAKE	-0.9	-0.9	0.7	0.0	0.0	0.0	0.0	0.0	0.0	15	18
RASCAL	-0.6	-0.1	1.9	0.0	-1.1	-1.2	-0.5	0.0	0.0	32	0
RAT	-1.3	-0.7	0.8	0.0	0.0	0.0	0.0	0.0	0.0	28	0
RATTLEBRAIN	-0.4	-1.5	0.4	0.0	0.0	0.0	0.0	0.0	0.0	29	5
RECEPTIONIST	1.1	-0.4	0.7	0.0	0.0	0.0	0.0	0.0	0.5	30	0
REFEREE	0.6	0.7	1.4	0.0	0.0	0.0	0.0	0.0	0.0	27	0
RELATION	0.9	0.5	0.6	0.0	0.0	0.0	0.0	0.0	0.0	30	2
REPORTER	0.6	0.7	2.3	0.0	0.0	0.0	0.0	0.0	0.0	27	0
RETARDATE	0.0	-1.2	-0.3	0.0	0.0	0.0	0.0	0.0	0.0	28	1
RINGLEADER	0.1	1.4	1.7	0.0	0.0	0.0	0.0	0.0	0.0	27	0
RIVAL	-0.6	1.0	1.4	0.0	0.0	0.0	0.0	0.0	0.0	32	0
ROGUE	-1.4	-0.3	0.7	0.0	0.0	0.0	0.0	0.0	0.0	25	6
ROOKIE COP	1.1	0.0	1.8	0.0	0.0	0.0	0.0	0.0	0.0	32	0
ROOMER	0.4	-0.3	0.5	0.0	0.0	0.0	-0.4	0.0	0.0	22	7
ROOMMATE	1.2	0.1	0.7	-0.9	0.0	0.0	0.0	0.0	0.0	32	0
ROUGHNECK	-2.0	0.6	1.8	0.0	0.0	0.0	0.0	0.0	0.0	27	0
ROWDY	-0.6	-0.5	1.8	0.0	0.0	0.0	-0.6	0.0	0.0	21	8
RUBE	0.3	-0.9	0.5	0.0	0.0	0.0	0.0	0.0	0.0	11	24
RUFFIAN	-0.4	0.4	1.4	-0.8	0.0	0.0	0.0	0.0	0.0	24	5
RUNAWAY	-0.5	-1.3	1.3	0.0	0.0	0.0	0.0	0.0	-0.5	31	0
SAFECRACKER	-2.0	-0.2	0.4	0.0	0.0	-1.2	-0.5	0.0	0.0	32	0
SALESGIRL	1.4	-0.4	1.2	0.0	0.0	0.0	0.0	0.0	0.0	27	0
SALESLADY	1.0	-0.4	-0.1	0.0	0.0	0.0	0.0	0.0	0.0	31	0
SALESMAN	0.6	0.9	1.5	0.0	-0.8	0.0	0.0	0.0	0.0	29	0
SALESWOMAN	0.8	-0.1	-0.1	0.0	0.0	1.5*	0.0	0.0	0.0	30	0
SALOON-KEEPER	0.7	-0.1	0.7	0.0	0.0	0.0	0.0	0.0	0.0	27	0
SAPHEAD	-1.1	-2.1	-1.0	0.0	0.0	0.0	0.0	0.0	0.0	22	11
SATYR	0.6	0.5	1.6	-1.4	0.0	0.0	0.0	0.0	0.0	13	16
SAWBONES	0.2	-0.4	0.2	0.0	0.0	0.0	0.0	0.0	0.0	10	22
SCAMP	-0.9	-1.6	0.0	0.0	1.1	1.2	0.0	0.0	0.0	27	4
SCAPEGOAT	-1.0	-1.5	-0.2	0.0	0.0	-0.9	-0.5	0.0	0.0	31	1
SCATTERBRAIN	-0.4	-1.2	1.4	0.0	0.0	0.0	0.0	0.0	0.0	32	0
SCHOLAR	1.6	1.0	0.1	0.0	-1.0	0.0	0.0	0.0	0.0	32	0
SCHOOLBOY	0.6	-0.3	1.8	0.0	0.0	0.0	0.4	0.0	0.0	31	0
SCHOOLGIRL	1.2	-0.4	1.5	0.0	0.0	0.0	0.0	0.0	0.0	34	0
SCHOOLMATE	1.4	0.4	1.8	0.0	0.0	0.0	0.0	0.0	0.0	27	0
SCHOOLTEACHER	1.3	0.9	0.6	0.0	0.0	0.0	0.3	0.0	0.0	32	0
SCOUNDREL	-2.0	-1.1	0.8	0.7	0.0	0.0	0.0	0.0	0.0	33	0
SCOUTMASTER	1.7	1.2	1.4	0.0	0.0	0.0	0.0	0.5	0.0	29	0
SCREWBALL	-0.7	-0.9	1.0	0.0	0.0	0.0	0.0	0.0	-0.5	34	0
SCROOGE	-1.7	-0.9	-1.5	0.0	0.0	0.0	0.0	0.0	0.0	31	1
SECONDSTORY MA	0.6	-0.2	0.6	-2.3*	0.0	0.0	1.0	0.0	0.0	14	17
SECRETARY	1.1	-0.1	0.7	0.0	0.0	0.0	0.0	0.0	0.0	31	0
SENIOR	1.1	1.4	2.0	0.0	-0.8	-1.4*	0.0	0.0	0.0	30	0

	1	2	3	4	5	6	7	8	9	10	11
SERVANT	1.2	-0.6	0.1	0.0	0.0	0.0	0.0	0.0	0.0	27	0
SEXPOT	-0.4	-0.8	2.4	0.0	0.0	0.0	-0.9*	0.0	0.0	29	0
SHARPIE	0.0	0.5	1.4	0.0	0.0	0.0	0.0	0.0	0.0	18	13
SHERIFF	1.3	1.6	0.5	0.0	0.0	0.0	0.0	0.0	0.0	31	0
SHOPLIFTER	-1.9	-1.5	1.2	0.0	0.0	0.0	0.0	0.0	0.5	31	0
SHREW	-1.4	-0.4	0.7	0.0	0.0	0.0	0.0	0.0	0.0	27	5
SHRIMP	-0.5	-1.9	-0.3	0.0	0.0	0.0	0.0	0.0	0.0	28	1
SHUT-IN	0.0	-1.6	-1.3	0.0	0.0	0.0	0.0	0.0	0.0	28	5
SHYSTER	-0.1	-0.6	-0.2	-1.7*	0.0	1.4	0.0	0.5	0.0	20	11
SIBLING	1.4	0.3	1.8	0.0	0.0	0.0	0.0	0.0	0.0	31	3
SIDEKICK	0.7	-0.7	0.9	0.0	0.0	0.0	-0.5	0.0	0.0	25	2
SIMPLETON	0.2	-1.2	-0.3	0.0	0.0	0.0	0.0	0.0	0.0	29	0
SISSY	-0.4	-1.7	-0.4	0.0	0.0	0.0	0.0	0.0	0.0	32	0
SISTER	2.3	0.8	2.6	0.0	0.0	-1.0	0.0	0.0	0.0	29	1
SISTER-IN-LAW	1.3	0.1	1.0	0.0	0.0	0.0	0.0	0.0	0.0	29	0
SKEPTIC	-0.7	-0.2	-0.2	0.0	0.0	0.0	-0.5	0.0	0.0	29	0
SLAVE	0.6	-1.6	-0.7	-1.2	0.0	0.0	0.0	0.0	0.0	32	0
SLAVEDRIVER	-2.3	0.8	0.8	0.0	0.0	0.0	0.0	0.6	0.0	30	1
SLEUTH	0.0	0.3	0.4	0.0	0.0	0.0	0.0	0.0	0.0	24	5
SLOB	-1.5	-1.9	-1.0	0.0	0.0	0.0	0.0	0.0	0.0	28	0
SLUGGARD	-2.2	-2.1	-1.5	1.2	1.6	0.0	0.0	0.0	0.0	19	10
SLUT	-1.8	-1.8	0.9	0.0	0.0	0.0	0.0	-0.4	0.0	29	0
SMART ALECK	-1.4	-1.4	1.3	0.0	0.0	0.0	0.0	0.0	0.0	31	0
SNEAK	-1.7	-1.6	0.2	0.0	0.0	0.0	0.0	0.0	-0.5	33	0
SNOB	-1.1	-0.2	-0.4	-0.9	-0.9	0.0	0.0	0.5	0.4	30	0
SNOOP	-2.1	-1.4	-0.3	0.0	0.0	0.0	0.0	0.0	0.0	32	0
SNOT	-1.7	-1.0	-0.1	0.0	0.0	0.0	0.0	0.0	0.0	30	4
SODOMITE	-1.8	2.7	0.0	0.0	-1.8	0.0	0.0	2.8*	0.0	14	15
SON	2.4	1.5	2.6	-0.7	0.0	0.0	0.5	0.4	0.0	30	0
SON-IN-LAW	1.3	0.8	1.6	0.0	0.0	0.0	0.5	0.7*	0.5	30	0
SOPHISTICATE	0.4	-0.2	0.4	0.0	0.0	0.0	0.0	0.0	0.0	27	2
SOPHOMORE	0.8	0.0	1.2	0.0	0.0	0.0	0.0	0.0	0.0	30	0
SOREHEAD	-1.7	-0.9	-1.0	0.0	0.0	1.7*	0.0	0.0	0.0	29	2
SOUSE	-1.4	-1.8	-0.1	0.0	0.0	0.0	0.5	0.0	0.0	12	16
SPECIALIST	2.0	1.8	1.1	0.0	0.0	0.0	0.0	0.0	0.0	29	0
SPECTATOR	0.9	-0.3	1.1	0.0	0.0	0.0	0.4	0.0	0.5	32	0
SPEEDER	-1.0	-0.5	2.2	0.0	0.0	0.0	-0.4	0.0	0.0	31	0
SPENDTHRIFT	-0.5	-1.1	0.4	0.0	0.0	0.0	0.0	-0.6	0.0	26	2
SPINSTER	0.4	-0.4	-0.7	-0.8	0.0	0.0	0.0	0.0	0.5	30	0
SPOILSPORT	-1.5	-1.5	-0.1	0.0	0.0	0.0	0.0	0.0	0.0	33	0
SPONGER	-2.1	-2.1	-0.5	0.0	0.0	0.0	0.0	0.0	0.0	22	11
SPOUSE	2.1	1.5	1.9	0.0	0.0	0.0	0.0	0.0	0.0	29	0
SPY	-0.2	0.7	1.0	0.0	-1.0	0.0	0.0	0.0	-0.4	33	0
SQUARE	0.0	-0.5	-0.9	0.0	0.0	0.0	0.0	0.0	0.0	31	0
SQUIRT	-0.1	-1.3	1.2	0.0	0.0	0.0	-0.6	-0.6	0.0	27	2
STAR	0.6	1.0	1.8	0.0	0.0	0.0	0.0	0.0	0.0	32	0
STARLET	0.7	-0.2	2.1	0.0	0.0	0.0	0.0	0.0	0.5	31	1
STATE TROOPER	1.0	1.1	0.7	-1.1	0.0	0.0	0.6	0.0	0.0	31	0
STENOGRAPHER	1.2	-0.3	0.6	0.0	0.0	0.0	0.0	0.0	0.0	30	1
STEPBROTHER	0.6	0.3	0.7	0.0	0.0	0.0	0.0	0.0	0.0	29	0
STEPDAUGHTER	0.8	-0.1	0.7	0.0	0.0	0.0	0.0	0.0	0.0	26	2
STEPFATHER	0.2	0.4	0.1	0.0	0.0	0.0	0.0	0.0	0.0	27	0
STEPMOTHER	0.5	0.0	0.2	0.0	0.0	0.0	0.0	0.0	0.0	33	0
STEPSISTER	0.6	-0.1	0.6	0.0	0.0	0.0	0.0	0.0	0.0	30	0
STEPSON	0.9	0.3	1.0	0.0	0.0	0.0	0.4	0.0	0.0	33	1
STEWARDESS	1.4	0.1	1.7	0.0	0.0	0.0	0.0	0.0	0.0	30	1

	1	2	3	4	5	6	7	8	9	10	11
STOOL PIGEON	-1.7	-1.7	-0.3	0.0	0.0	0.0	0.0	0.0	0.0	32	
STRAIGHT	0.9	-0.1	-0.3	0.0	0.0	0.0	0.6*	0.4	0.5	31	
STRANGER	0.1	-0.3	-0.1	0.0	0.0	0.0	0.0	0.0	0.0	30	
STREETWALKER	-0.7	-0.8	0.8	0.0	0.0	0.0	0.0	0.0	0.0	28	
STRIPPER	0.1	0.0	2.5	0.0	0.0	0.0	-0.8*	0.0	0.0	30	
STRUMPET	-0.6	-0.4	0.9	0.0	-1.5	0.0	0.0	0.0	0.0	12	1
STUDENT	1.4	0.4	2.4	0.0	0.0	0.0	0.0	0.0	0.0	29	
STUFFED SHIRT	-0.8	-1.0	-1.1	0.0	0.0	0.0	0.0	0.0	0.0	29	
SUBORDINATE	0.2	-0.9	-0.1	0.0	0.0	0.0	0.0	0.0	0.0	27	
SUCKER	-0.5	-2.1	-0.6	0.0	0.0	0.0	-0.6*	0.0	0.0	31	
SUPERIOR	0.7	1.3	0.5	0.0	0.0	0.0	0.0	0.0	0.0	27	
SUPERSTAR	1.2	1.6	2.6	0.0	0.0	0.0	0.0	0.0	0.0	30	
SUPERVISOR	1.0	1.1	0.4	0.0	0.0	0.0	0.4	0.0	0.0	31	
SURGEON	2.5	2.7	1.5	-0.8	-1.5*	-1.1	0.0	0.0	0.0	32	
SUSPECT	-0.3	-0.6	0.5	0.0	0.0	0.0	0.0	0.0	0.6	29	
SWEETHEART	2.2	1.1	2.4	0.8	0.0	0.0	0.0	0.0	0.4	26	
SWINGER	0.4	0.1	2.6	0.0	0.0	0.0	0.0	0.0	0.0	32	
TACKLE	0.5	1.8	2.1	0.0	0.0	0.0	0.0	0.0	0.0	30	
TEACHER	1.9	0.9	0.7	0.0	0.0	0.0	0.0	0.0	0.0	32	
TEAMMATE	1.4	1.2	1.8	0.0	0.0	0.0	0.0	0.0	0.0	29	
TEASE	-1.3	-0.6	1.6	0.0	0.0	-1.1	0.0	0.0	0.0	31	
TECHNICIAN	1.9	0.7	1.0	-0.7	0.0	0.0	0.4	0.0	0.0	30	
TEENYBOPPER	0.3	-0.8	2.1	0.0	0.0	0.0	0.0	0.0	0.0	31	
TEETOTALER	0.0	-0.2	-0.3	0.0	0.0	0.0	0.3	0.0	0.0	30	
TENANT	0.4	-0.6	-0.1	0.0	0.0	0.0	0.0	0.0	0.0	29	
THIEF	-2.3	0.4	0.7	0.0	-2.0*	0.0	-0.4	0.0	0.0	27	
THUG	-2.7	-0.3	0.2	0.0	0.0	0.0	0.0	0.0	0.0	26	
TIGHTWAD	-1.0	-0.6	-0.5	0.0	0.0	0.0	0.0	-0.7	0.0	28	
TOMBOY	0.9	1.1	2.6	0.0	0.0	0.0	0.0	0.0	0.0	32	
TOT	1.2	-1.3	2.0	0.0	0.0	0.0	0.0	0.0	0.0	27	
TOUGH	-1.5	0.6	1.7	0.0	0.0	-1.1	0.0	0.0	0.0	26	
TOWNSMAN	1.1	0.6	0.4	-0.8	0.0	0.0	0.0	0.0	0.0	29	
TRAINEE	0.8	-0.9	1.2	0.0	0.0	0.0	0.0	0.0	0.0	27	
TRAITOR	-2.8	-1.3	-0.1	0.0	-1.2	0.0	0.0	0.0	0.0	30	
TRAMP	-1.5	-1.9	-0.2	0.0	0.0	-1.1	-0.5	0.0	0.0	30	
TROLLOP	-0.4	-1.1	0.2	0.0	0.0	0.0	0.0	0.0	0.0	12	1
TROUBLEMAKER	-2.7	-0.7	1.7	0.9	0.0	-0.8	0.0	0.0	0.0	33	
TRUANT	-0.6	-0.7	1.0	0.0	0.0	0.0	0.0	0.0	0.0	25	
TRUELOVE	2.6	2.1	2.4	0.0	0.0	0.0	0.5	0.0	0.0	34	
TURNCOAT	-1.4	-0.7	0.8	0.0	-1.5	-1.7	0.0	0.0	0.0	18	1
TUTOR	1.8	0.8	0.7	0.0	0.0	0.0	0.0	0.0	0.0	29	
TYPIST	1.0	-0.6	0.4	0.0	0.0	0.0	0.0	0.0	0.0	30	
UNCLE	1.3	0.6	0.3	0.0	0.0	0.0	0.0	0.5	0.0	27	
UNDERDOG	0.7	-0.9	-0.1	0.0	0.0	0.0	0.0	0.0	0.0	30	
UNDERGRADUATE	1.1	-0.2	2.4	0.0	0.0	0.0	0.0	0.0	0.0	27	
URCHIN	-0.3	-0.3	0.5	0.0	-1.2	0.0	0.0	0.0	0.0	23	
V.I.P.	0.5	1.4	0.7	0.0	0.0	0.0	0.0	0.0	0.0	26	
VAGABOND	-0.4	-0.9	0.2	0.0	0.0	0.0	0.0	0.0	0.0	24	
VAGRANT	-0.9	-1.5	-0.2	0.0	0.0	0.0	-0.4	0.0	0.5	30	
VAMP	-1.1	-0.5	1.9	0.0	0.0	-1.3	-0.4	0.0	-0.6	23	
VAMPIRE	-2.2	1.3	0.5	0.0	0.0	0.0	0.0	0.0	0.5	30	
VANDAL	-2.1	-0.3	1.3	0.0	-1.0	0.0	0.0	0.0	0.0	33	
VICTIM	-0.3	-1.8	-1.2	0.0	0.0	1.5*	-0.7	0.0	0.0	28	
VIGILANTE	-1.0	1.0	1.6	-0.9	0.0	0.0	0.0	0.0	0.0	22	
VILLAIN	-2.4	1.2	1.5	0.0	-1.0	0.0	0.0	0.0	0.0	31	
VIRGIN	1.2	0.6	0.5	0.0	0.0	0.0	0.8*	1.3*	0.9*	34	

	1	2	3	4	5	6	7	8	9	10	11
VISITOR	1.0	0.1	0.7	0.0	0.0	0.0	0.0	0.0	0.0	32	0
VIXEN	-1.9	0.2	1.6	1.8*	0.0	0.0	0.0	0.0	-0.6	20	11
VOYEUR	-0.2	-0.8	0.9	0.0	0.0	0.0	0.0	0.0	0.0	16	17
WAGE EARNER	1.8	0.6	0.8	0.0	0.0	0.0	0.0	0.0	0.4	32	0
WAIF	0.3	-1.6	-0.5	0.0	0.0	1.9	0.0	0.6	0.0	15	14
WAITER	1.3	-0.3	0.6	0.0	0.0	0.0	0.0	0.0	0.0	32	0
WAITRESS	1.3	0.0	1.2	0.0	0.0	0.0	0.0	0.0	0.0	29	0
WALLFLOWER	-0.1	-2.0	-1.2	0.0	0.0	0.0	0.0	0.0	0.0	32	2
WARDEN	-0.1	1.2	-0.2	0.0	0.0	0.0	0.0	0.0	0.0	27	0
WATCHMAN	1.2	0.7	-0.5	0.0	-1.0	0.0	-0.4	0.0	0.0	28	0
WEAKLING	-0.4	-2.2	-0.7	0.0	0.0	0.0	0.0	0.0	0.0	31	0
WEIRDO	-0.1	-0.5	0.7	0.0	0.0	0.0	0.0	0.0	0.0	28	1
WENCH	-0.8	-0.6	0.7	0.0	0.0	0.0	-0.5	0.0	0.0	24	5
WHIZ KID	1.0	0.5	1.7	0.0	0.0	0.0	0.0	0.0	0.0	32	0
WHORE	-1.3	-0.5	1.5	0.0	-0.8	0.0	-1.1*	-0.8*	0.0	34	0
WIDOW	0.7	-0.4	-0.3	0.0	0.0	0.0	0.0	0.0	0.0	31	0
WIDOWER	0.9	-0.5	-0.9	0.0	0.0	0.0	-0.4	0.0	0.0	29	0
WIFE	2.2	1.4	2.0	0.0	0.0	0.0	0.0	0.7	0.5	32	0
WINDBAG	-1.0	-1.2	0.4	0.0	0.0	0.0	0.0	0.0	0.0	24	3
WINNER	1.3	1.9	1.9	0.0	0.0	0.0	0.4	0.6	0.0	29	0
WINO	-1.0	-1.5	-1.3	0.0	0.0	0.0	0.0	0.0	0.0	29	1
WIT	1.4	1.2	1.9	0.0	-1.2	0.0	0.0	0.0	0.0	32	2
WITCH	-1.2	1.1	0.8	0.0	0.0	0.0	-0.4	0.0	0.0	30	0
WITNESS	1.6	1.1	0.4	0.0	0.0	0.0	0.0	0.6	0.0	32	0
WIZARD	0.7	1.2	1.6	0.0	0.0	-1.2	0.0	0.0	-0.4	32	1
WOMAN	2.2	1.2	2.5	0.0	-0.9	-0.9	0.0	-0.4	0.0	30	0
WORKER	1.6	0.9	1.6	0.0	0.0	0.0	0.5	0.6	0.5	34	0
WORKMAN	1.0	0.8	0.9	0.0	0.0	0.0	0.0	0.0	0.0	30	0
WRETCH	-0.8	-0.8	-0.3	-1.1	-1.5	-1.3	0.0	0.0	0.0	24	3
WRONGDOER	-0.7	-1.2	0.7	0.0	0.0	0.0	0.4	0.0	0.0	29	0
YOKEL	0.6	-1.1	0.1	0.0	0.0	0.0	0.0	0.0	0.7	16	15
YOUNGSTER	1.3	-0.2	3.2	0.0	-1.0	0.0	0.0	0.0	0.0	30	0
YOUTH	1.7	0.8	3.1	0.0	0.0	0.0	0.0	0.5	0.0	29	0
ZOMBIE	-1.2	-1.2	-1.4	0.0	0.0	0.0	0.0	0.0	0.0	31	1

	1	2	3	4	5	6	7	8	9	10	11
ABANDON	-2.3	-0.6	-0.4	0.0	-1.4	0.0	0.0	0.0	0.0	28	
ABUSE	-2.8	-1.6	0.7	0.0	1.4	0.0	0.0	0.0	0.0	32	‡
ACCLAIM	1.7	0.9	1.2	0.0	0.0	0.0	0.0	0.0	0.0	30	
ACCOMMODATE	2.0	1.2	0.5	0.0	0.0	0.0	0.0	0.0	0.0	28	
ACCUSE	-1.2	0.2	0.6	0.0	0.0	0.0	0.0	0.0	0.0	33	
ADDRESS	0.7	0.6	0.4	0.0	0.0	0.0	0.0	0.0	0.0	30	
ADMIRE	1.8	0.5	0.5	0.0	0.0	0.0	0.0	0.0	0.0	33	
ADMONISH	0.7	0.6	0.2	0.0	0.0	0.0	0.0	0.6	0.0	19	1
ADOPT	2.3	1.6	1.0	0.0	0.0	0.0	0.0	0.0	0.0	32	
ADORE	2.0	1.5	1.1	0.0	0.0	0.0	0.0	0.0	0.0	31	
ADORN	1.4	0.9	0.7	0.0	0.0	0.0	0.0	0.0	0.0	30	
ADVISE	2.0	1.2	0.8	0.0	0.0	0.0	0.0	0.0	0.0	30	
AFFRONT	-0.5	0.0	0.9	0.0	0.0	0.0	0.4	0.0	0.0	28	
AGGRAVATE	-1.6	0.3	0.8	0.0	-1.5	0.0	0.0	0.0	0.0	28	
AGITATE	-1.1	0.2	1.6	0.0	0.0	0.0	0.0	0.0	0.0	30	
AID	2.8	1.9	1.1	0.0	0.0	0.0	0.0	0.0	0.0	29	
ALERT	1.9	1.6	1.8	0.0	0.0	0.0	0.0	0.0	0.0	34	
AMAZE	0.9	1.0	1.5	0.0	0.0	0.0	0.0	0.0	0.0	31	
AMUSE	2.0	0.6	1.7	0.0	0.0	0.0	0.0	0.0	0.0	33	
ANALYZE	0.7	0.6	0.6	0.0	0.0	-1.0	0.0	0.0	0.0	33	
ANGER	-1.5	0.6	0.9	0.0	0.0	0.0	0.0	0.0	0.0	30	
ANNIHILATE	-3.0	1.3	1.9	0.0	1.8*	0.0	0.0	0.5	0.0	27	
ANNOY	-1.9	-0.8	0.6	0.0	0.0	0.0	0.0	0.0	0.0	32	
ANSWER	2.0	1.0	0.8	0.0	0.0	0.0	0.0	0.0	0.0	32	
ANTAGONIZE	-1.6	0.1	0.9	0.0	-1.4	0.0	0.0	0.0	0.0	28	
APE	-0.3	-0.4	0.1	-1.0	0.0	1.2	-0.6	0.0	0.0	17	1
APPEASE	1.0	-0.8	-0.5	-1.8*	0.0	0.0	0.0	0.0	0.0	24	
APPLAUD	2.1	1.5	2.2	0.0	0.0	0.0	0.0	0.0	0.0	34	
APPOINT	1.4	1.9	0.8	0.0	0.0	0.0	0.0	0.0	0.0	34	
APPRECIATE	2.6	1.7	1.0	0.0	0.0	0.0	0.0	0.0	0.0	31	
APPROACH	0.6	1.1	0.6	0.0	-1.2	0.0	0.0	0.0	0.0	32	
ARM	-0.7	0.1	0.7	0.0	0.0	0.0	0.0	0.0	0.0	30	
AROUSE	1.5	1.6	1.7	-0.9	0.0	0.0	0.0	0.0	0.0	32	
ARREST	0.1	0.9	0.6	0.0	0.0	0.0	0.6*	0.0	0.0	30	
ASK	1.3	0.6	0.6	0.0	0.0	0.0	0.0	0.0	0.0	30	
ASSAIL	-1.0	1.1	1.1	0.0	0.0	1.0	0.0	0.0	0.0	25	
ASSAULT	-2.6	-0.1	0.9	0.0	0.0	0.0	0.0	0.0	0.0	32	
ASSIST	2.4	1.6	1.3	0.0	0.0	0.0	0.0	0.0	0.0	28	
ASTONISH	0.5	0.8	1.7	0.0	0.0	0.0	-0.5	0.0	0.0	29	
ASTOUND	0.8	1.2	1.4	0.0	0.0	0.0	-0.6	0.0	0.0	28	
ATTACK	-2.1	1.8	2.3	0.0	0.0	0.0	0.0	0.0	0.0	34	
AVOID	-1.0	-1.0	-0.3	0.0	0.0	0.0	0.0	0.0	0.0	31	
AWAKE	0.2	0.2	1.0	0.0	0.0	0.0	0.0	0.0	0.0	33	
AWE	0.9	1.3	0.7	-0.8	0.0	0.0	0.0	0.0	0.0	32	
BABY	-1.1	-0.7	-0.4	0.0	0.0	0.0	0.0	0.6	0.0	30	
BACK	2.2	1.6	1.9	0.0	0.0	0.0	0.0	0.0	0.5	31	
BADGER	-1.8	-0.9	0.5	0.0	0.0	1.2	0.0	0.0	0.0	30	
BAIT	-1.3	-0.6	0.3	0.0	0.0	0.0	0.0	0.0	0.0	27	
BAMBOOZLE	-1.2	0.1	0.7	0.0	0.0	0.0	0.0	0.8	0.0	17	1
BANTER	-1.1	-0.9	1.6	0.0	0.0	0.0	0.0	0.0	0.0	14	1
BATHE	1.7	0.7	1.0	0.0	0.0	0.0	0.0	0.0	0.0	34	
BATTER	-1.7	0.6	0.8	0.0	0.0	0.0	0.0	-0.7	0.0	25	
BAWL OUT	-1.4	-0.1	1.5	0.0	0.0	0.0	0.0	0.0	0.0	33	
BECKON	0.1	0.3	0.5	0.0	0.0	0.0	0.0	0.0	0.0	32	
BED	1.2	1.6	2.0	0.0	0.0	-1.0	0.0	0.0	0.0	24	
BEFRIEND	1.8	1.4	1.2	0.0	0.0	0.0	0.0	0.0	0.0	30	

	1	2	3	4	5	6	7	8	9	10	11
BEFUDDLE	-1.4	-1.0	0.5	0.0	0.0	0.0	0.0	-0.6	0.0	23	9
BEG	-0.8	-1.1	-0.3	0.0	0.0	0.0	0.0	0.0	0.0	28	0
BELIEVE	2.2	1.2	0.8	0.0	0.0	0.0	0.0	0.0	0.0	31	0
BELITTLE	-2.0	-1.1	0.1	0.0	0.0	0.0	0.0	0.0	0.0	30	3
BELT	-2.1	0.5	1.5	0.0	0.0	0.0	0.0	0.0	0.0	29	0
BERATE	-1.3	0.7	0.7	0.0	-1.5	0.0	0.0	0.0	0.0	23	11
BESEECH	-0.1	-0.6	0.4	0.0	0.0	0.0	0.0	0.6	0.0	26	5
BETRAY	-2.7	-1.7	-0.1	0.0	0.0	0.0	0.0	0.0	0.0	33	0
BEWILDER	-1.1	-0.2	0.7	0.0	0.0	0.0	0.0	0.7	0.6	30	0
BEWITCH	-0.9	0.6	0.5	0.0	0.0	0.0	0.0	0.0	0.0	29	1
BIAS	-1.3	-0.7	0.8	0.0	0.0	0.0	0.0	0.5	0.4	30	1
BIND	-1.7	-0.1	-0.2	0.0	1.5	1.4	0.0	0.0	0.0	28	4
BITE	-1.9	-0.3	0.7	0.0	-1.5	0.0	0.0	0.0	0.0	28	0
BLACKMAIL	-2.6	-1.0	0.2	0.0	0.0	0.0	0.0	-0.7	0.0	28	0
BLAME	-1.3	-0.4	0.4	0.0	0.0	0.0	0.0	0.0	0.0	29	0
BLESS	2.4	1.5	0.5	0.0	0.0	0.0	0.4	0.0	0.0	34	0
BLUFF	-0.8	0.0	0.6	0.0	0.0	0.0	0.0	0.0	0.0	31	0
BOOTLICK	-1.2	-1.0	0.0	0.0	0.0	0.0	0.0	0.0	0.0	13	19
BOP	-0.5	0.3	1.2	0.0	0.0	0.0	0.0	0.0	0.0	29	2
BOSS	-1.6	-0.3	0.8	0.0	1.4	0.0	0.0	0.0	0.0	30	0
BOTHER	-1.6	0.2	1.1	0.0	0.0	0.0	0.0	0.0	0.0	31	0
BRIBE	-2.1	-1.1	-0.1	0.0	0.0	0.0	0.0	0.0	0.5	32	0
BRIEF	1.1	0.3	0.5	0.0	0.0	0.0	0.0	0.0	0.0	27	1
BROWBEAT	-1.9	-0.6	0.7	0.9	0.0	0.0	0.0	-0.8	0.0	24	8
BULLY	-1.9	-1.7	1.0	0.0	1.3	0.0	-1.0*	0.0	0.0	29	0
BUTT	-1.5	0.6	1.2	0.0	0.0	0.0	0.0	0.0	0.0	28	6
CAJOLE	-0.4	0.0	1.0	0.0	0.0	0.0	0.0	0.0	0.0	19	12
CALL	0.7	0.5	0.5	0.0	0.0	0.0	0.0	0.0	0.0	32	0
CALM	2.4	1.4	0.1	0.0	0.0	-1.0	0.0	0.0	0.0	33	0
CAPTIVATE	0.7	1.6	1.3	0.0	0.0	0.0	0.0	0.0	0.0	32	0
CAPTURE	-1.2	1.1	1.5	0.0	0.0	0.0	0.0	0.0	0.0	30	0
CARESS	2.7	1.6	1.4	0.0	0.0	0.0	0.0	0.0	0.0	31	0
CARRY	1.7	1.8	1.3	0.0	0.0	0.0	0.0	0.0	0.0	33	0
CATCH	0.2	0.9	1.3	0.0	0.0	0.0	0.0	0.0	0.0	32	0
CAUTION	2.0	1.0	0.4	0.0	0.0	0.0	0.0	0.0	0.0	32	0
CHALLENGE	0.8	1.3	1.5	0.0	0.0	0.0	0.0	0.0	0.0	27	1
CHARM	1.3	1.2	1.2	0.7	0.0	0.0	0.0	0.0	0.0	32	0
CHASE	-0.6	0.7	1.8	0.0	0.0	0.0	0.0	-1.0*	-0.6	29	0
CHEAT	-2.4	-1.0	0.3	0.0	0.0	0.0	-0.5	0.0	0.0	32	0
CHIDE	-0.9	-0.2	0.6	0.0	0.0	0.0	0.0	0.0	0.0	24	10
CHOKE	-2.9	0.9	1.3	0.0	0.0	0.0	0.0	0.0	0.0	31	0
CLASSIFY	-0.9	-0.9	0.3	0.0	0.0	-0.8	0.3	0.0	0.0	33	0
CLAW	-1.8	0.0	1.9	0.0	0.0	0.0	0.0	0.0	0.0	32	0
CLUB	-2.6	2.0	2.0	0.0	-0.9	0.0	0.0	0.4	0.4	31	0
CLUTCH	0.3	0.6	0.8	0.0	0.0	0.0	0.0	0.0	0.0	32	0
COACH	1.3	1.0	1.4	0.0	0.0	0.0	0.0	0.0	0.0	27	1
COAX	0.0	0.5	0.6	0.0	0.0	0.0	-0.5	0.0	0.0	32	0
CODDLE	1.0	0.1	0.0	0.0	0.0	0.0	0.0	0.0	0.7	24	5
COERCE	-1.1	1.0	1.2	0.0	0.0	0.0	0.5	0.0	0.0	31	3
COMBAT	-1.1	1.6	1.6	0.0	0.0	0.0	0.0	0.0	0.0	31	0
COMFORT	2.7	1.6	0.4	0.0	0.0	0.0	0.0	0.0	0.0	33	0
COMMAND	-0.6	1.4	0.6	0.0	0.0	0.9	0.0	0.0	0.0	31	0
COMPLIMENT	2.7	1.5	0.7	0.0	0.0	0.0	0.0	0.0	0.0	30	0
CON	-2.2	0.9	1.6	0.0	-1.3	0.0	0.0	0.0	0.5	31	0
CONDEMN	-2.0	-0.4	0.2	0.0	0.0	0.0	0.0	0.0	0.0	32	0
CONFINE	-1.7	0.0	-0.5	0.0	0.0	0.0	0.0	0.0	0.0	28	0

	1	2	3	4	5	6	7	8	9	10	1
CONFOUND	-0.6	0.2	1.0	0.0	0.0	0.0	0.0	0.0	0.0	23	
CONFRONT	1.4	1.6	0.9	-1.2	0.0	0.0	0.0	0.0	0.0	28	
CONFUSE	-1.7	-0.3	0.6	0.0	0.0	0.0	0.0	0.0	0.0	34	
CONGRATULATE	2.4	1.6	1.3	0.0	0.0	0.0	0.0	0.0	0.0	31	
CONK	-1.7	0.2	1.0	0.0	0.0	0.0	0.0	0.0	0.0	30	
CONSIDER	1.8	1.3	0.5	-1.2	0.0	0.0	0.0	0.0	0.0	31	
CONSOLE	2.6	2.0	0.2	0.0	0.0	0.0	0.0	0.0	0.0	32	
CONSTRAIN	-0.8	0.9	0.4	0.0	0.0	-0.9	0.0	0.0	0.0	28	
CONTEMPLATE	1.0	0.4	-0.5	0.0	1.0	0.0	0.0	0.0	0.0	30	
CONTRADICT	0.1	0.6	0.6	0.0	0.0	0.0	0.0	0.0	0.0	32	
CONTROL	-1.3	1.4	0.6	0.0	-1.1	0.0	0.0	-0.6	0.0	32	
CONVICT	-0.3	1.0	-0.1	0.0	0.0	0.0	0.0	0.0	0.0	28	
CONVINCE	0.9	1.8	1.6	0.0	0.0	0.0	0.0	0.0	0.0	30	
CORNER	-1.3	-0.3	0.4	0.0	1.3	0.0	0.0	-0.8	0.0	28	
CORRECT	1.4	1.1	0.6	0.0	-1.0	0.0	0.0	0.0	0.0	34	
CORRUPT	-2.4	0.3	0.6	0.0	0.0	0.0	-0.5	0.0	0.0	31	
COUNSEL	2.5	1.3	0.2	-0.8	0.0	0.0	0.0	0.0	0.0	33	
COURT	1.8	1.0	1.9	0.0	0.0	-0.8	0.0	0.0	0.0	32	
COVER	0.8	0.6	0.3	0.0	0.0	0.0	0.4	0.0	0.0	31	
CRITICIZE	-0.5	-0.1	0.0	0.9	0.0	1.3	0.0	0.0	0.0	30	
CROSSEXAMINE	-1.3	1.1	0.1	0.8	0.0	1.3	0.0	0.5	0.0	29	
CUCKOLD	-1.5	-0.7	0.3	0.0	0.0	0.0	0.0	0.0	0.0	10	2
CUDDLE	2.0	1.1	0.6	0.0	0.0	0.0	0.0	-0.6	0.0	27	
CUE	1.2	0.7	1.0	0.0	0.0	0.0	0.0	0.0	0.0	28	
CUFF	-1.4	-0.6	1.5	0.0	1.9	0.0	0.0	0.0	0.0	20	1
CURE	2.8	2.2	1.3	0.0	0.0	0.0	0.0	0.0	0.0	33	
CUSS	-1.9	-0.9	1.4	0.0	0.0	0.0	0.0	0.0	-0.8*	31	
DAMN	-1.9	0.6	1.3	0.0	-1.3	-0.9	-0.3	0.0	0.0	33	
DANCE WITH	1.4	0.6	1.6	0.0	0.0	0.0	-0.3	0.0	0.0	33	
DARE	-0.9	-0.5	1.2	0.0	0.0	0.0	0.0	0.0	0.0	30	
DAZZLE	1.2	0.4	2.1	0.0	0.0	0.0	0.0	0.0	0.0	30	
DEBAUCH	-1.2	1.6	0.7	0.0	-1.9	0.0	0.0	0.8	0.0	14	19
DECEIVE	-2.6	-1.0	-0.2	0.0	0.0	0.0	0.0	0.0	0.0	32	
DEFEND	2.2	1.7	1.4	0.0	0.0	0.0	0.0	0.0	0.0	30	
DEFILE	-1.4	-0.5	0.3	0.0	0.0	0.0	-0.7	0.0	0.0	22	1
DEFLATE	-1.3	-1.1	0.1	0.0	0.0	0.0	-0.7	0.0	0.0	29	
DEFLOWER	-1.7	0.5	1.2	1.6*	0.0	0.0	-0.6	0.0	0.0	26	8
DEFY	-0.6	1.8	1.5	0.0	0.0	0.0	0.0	0.0	0.0	31	
DEGRADE	-2.3	-1.0	0.1	0.0	0.0	0.0	0.0	0.0	0.0	33	
DELIGHT	2.9	1.8	2.2	0.0	0.0	0.0	0.0	0.0	0.0	30	
DELUDE	-1.5	-0.7	0.1	0.0	0.0	0.0	0.0	0.0	0.0	25	5
DEMEAN	-1.9	-0.3	0.0	0.0	0.0	0.0	0.0	0.0	0.0	26	6
DEMORALIZE	-2.6	-0.7	-0.1	0.0	0.0	0.0	0.0	0.0	0.0	30	
DENOUNCE	-1.2	0.5	0.2	0.0	-1.3	0.0	0.0	0.0	0.0	27	1
DEPRAVE	-1.7	-0.5	-0.1	0.0	0.0	0.0	0.0	0.0	0.0	26	6
DEPRECATE	-1.5	-1.4	-0.1	0.0	0.0	0.0	0.0	0.0	0.0	21	9
DEPRIVE	-1.7	-0.2	0.1	0.0	0.0	0.0	0.0	0.0	0.0	34	
DERIDE	-1.5	-0.1	0.5	0.0	-1.0	0.0	0.0	0.0	0.0	18	14
DESERT	-2.1	-0.6	0.2	0.0	-1.1	0.0	0.0	0.0	0.0	32	
DESIRE	1.8	2.1	2.1	-1.0	-1.2	0.0	0.0	0.0	0.0	33	
DESPISE	-2.2	-0.2	0.7	0.0	0.0	0.0	0.0	0.0	0.0	33	
DESTROY	-2.8	0.1	0.5	0.0	0.0	0.0	0.0	-1.0*	0.0	31	
DETAIN	-1.0	0.1	0.0	0.0	0.0	0.0	0.0	0.0	0.5	30	
DETER	-0.9	0.5	0.7	0.0	0.0	0.0	-0.6*	0.0	0.0	27	3
DETEST	-2.0	-0.4	0.1	0.0	0.0	0.0	0.0	0.0	0.0	32	
DIAPER	1.2	0.2	0.8	0.0	0.0	0.0	0.0	0.0	0.0	29	3

	1	2	3	4	5	6	7	8	9	10	11
IRECT	1.6	1.4	1.2	0.0	0.0	0.0	0.0	0.0	0.0	32	0
ISABLE	-2.7	-1.8	0.3	0.0	2.1*	0.0	0.0	-0.7	0.0	29	0
ISBELIEVE	-0.7	0.0	0.4	0.0	0.0	0.0	0.0	-0.5	0.0	34	0
ISCIPLINE	1.0	1.4	0.9	0.6	0.0	0.0	0.0	0.0	0.0	31	0
ISCONCERT	-1.0	-0.5	0.5	0.0	0.0	0.0	0.0	0.0	0.0	20	12
ISCOURAGE	-1.0	-0.3	-0.2	0.0	0.0	0.0	0.0	0.0	0.0	32	0
ISCREDIT	-2.2	-1.1	-0.1	0.0	0.0	0.0	0.0	0.0	0.0	30	0
ISENCHANT	-1.2	0.0	0.3	0.0	0.0	-1.0	0.0	0.0	0.0	31	0
ISGRACE	-2.0	-1.2	0.0	-1.1	0.0	0.0	0.0	0.0	0.0	28	0
ISILLUSION	-1.9	-1.1	-0.3	0.0	0.0	0.0	0.0	0.0	0.0	32	0
ISLIKE	-1.2	0.2	0.2	0.0	-1.3	0.0	0.0	-0.7	0.0	30	0
ISOBEY	-0.9	-0.6	0.7	-1.0	0.0	0.0	0.0	0.0	0.0	29	0
ISPARAGE	-1.2	-0.2	0.4	0.0	0.0	0.0	0.0	0.0	0.0	11	23
ISPLEASE	-1.4	-0.3	0.1	0.0	0.0	0.0	0.0	0.0	0.0	31	0
ISREGARD	-1.3	-0.7	-0.5	0.0	0.0	0.0	0.0	0.0	0.0	32	1
ISRESPECT	-1.4	-0.7	0.1	0.0	0.9	0.0	0.0	0.0	0.0	32	0
ISROBE	0.3	1.1	1.3	1.5*	0.0	0.0	0.0	0.0	0.0	29	1
ISSUADE	0.1	1.1	0.5	0.0	0.0	0.0	0.0	0.0	0.0	26	5
ISTRESS	-1.9	-1.1	0.4	0.0	0.0	0.0	-0.3	0.0	0.0	31	0
ISTRUST	-1.6	-0.1	0.0	0.0	0.0	0.0	0.0	0.0	0.0	28	0
ISTURB	-1.5	-0.5	0.6	1.0	0.0	0.0	0.0	0.0	0.0	29	0
IVERT	-0.7	0.4	0.6	0.0	0.0	0.0	0.6	0.0	-0.6	29	0
IVORCE	-1.0	0.1	0.6	0.0	0.0	0.0	0.0	0.0	0.0	34	0
OG	-1.4	-0.4	0.7	0.0	0.0	0.0	0.0	0.9	0.0	20	11
OMINATE	-1.7	1.3	0.7	0.0	0.0	0.0	0.0	0.0	0.0	33	0
OPE	-1.8	0.0	0.0	0.0	0.0	0.0	0.0	0.0	0.0	28	4
OUBLECROSS	-2.7	-1.6	0.3	0.0	1.3	0.0	0.0	0.0	0.0	30	0
OUBT	-1.1	-0.3	-0.3	0.0	0.0	0.0	0.0	0.0	0.0	31	0
REAM OF	1.6	0.7	0.3	-0.8	0.0	0.0	0.0	0.0	0.0	28	0
RESS	1.7	0.4	0.5	0.0	0.0	0.0	0.0	0.0	0.0	32	0
RUG	-1.4	-0.7	-0.6	0.0	0.0	0.0	-0.5	-0.5	0.0	28	0
UPE	-1.8	-0.4	0.4	0.0	0.0	0.0	0.0	0.0	0.0	19	13
EDUCATE	2.7	1.7	0.8	0.0	0.0	0.0	0.0	0.0	0.0	28	0
ELUDE	-0.4	-0.5	0.3	0.0	0.9	1.1	0.0	0.0	0.0	32	2
EMBARRASS	-1.8	-1.1	0.1	0.0	0.0	0.0	0.0	0.0	0.0	31	0
EMBRACE	2.0	1.5	1.7	0.0	0.0	0.0	0.0	0.0	0.0	33	0
EMULATE	0.4	-0.3	0.7	0.0	0.0	0.0	0.0	0.0	0.0	22	10
ENCOURAGE	2.7	1.8	1.4	0.0	0.0	0.0	0.0	0.0	0.0	30	0
ENDANGER	-2.2	0.9	1.1	0.0	0.0	0.0	0.0	0.4	0.0	31	0
ENDURE	1.0	1.1	0.1	0.0	0.0	0.0	0.0	0.0	0.0	29	2
ENGAGE	1.1	0.7	1.0	0.0	0.0	0.0	0.0	0.0	0.0	28	0
ENJOY	2.6	1.6	1.9	0.0	0.0	0.0	0.0	0.0	0.0	31	0
ENRAGE	-1.7	0.4	1.5	0.0	0.0	0.0	0.0	0.0	0.0	32	0
ENRAPTURE	1.4	2.1	1.4	0.0	0.0	0.0	0.0	0.0	0.0	23	6
ENSLAVE	-1.9	1.0	0.6	-0.8	0.0	0.0	0.0	0.0	0.0	34	0
ENSNARE	-1.3	0.6	0.8	0.0	0.0	0.0	0.0	0.0	0.0	25	6
ENTERTAIN	1.8	1.0	1.7	0.0	0.0	0.0	0.0	0.0	0.0	33	0
ENTHRALL	1.1	1.4	1.1	0.0	0.0	0.0	0.0	0.0	0.0	27	6
ENTICE	0.6	0.8	1.6	0.0	0.0	-1.1	0.0	0.0	0.0	30	0
ENTRAP	-1.6	1.4	1.1	0.0	0.0	0.0	0.0	0.0	0.0	28	3
ENTREAT	0.3	0.0	0.9	0.0	0.0	0.0	0.0	0.0	0.0	21	7
ENVY	-1.4	-1.1	0.2	0.0	0.0	-0.7	0.0	0.0	0.0	28	0
ESCAPE	1.0	0.9	1.7	0.0	0.0	0.0	0.0	0.0	0.0	30	0
ESTEEM	1.8	1.1	0.8	0.0	0.0	0.0	0.0	0.0	0.0	28	4
EVADE	-1.1	-1.0	0.5	0.0	0.0	0.0	0.0	0.0	0.0	28	1
EVALUATE	0.8	0.6	0.5	0.0	0.0	0.0	0.0	0.0	0.0	34	0

	1	2	3	4	5	6	7	8	9	10	11
EXALT	0.9	0.9	1.0	0.0	0.0	0.0	0.0	0.0	0.0	25	
EXAMINE	0.5	0.2	0.2	0.0	0.0	0.0	0.0	0.0	0.0	33	
EXCITE	1.7	1.6	2.4	-0.7	0.0	0.0	0.0	0.0	0.0	32	
EXCLUDE	-2.2	-1.7	0.0	0.0	1.3	0.0	0.0	0.0	0.0	30	
EXCUSE	2.1	1.2	0.1	0.0	0.0	0.0	0.5*	0.0	0.0	31	
EXECUTE	-2.5	-0.3	0.5	0.0	0.0	-1.9	0.5	0.0	0.0	28	
EXHAUST	-0.5	0.4	1.2	0.0	0.0	0.0	-0.4	0.0	0.0	32	
EXHIBIT	-0.9	-0.1	0.3	0.0	0.0	0.0	0.0	0.0	0.0	31	
EXHORT	-2.0	-1.2	-0.3	1.8*	2.0	1.3	0.0	-1.2	0.0	15	19
EXONERATE	1.6	1.5	0.6	0.0	0.0	0.0	0.5	0.0	0.0	21	1
EXPERIENCE	1.7	1.4	1.2	0.0	0.0	0.0	0.0	0.0	0.4	30	
EXPLOIT	-2.1	-0.5	0.5	0.0	0.0	0.0	0.0	0.0	0.0	33	
EXPOSE	-0.3	0.3	0.6	0.0	0.0	0.0	0.0	0.6	0.0	32	
EXTOL	1.0	0.7	0.4	0.0	0.0	0.0	0.0	0.0	0.0	20	1
EYE	0.2	0.4	0.5	0.0	0.0	0.0	0.0	0.0	0.0	30	
FACE	1.8	1.9	0.9	0.0	-1.1	0.0	0.0	0.0	0.0	32	
FAVOR	0.6	0.0	0.6	0.0	0.0	0.0	0.0	0.0	0.0	32	
FEAR	-1.2	-0.1	0.0	0.0	0.0	0.0	0.0	0.0	0.0	28	
FEED	2.6	0.5	1.3	0.0	0.0	-1.2	0.0	0.0	0.0	32	
FEEL	2.0	1.7	1.3	0.0	0.0	0.0	0.0	0.0	0.4	29	
FETTER	-0.5	0.0	-0.9	0.0	0.0	0.0	-0.8	-0.8	0.0	14	1
FIGHT	-1.8	-0.1	1.7	0.0	0.0	0.0	0.6	0.0	0.0	30	
FIX	-1.0	0.2	0.6	0.0	0.0	0.0	0.0	0.0	0.6	25	5
FLAGELLATE	-1.6	1.0	1.2	0.0	0.0	0.0	0.0	0.0	0.0	17	17
FLAIL	-1.4	-0.1	1.7	-1.1	0.0	0.0	0.0	-0.7	-0.6	20	11
FLATTER	1.8	0.6	1.0	-0.9	0.0	0.0	0.4	0.0	0.0	33	
FLEE	-0.1	0.7	1.9	0.0	-1.0	0.0	0.0	0.0	0.4	31	
FLOG	-2.2	0.3	1.1	0.0	0.0	0.0	0.0	0.0	0.0	26	
FLUNK	-1.7	0.2	-0.1	0.9	0.0	0.0	0.6*	0.0	0.4	30	
FLUSTER	-1.2	-0.1	0.9	0.0	0.0	0.0	0.0	0.0	0.0	30	
FOIL	-0.4	0.4	0.2	0.0	0.0	0.0	0.0	0.0	0.0	24	
FOLLOW	-0.2	-0.5	0.2	0.0	0.0	0.0	0.0	0.0	0.7*	30	
FONDLE	1.9	1.2	1.2	0.0	0.0	0.0	0.0	0.0	0.0	29	
FOOL	-1.0	-0.9	1.5	0.0	0.0	-1.2	-0.6	0.0	-0.6	29	
FORCE	-2.0	1.3	1.1	0.0	0.0	0.0	0.0	0.0	0.0	29	
FORGET	-1.3	-0.8	-0.8	0.0	0.0	0.0	0.0	0.0	0.0	34	
FORGIVE	2.6	2.6	0.6	0.0	0.0	0.0	0.7*	0.0	0.0	34	
FORSAKE	-2.4	-1.7	-0.5	0.0	0.0	0.0	0.0	0.0	0.0	30	
FOX	-1.1	-0.3	0.5	0.0	0.0	0.0	0.0	0.0	0.0	29	
FRAME	-1.7	-0.5	0.4	-0.8	0.0	0.0	0.0	0.0	0.0	32	
FREAK-OUT	-0.3	0.2	1.9	0.0	0.0	0.0	-0.5	0.0	0.0	30	
FRISK	-0.7	0.6	1.6	0.0	0.0	0.0	0.7*	0.0	0.0	31	
FRUSTRATE	-1.4	-0.3	0.7	-0.9	0.0	-1.0	0.0	0.0	0.0	28	
GIBE	-0.6	-0.8	0.3	0.0	0.0	0.0	0.0	0.0	0.0	13	20
GLORIFY	0.9	0.9	0.9	0.0	0.0	0.0	0.0	0.0	0.0	29	
GOAD	-1.2	0.2	0.8	0.0	0.0	0.0	0.0	0.0	0.0	21	13
GRAB	-0.5	1.0	1.7	0.0	0.0	0.0	0.0	0.0	-0.5	33	
GRASP	0.1	0.9	2.1	0.0	0.0	-0.8	0.0	0.0	0.0	31	
GRATIFY	2.0	1.6	0.6	0.0	0.0	0.0	-0.4	0.0	0.0	27	3
GREET	1.9	1.4	1.3	0.0	0.0	0.0	0.0	0.0	0.0	31	
GRIEVE FOR	0.1	0.6	-1.1	0.0	0.0	0.0	0.0	0.0	0.0	29	
GUARD	1.4	1.9	0.6	0.0	0.0	0.0	0.0	0.0	0.4	27	
GUIDE	1.9	1.5	0.7	0.0	0.0	0.0	0.0	0.0	0.0	28	
GYP	-2.2	-0.6	0.3	0.0	0.0	0.0	0.0	0.0	0.0	30	2
HAIL	1.0	0.6	1.3	0.0	0.0	0.0	0.0	0.0	0.0	29	
HALT	-0.4	0.9	1.1	0.0	0.0	0.0	0.0	0.0	-0.5	33	0

	1	2	3	4	5	6	7	8	9	10	11
HANDCUFF	-0.8	0.7	0.7	0.7	0.0	0.0	0.0	0.0	0.0	30	1
HARANGUE	-1.6	0.8	1.6	1.0	-1.8	0.0	0.0	0.0	0.0	20	13
HARASS	-2.0	-0.4	1.6	0.0	0.0	0.0	0.0	0.0	0.0	33	0
HARM	-2.6	-0.6	0.7	0.0	0.0	0.0	0.0	0.0	0.0	30	0
HASSLE	-1.8	-0.5	1.4	0.0	1.1	0.0	0.0	0.0	0.0	31	0
HATE	-2.7	0.5	1.4	0.7	-1.2	-1.3*	0.0	0.0	0.0	34	0
HAZE	-1.3	-0.6	0.5	0.0	0.0	1.7	0.0	0.0	0.0	18	14
HEAL	2.5	2.5	0.9	1.0	0.0	0.0	0.0	0.0	0.0	27	1
HECKLE	-1.8	-0.7	1.0	0.0	0.0	0.0	0.0	0.0	0.0	30	2
HELP	2.8	1.8	1.4	0.0	0.0	0.0	0.0	0.0	0.0	31	0
HIDE	0.1	0.5	0.3	0.0	0.0	0.0	0.0	0.0	0.0	28	0
HIDE FROM	-0.8	-0.8	0.5	0.0	0.0	-0.9	0.0	0.0	0.0	34	0
HINDER	-1.8	-0.7	-0.3	0.0	0.0	0.0	0.0	0.0	0.0	29	0
HIRE	2.2	1.4	0.7	0.0	0.0	0.0	0.0	0.0	0.0	34	0
HIT	-2.1	1.4	1.4	0.0	0.0	0.9	0.0	0.6	0.0	30	0
HOGTIE	-1.3	0.7	0.9	0.0	0.0	0.0	0.0	0.0	0.0	23	8
HOLD	2.1	1.7	1.3	-1.0	0.0	-1.1	0.4	0.0	0.8*	29	0
HONOR	2.4	1.3	0.5	-0.9	0.0	0.0	0.0	0.0	0.0	33	0
HOODWINK	-1.4	-0.1	0.7	0.0	0.0	0.0	0.0	0.0	0.0	20	14
HORRIFY	-2.4	0.0	0.7	0.0	1.0	0.0	0.0	0.0	0.0	30	0
HOUND	-1.4	0.2	1.7	0.0	0.0	0.0	0.0	0.0	0.6*	30	0
HUG	2.4	1.6	1.3	0.0	0.0	0.0	0.0	0.0	0.0	28	0
HUMBLE	-0.6	0.5	0.1	1.1	0.0	0.0	0.5	0.0	0.0	27	1
HUMILIATE	-2.4	-1.1	0.5	0.0	0.0	0.0	0.0	0.0	0.0	32	0
HUMOR	1.1	0.6	1.3	0.0	0.0	-1.0	0.0	-0.6	-0.6	29	0
HURRY	-0.2	0.5	1.8	0.0	0.0	0.0	0.0	0.0	0.0	31	0
HURT	-2.4	-0.8	0.1	0.0	0.0	0.0	0.0	0.0	0.0	33	0
HUSH	-0.2	0.8	-0.3	0.8	0.0	1.0	0.4	0.0	0.0	32	0
HUSTLE	-0.5	0.4	1.1	-0.9	0.0	0.0	0.4	0.0	0.0	29	1
IDEALIZE	0.5	-0.3	0.5	0.0	1.0	0.0	0.0	0.0	0.0	31	0
IDOLIZE	-0.6	-1.1	0.7	0.0	0.0	-1.7*	0.0	0.0	0.0	31	0
IGNORE	-1.8	-1.0	-0.3	0.0	0.0	0.0	0.0	0.0	0.0	28	0
IMITATE	-0.4	-0.5	0.6	0.0	0.0	0.0	0.0	0.0	0.0	32	0
IMPEDE	-2.0	-0.5	1.0	0.0	1.3	0.0	0.0	-0.7	-0.6	25	4
IMPLORE	0.1	0.4	0.2	0.0	0.0	0.9	0.0	0.0	0.0	32	2
INCITE	-0.6	0.8	1.6	0.0	0.0	0.0	0.0	0.0	0.0	22	9
INCRIMINATE	-1.6	-0.2	0.4	0.0	0.0	0.0	0.0	0.0	0.0	33	0
INDOCTRINATE	0.1	0.8	0.7	0.0	0.0	0.0	0.0	0.0	0.0	27	5
INDULGE	0.8	-0.2	0.1	-0.9	0.0	0.0	0.0	0.0	0.0	26	4
INFLUENCE	0.5	1.3	0.8	0.0	0.0	0.0	0.0	0.0	0.0	32	0
INFORM	1.5	1.1	1.0	0.0	0.0	0.0	0.0	0.0	0.0	31	0
INFURIATE	-1.9	0.0	1.7	0.0	0.0	0.0	0.0	0.0	0.0	31	1
INITIATE	0.9	0.8	0.8	0.0	0.0	0.0	0.0	0.0	0.0	28	0
INJURE	-2.4	0.0	0.8	0.0	0.0	0.0	0.0	0.0	0.0	30	0
INSPECT	-0.2	0.5	0.1	0.0	0.0	0.0	0.0	0.0	0.0	28	1
INSPIRE	2.4	2.2	1.6	0.0	0.0	0.0	0.0	0.0	0.0	34	0
INSTRUCT	2.1	1.5	1.0	0.0	0.0	0.0	0.0	0.0	0.5	31	0
INSULT	-1.9	-0.9	0.6	0.0	0.0	0.0	0.0	0.0	0.0	33	0
INTEREST	2.0	1.1	1.0	0.0	0.0	0.0	0.0	0.0	0.0	28	0
INTERROGATE	-0.7	1.1	1.2	0.0	0.0	-0.8	0.0	0.0	-0.4	31	0
INTERRUPT	-1.7	-0.9	1.6	0.0	0.0	0.0	0.0	0.0	0.0	30	0
INTERVIEW	0.8	0.8	0.5	0.0	0.0	0.0	0.0	0.0	0.0	31	0
INTIMIDATE	-2.2	-1.1	0.3	0.0	1.3	0.0	0.0	0.0	0.0	31	0
INVITE	1.9	1.3	1.4	0.0	0.0	0.0	0.0	0.0	0.0	34	0
IRRITATE	-1.7	0.3	0.6	0.0	-1.4	0.0	0.0	0.0	0.0	28	0
JEER	-1.5	-0.6	0.3	0.0	0.0	0.0	0.0	0.0	0.0	28	4

	1	2	3	4	5	6	7	8	9	10	11
JERK	-1.7	0.3	1.6	0.0	0.0	0.0	0.0	-0.9	-0.6	29	
JEST	-0.2	0.0	1.4	0.0	0.0	0.0	0.0	0.0	0.0	34	
JOGGLE	-0.4	0.3	1.0	0.0	0.0	0.0	0.0	0.0	0.0	17	14
JOIN	1.6	0.8	0.6	0.0	0.0	0.0	0.0	0.0	0.0	28	
JOLT	-0.6	0.7	1.2	-0.7	0.0	0.0	0.0	0.0	0.0	33	
JOSH	0.4	0.2	1.1	0.0	0.0	0.0	0.0	0.0	0.0	33	
JOSTLE	-0.3	0.4	1.2	0.0	0.0	0.0	0.0	0.0	0.0	26	
JUDGE	-1.3	0.1	0.3	0.0	0.0	0.0	-0.4	0.0	0.5	31	
KICK	-2.5	-0.5	1.0	0.0	1.2	0.0	0.0	0.0	0.0	31	
KID	0.0	0.1	1.3	0.0	0.0	0.0	0.0	0.0	0.0	28	
KILL	-3.2	0.4	0.8	0.0	0.0	0.0	0.0	0.0	0.0	32	
KISS	2.5	1.4	1.5	0.0	0.0	0.0	0.0	0.0	0.0	28	
LAUD	1.8	1.2	0.9	-1.3	0.0	0.0	0.0	0.0	0.0	23	
LAUGH AT	-1.5	-0.9	1.1	0.0	0.0	0.0	0.0	0.0	0.0	31	
LAUGH WITH	3.0	1.5	2.6	-0.9	0.0	0.0	0.0	0.0	0.0	31	
LEAD	1.7	1.4	0.8	0.0	0.0	0.0	0.4	0.0	0.0	31	
LEAVE	-0.9	0.5	0.5	0.0	0.0	0.0	0.0	0.0	0.0	31	
LIBERALIZE	1.6	1.3	1.9	0.0	0.0	0.0	-0.4	0.0	0.0	28	
LIFT	1.3	1.4	1.3	0.0	0.0	0.0	0.0	0.0	0.0	28	
LIKE	2.4	1.2	2.3	0.0	0.0	-1.1	0.0	0.0	0.0	31	0
LOATHE	-1.7	-0.9	0.0	0.0	0.0	0.0	0.0	0.0	0.0	31	2
LOVE	2.8	2.7	2.4	0.0	0.0	0.0	0.0	0.0	0.0	29	0
LULL	0.3	0.4	-0.3	0.0	0.0	-1.2	0.0	0.0	0.0	31	1
LURE	-1.0	1.1	0.7	0.0	0.0	-1.1	0.0	0.5	0.6	30	0
MACE	-2.6	-0.1	0.9	0.0	0.0	0.0	0.0	0.7	0.0	20	11
MAIM	-2.7	-1.4	0.4	0.0	0.0	0.0	0.0	0.0	0.0	28	4
MALIGN	-1.9	-0.5	0.2	0.0	0.0	0.0	0.5	0.0	0.0	23	5
MANHANDLE	-2.0	0.4	0.5	0.8	0.0	1.3	0.0	0.0	0.0	30	0
MANIPULATE	-1.7	-0.3	0.4	0.0	1.6	0.0	0.0	-0.8	0.0	29	0
MARRY	1.8	1.7	1.8	0.0	0.0	0.0	0.0	0.0	0.0	32	0
MASSAGE	2.2	1.4	1.0	0.0	0.0	0.0	0.0	0.0	0.0	34	0
MASTER	-1.1	0.8	0.7	0.0	0.9	0.0	0.0	0.0	0.0	31	0
MEDICATE	2.3	1.4	0.5	0.0	0.0	0.0	0.0	0.0	0.0	30	2
MENACE	-1.9	0.5	1.1	0.0	0.0	0.0	0.0	0.0	0.0	29	1
MIMIC	-0.7	-0.7	1.0	0.0	0.0	0.0	0.0	0.0	0.0	31	0
MISLEAD	-1.8	-0.7	-0.4	0.0	0.0	0.0	0.0	0.0	0.0	32	0
MISS	0.5	1.3	0.7	0.0	0.0	-1.0	0.5	0.0	0.6	29	1
MISUNDERSTAND	-1.3	-0.3	-0.4	0.0	0.0	0.0	0.0	0.0	0.0	28	0
MOCK	-1.3	-1.3	0.6	0.0	0.0	0.0	0.0	0.0	0.0	30	0
MOLEST	-2.4	-1.1	0.6	0.0	1.2	0.0	-1.0*	-1.6*	0.0	29	0
MOLLIFY	-0.3	-0.4	0.1	0.0	0.0	0.0	0.0	0.0	0.0	13	21
MOLLYCODDLE	-0.8	-0.1	0.3	0.0	0.0	0.0	0.0	0.0	0.0	12	19
MONITOR	-0.4	-0.2	-0.2	0.0	0.0	0.0	0.6*	0.0	0.0	31	2
MONOPOLIZE	-1.7	0.8	0.5	0.0	0.0	0.0	0.0	0.5	0.0	33	0
MORTIFY	-2.1	-0.8	0.4	0.0	1.2	0.0	0.0	0.0	0.0	27	3
MOTHER	1.4	1.3	0.1	0.0	0.0	0.0	0.0	0.0	0.0	31	0
MUG	-2.8	-0.9	0.7	0.0	0.0	0.0	0.0	0.0	0.0	32	0
MURDER	-3.3	0.9	0.5	0.0	-2.3*	0.0	0.0	0.0	0.0	27	0
MUTILATE	-3.0	0.5	1.1	0.0	0.0	0.0	0.0	-0.7	0.0	31	0
MYSTIFY	0.4	0.7	0.5	0.0	0.0	0.0	0.0	0.0	0.0	29	0
NAB	-0.6	0.8	1.2	-0.9	0.0	0.0	0.0	-0.4	-0.5	33	1
NAG	-2.1	-0.7	0.4	0.0	0.0	0.0	0.0	0.0	-0.4	31	0
NAIL	-1.5	0.3	0.9	0.0	0.0	-0.8	0.0	0.0	0.0	28	4
NEED	2.1	0.8	0.7	0.0	0.0	0.0	0.0	0.0	0.0	30	0
NEEDLE	-1.2	-0.4	0.8	0.0	0.0	0.0	0.4	0.0	0.0	31	1
NEGLECT	-2.4	-1.6	-1.0	0.0	0.0	1.0	0.0	0.0	0.0	30	0

	1	2	3	4	5	6	7	8	9	10	11
NESTLE	1.8	1.4	0.2	0.0	0.0	0.0	0.0	0.0	0.0	27	4
NOTICE	1.7	0.7	0.6	0.0	0.0	0.0	0.0	0.0	0.0	29	0
NUDGE	0.3	0.1	0.6	0.0	0.0	0.0	0.0	0.0	0.0	32	0
NURSE	2.5	1.5	0.6	0.0	0.0	0.0	0.0	0.0	0.0	28	0
NUZZLE	1.2	0.4	0.6	0.0	0.0	0.0	0.0	0.0	0.0	19	12
OBEY	1.4	0.8	0.5	0.0	0.0	0.0	0.0	0.0	0.0	29	0
OBLIGE	2.1	1.2	0.7	0.0	0.0	0.0	0.0	0.0	0.0	33	1
OBSERVE	0.2	0.2	0.1	0.9	0.0	0.0	0.4	0.0	0.0	28	0
OBSTRUCT	-1.6	0.0	0.7	0.0	0.0	0.0	0.0	0.0	0.0	28	3
OFFEND	-1.7	-0.8	0.6	0.0	0.0	0.0	0.0	0.0	0.0	33	0
OGLE	-0.5	-0.1	0.7	0.0	0.0	0.0	0.0	0.0	0.0	21	12
OPPOSE	0.0	1.6	1.5	0.0	0.0	0.0	0.0	0.0	0.0	30	0
OPPRESS	-2.7	0.7	-0.4	0.0	1.1	0.0	0.0	0.0	0.0	30	0
OSTRACIZE	-2.1	0.7	1.3	0.0	0.0	0.0	0.0	0.7	0.5	27	5
OUTDO	0.1	0.5	1.3	0.0	1.4	0.0	0.0	0.0	0.0	31	0
OUTRAGE	-1.5	0.8	1.4	0.0	0.0	0.0	0.0	0.0	0.0	28	0
OUTWIT	0.2	0.9	1.2	0.0	0.0	0.0	0.0	0.0	0.0	32	0
OVERDOSE	-2.6	-2.4	0.2	0.9	2.6*	0.0	-0.9*	0.0	-0.6	29	0
OVERHEAR	-0.6	-0.5	0.0	0.0	0.0	0.0	0.0	0.0	0.0	34	0
OVERLOOK	-1.9	-1.3	0.0	0.0	0.0	0.0	0.0	0.0	0.0	31	0
OVERRATE	-0.3	-0.3	0.4	0.0	0.0	0.0	0.0	0.0	0.0	33	0
OVERWHELM	0.4	1.8	1.8	-0.8	0.0	0.0	0.0	0.0	0.0	32	0
OVERWORK	-2.1	0.3	0.6	0.0	0.0	0.0	0.0	0.0	0.4	30	0
PACIFY	1.1	0.1	-0.5	0.0	0.0	0.0	-0.4	-0.5	0.0	30	0
PADDLE	-0.4	0.5	0.5	0.0	0.0	0.0	0.0	0.6	0.5	32	0
PAMPER	-0.5	-1.0	-0.2	0.0	0.0	0.0	0.0	0.0	0.0	28	0
PARODY	0.1	-0.2	0.7	0.0	0.0	0.0	0.7	0.0	0.0	16	15
PASS	0.0	0.1	1.1	0.0	0.0	0.0	0.0	0.0	0.0	24	4
PAT	1.3	0.5	0.4	0.0	0.0	0.0	0.0	0.0	0.0	28	1
PATRONIZE	1.2	0.4	0.3	0.0	0.0	0.0	0.0	0.0	0.0	30	4
PAW	-1.2	0.2	0.9	0.0	-1.1	0.0	0.0	0.0	0.0	25	6
PAY	1.6	1.0	0.5	0.0	0.0	0.0	0.4	0.0	0.0	34	0
PENALIZE	0.0	0.3	0.0	0.0	0.0	0.0	0.4	0.4	0.0	32	1
PERSECUTE	-2.0	0.0	0.4	0.0	0.0	0.0	0.0	0.0	0.0	32	0
PERSUADE	0.5	1.6	0.8	0.0	0.0	0.0	0.0	0.0	0.0	30	0
PERVERT	-1.9	0.0	0.7	0.0	0.0	0.0	0.0	0.0	0.0	31	1
PESTER	-1.8	-1.1	1.1	0.0	0.0	0.0	0.0	0.0	0.0	31	1
PET	1.0	0.5	1.1	1.1	0.0	0.0	-0.4	0.0	0.0	28	0
PINCH	-0.2	0.1	1.5	0.0	0.0	0.0	0.0	0.0	0.0	30	0
PLACATE	1.1	0.4	-0.4	-1.7	0.0	0.0	0.0	0.0	0.0	18	12
PLAY WITH	1.5	0.6	2.0	0.0	0.0	0.0	0.0	0.0	0.0	32	0
PLEASE	2.5	1.5	1.0	0.0	0.0	0.0	0.3	-0.0	0.0	34	0
POISON	-3.1	0.2	0.6	0.0	-1.4	-1.6*	0.0	0.0	0.0	31	0
POKE	-0.7	-0.2	0.8	0.0	0.0	0.0	0.0	0.0	0.0	33	0
POOH-POOH	-1.2	-1.1	0.1	0.0	0.0	0.0	0.0	0.0	0.0	22	10
PRAISE	2.8	1.8	1.2	0.0	0.0	0.0	0.0	0.6	0.0	30	0
PROD	-0.5	0.3	0.6	0.7	0.0	0.0	0.0	0.0	0.0	29	1
PROMPT	1.3	0.7	0.8	0.0	0.0	0.0	0.0	0.0	0.0	31	0
PROTECT	2.3	2.1	1.1	0.0	0.0	0.0	0.0	0.0	0.0	28	0
PROVOKE	-1.2	0.3	0.7	0.0	0.0	0.0	0.0	0.0	0.0	32	0
PSYCHOANALYZE	0.7	0.9	0.0	0.0	0.0	0.0	0.0	0.0	0.0	29	0
PUNCH	-1.8	1.4	1.8	0.0	0.0	0.0	0.0	0.0	0.0	34	0
PUNISH	-0.4	0.8	0.7	0.0	0.0	0.0	0.0	0.0	0.0	31	0
PURSUE	0.1	0.9	1.9	0.0	0.0	0.0	0.0	0.0	0.0	32	0
PUSH	-0.9	0.4	1.4	0.0	0.0	0.0	0.0	0.0	0.0	32	0
QUERY	0.3	0.6	0.9	0.0	0.0	0.0	0.0	0.0	0.0	19	11

	1	2	3	4	5	6	7	8	9	10	11
QUESTION	0.3	0.7	0.4	0.0	0.0	0.0	0.0	0.6	0.0	29	1
QUIET	1.1	0.7	-0.2	0.0	0.0	0.0	0.0	0.0	0.0	31	0
QUIZ	-0.1	0.1	0.6	0.0	0.0	0.0	0.0	0.0	0.0	28	0
RADICALIZE	-0.4	1.3	1.6	0.0	0.0	0.0	0.0	0.0	0.0	28	3
RALLY	0.9	1.0	2.2	0.0	0.0	0.0	0.0	0.0	-0.6	26	2
RAM	-1.4	1.0	1.9	0.0	0.0	0.0	0.0	0.0	0.0	31	3
RANKLE	-1.4	-0.4	0.5	0.0	0.0	0.0	0.0	0.0	0.0	16	15
RAPE	-3.6	-1.0	2.1	1.0	0.0	-1.1	0.0	0.6	0.0	33	0
RATTLE	-1.0	0.0	1.3	0.0	0.0	0.0	0.0	0.0	0.0	32	0
RAVISH	0.2	1.1	1.8	1.2	0.0	0.0	0.7	0.5	0.0	24	6
REASSURE	2.6	1.9	0.4	0.0	0.0	0.0	0.4	0.0	0.0	31	0
REBUFF	-0.4	0.3	0.5	0.0	0.0	0.0	0.0	0.0	0.0	25	7
REBUKE	-0.4	0.4	0.4	0.0	0.0	0.0	0.0	0.0	0.0	26	2
REFORM	2.0	1.1	1.0	0.0	0.0	0.0	0.0	0.0	0.5	30	0
REFUSE	-0.4	0.6	0.6	0.0	0.0	0.0	0.0	0.0	0.0	29	2
REGARD	0.8	0.5	0.1	0.0	0.0	0.0	0.0	0.0	0.0	27	1
REHABILITATE	3.0	1.8	1.4	-0.7	0.0	-1.1	0.0	0.0	0.0	29	0
REJECT	-1.9	0.0	0.4	0.0	0.0	0.0	0.0	0.0	0.0	34	0
RELEASE	1.4	0.9	0.5	0.0	0.0	0.0	0.0	0.0	0.0	31	0
RELIEVE	2.3	1.2	0.5	0.0	0.0	0.0	0.0	0.0	0.0	33	0
RELISH	0.9	1.1	1.2	0.0	0.0	0.0	0.0	0.0	0.0	33	0
REMEMBER	2.0	1.1	0.2	0.0	0.0	0.0	0.4	0.6	0.6	31	0
REMIND	1.8	0.9	0.4	0.0	0.0	0.0	0.0	0.0	0.0	30	0
RENOUNCE	-1.5	0.6	0.7	0.0	0.0	0.0	0.0	0.0	0.0	30	2
REPEL	-1.1	-0.5	0.5	0.0	1.0	0.0	0.0	0.0	0.0	30	2
REPRIMAND	0.7	0.8	0.5	0.0	0.0	0.0	0.0	0.0	0.0	30	2
REPROACH	-0.5	0.1	0.3	0.0	0.0	0.0	0.0	0.0	0.0	24	6
REPULSE	-2.1	-0.8	0.3	0.0	1.9*	0.0	0.0	-0.7	0.0	26	3
RESCUE	2.8	2.5	2.3	0.0	0.0	0.0	0.4	0.0	0.0	34	0
RESPECT	2.4	2.0	0.5	0.0	0.0	0.0	0.0	0.0	0.0	34	0
RESTRAIN	-0.9	1.1	0.3	0.7	0.0	0.0	0.0	0.0	0.0	31	0
REVERE	0.9	0.4	0.2	0.0	0.0	0.0	0.0	0.0	0.0	23	10
REVILE	-1.1	1.0	1.0	0.0	-1.3	0.0	0.0	0.0	0.0	17	17
RIB	-0.7	-0.6	0.9	0.0	0.0	0.0	0.8*	0.0	0.6	27	3
RIDE	-1.4	-0.1	0.7	0.0	0.0	0.8	0.0	0.5	0.0	30	0
RIDICULE	-2.4	-1.8	0.9	0.0	1.0	0.0	0.0	0.0	0.0	30	0
RILE	-1.4	0.0	1.3	0.0	0.0	0.0	0.0	0.0	0.0	30	2
ROB	-3.1	-1.1	0.5	0.0	1.9*	0.0	0.0	0.0	0.0	32	0
ROOK	-1.8	-1.1	0.1	0.0	0.0	0.0	0.0	0.0	0.0	23	8
ROUSE	0.3	0.3	0.9	-0.9	0.0	0.0	0.0	0.0	-0.5	28	2
SATISFY	2.4	1.4	1.1	0.0	0.0	0.0	0.0	0.0	0.0	30	0
SAVE	3.0	2.4	1.5	0.0	0.0	0.0	0.0	0.0	0.5	29	0
SCARE	-1.5	1.3	1.7	0.0	-0.9	0.0	0.0	-0.5	0.0	34	0
SCOLD	-0.8	0.6	0.7	0.0	0.0	0.0	0.0	0.0	0.0	31	0
SCORN	-1.1	-0.4	0.1	0.0	0.0	0.0	0.0	0.0	0.0	33	0
SCRUTINIZE	-0.2	0.3	0.1	0.0	0.0	0.0	0.0	0.0	0.0	26	5
SEARCH	-1.4	0.8	1.1	0.0	0.0	0.0	0.0	0.0	0.0	31	0
SEDUCE	-0.2	0.5	0.7	2.0*	1.1	1.4	-0.4	0.0	0.0	28	0
SEIZE	-0.9	1.4	1.4	-1.2	0.0	0.0	0.0	0.0	0.0	31	1
SENTENCE	-0.4	1.2	0.0	0.0	0.0	0.0	0.0	0.0	0.0	32	0
SERENADE	2.1	1.2	1.6	0.0	0.0	-0.7	0.0	0.0	0.0	29	0
SERVE	1.3	-0.1	0.2	0.0	0.0	0.0	0.0	0.5	0.0	33	0
SHACKLE	-1.4	0.4	0.3	0.0	0.0	0.0	0.0	0.0	0.0	28	6
SHAFT	-2.4	1.0	0.8	0.0	-1.1	0.0	0.0	-0.6	0.0	28	3
SHAKE	-0.4	0.9	1.2	0.0	0.0	0.0	0.0	0.0	0.0	32	1
SHIELD	0.9	1.3	0.4	0.0	0.0	0.0	0.4	0.0	0.0	33	0

	1	2	3	4	5	6	7	8	9	10	11
SHOCK	-1.2	0.4	1.4	0.0	0.0	0.0	0.0	0.0	0.0	30	0
SHOOT	-3.2	-0.4	1.5	0.6	0.0	0.0	0.0	0.6	0.0	33	0
SHOVE	-1.9	0.8	1.7	0.0	0.0	0.0	0.0	0.0	0.0	31	0
SHUSH	-0.3	-0.2	-0.2	0.0	0.0	0.0	0.0	0.0	0.0	27	1
SIGNAL	0.8	0.6	0.5	0.0	0.0	0.0	0.0	0.0	0.0	28	0
SILENCE	-0.4	0.8	0.0	-0.9	0.0	0.0	0.0	0.0	0.0	31	1
SING TO	1.8	1.0	1.6	0.0	0.0	0.0	0.5	0.0	0.4	34	0
SLAP	-1.9	0.3	1.8	0.0	0.0	0.0	0.0	0.0	0.0	29	0
SLAY	-2.8	1.0	1.1	0.0	0.0	0.0	0.0	0.0	-0.6*	33	0
SLIGHT	-2.0	-1.2	-0.4	0.0	0.0	0.0	0.0	0.0	0.0	28	3
SLUG	-1.6	0.7	1.8	0.0	0.0	0.0	0.0	0.0	0.0	33	0
SNUB	-1.9	-0.7	0.2	0.0	0.0	0.0	0.0	0.0	0.0	32	1
SNUGGLE	2.3	1.2	0.7	0.0	0.0	0.0	0.0	0.0	0.0	31	0
SOCK	-2.2	1.9	2.4	0.0	0.0	0.0	0.0	0.6	0.6	30	1
SOFT-SOAP	-1.2	-1.0	-0.3	0.0	0.0	0.0	0.0	0.0	0.0	22	10
SOOTHE	2.3	1.5	0.0	0.0	0.0	0.0	0.0	0.0	0.0	28	0
SPANK	0.0	0.5	1.2	0.0	0.0	0.0	0.0	0.0	0.0	32	0
SPIT ON	-2.8	-1.5	0.5	0.0	-1.4	0.0	0.0	0.0	0.0	31	0
SPOIL	-1.2	-0.6	0.3	0.0	0.0	0.0	0.0	0.0	0.0	30	0
SPOOF	-0.4	0.0	0.9	0.0	0.0	0.0	0.0	0.0	0.0	21	7
SPOOK	-0.9	0.3	1.1	0.0	0.0	0.0	0.0	0.0	0.0	33	1
SPURN	-1.6	0.0	0.3	0.0	0.0	0.0	0.0	0.0	0.0	23	7
SQUEEZE	0.9	0.9	2.0	0.0	0.0	-1.2	0.0	0.0	0.0	33	0
STAB	-3.0	-0.8	1.2	0.0	2.0*	0.0	0.0	0.0	-0.5	29	0
STALL	-0.7	0.1	0.2	0.0	0.0	0.0	0.6	0.0	0.0	30	0
STARTLE	-0.7	-0.1	1.5	0.0	0.0	0.0	0.0	0.0	0.0	33	0
STRANGLE	-3.2	0.7	0.6	0.0	0.0	0.0	0.0	-0.6	0.6	32	0
STRIKE	-2.1	1.0	1.2	0.0	-1.7	0.0	0.0	0.0	0.0	28	0
STRIP	-1.1	0.7	1.5	0.0	0.0	0.0	-0.5	-0.7	0.0	31	1
STROKE	2.0	0.6	0.7	0.0	0.0	0.0	0.0	0.0	0.0	27	3
STUDY	0.7	0.5	0.1	0.0	0.0	0.0	0.0	0.0	0.0	29	0
STUN	-0.6	1.2	1.2	0.0	0.0	0.0	0.0	0.0	0.0	34	0
STYMIE	-1.0	0.2	-0.2	0.0	0.0	0.0	0.0	0.0	0.0	19	11
SUBDUE	0.0	1.0	-0.4	0.0	0.0	1.3	0.0	0.0	0.0	33	0
SUBJUGATE	-1.3	1.1	0.6	0.0	-1.3	0.0	0.0	0.0	0.0	21	11
SUCKLE	1.1	0.5	0.6	0.8	0.0	-1.0	0.0	0.0	0.0	21	10
SUMMON	0.2	0.5	0.2	0.0	0.0	0.0	0.0	0.0	0.0	32	1
SUPERVISE	1.1	1.4	0.6	0.0	0.0	0.0	0.0	0.0	0.0	32	0
SUPPORT	2.3	1.9	1.2	0.0	0.0	0.0	0.4	0.0	0.5	31	0
SURPRISE	1.3	1.2	1.9	0.0	0.0	0.0	0.0	0.0	0.0	30	0
SUSPECT	-0.5	-0.2	0.3	0.0	0.0	0.0	0.0	0.0	0.0	28	0
SWAT	-1.1	0.4	1.1	0.0	0.0	0.0	0.0	0.0	0.0	32	0
SWEET-TALK	0.1	-0.6	0.4	0.0	0.0	0.0	0.0	0.0	0.0	29	0
SWINDLE	-2.1	0.1	1.0	0.0	0.0	0.0	0.0	0.0	0.0	33	0
TACKLE	-0.3	1.6	1.8	0.0	0.0	0.0	0.0	0.0	0.0	29	2
TANTALIZE	-0.1	0.1	1.1	0.0	0.0	0.0	0.0	0.0	-0.5	32	1
TAP	0.4	0.0	0.4	0.0	0.0	0.0	0.0	0.0	0.0	31	1
TAUNT	-2.0	-0.9	0.7	0.0	0.0	1.0	0.0	0.0	0.0	25	5
TEACH	2.1	1.9	1.3	0.0	0.0	0.0	0.0	0.0	0.0	32	0
TEASE	-0.5	-0.7	1.1	0.0	0.0	0.0	0.4	0.0	0.0	33	0
TEMPT	-1.0	0.1	0.9	0.0	0.0	0.0	-0.5	-0.4	0.0	32	0
TERRORIZE	-2.7	-0.3	0.9	0.0	0.0	-0.8	0.0	0.0	0.0	27	1
TEST	0.4	0.5	0.4	0.0	0.0	0.0	0.5	0.0	0.0	29	1
THANK	2.9	1.9	0.7	0.0	0.0	0.0	0.0	1.2*	0.0	29	0
THREATEN	-2.1	0.6	1.6	0.0	0.0	0.0	0.0	0.0	0.0	33	0
THRILL	2.2	1.8	2.2	0.0	0.0	0.0	0.0	0.0	0.0	31	0

	1	2	3	4	5	6	7	8	9	10	11
TICKLE	0.6	0.2	1.9	0.0	0.0	0.0	0.0	0.0	-0.4	33	0
TITILLATE	1.0	0.9	1.7	-1.1	0.0	0.0	0.0	0.0	0.0	21	12
TOAST	2.1	0.9	1.4	0.0	0.0	0.0	0.0	0.0	0.0	30	0
TORMENT	-2.6	-0.1	1.4	0.0	0.0	0.0	-0.4	0.0	0.0	30	0
TORTURE	-3.1	-1.1	-0.1	0.0	0.0	0.0	0.0	0.0	0.0	31	0
TOUCH	2.2	1.8	1.1	0.0	-1.1	0.0	0.0	0.0	0.0	32	0
TRAIN	1.9	1.6	0.9	0.0	0.0	0.0	0.0	0.0	0.0	29	0
TRAP	-1.7	0.5	0.4	0.0	0.0	0.0	0.0	-1.2*	0.0	29	0
TREAT	1.9	0.9	0.7	0.0	0.0	1.1	0.0	0.0	0.0	32	2
TRICK	-1.6	-0.9	0.1	0.0	0.0	1.0	-0.3	0.0	0.0	31	0
TRUST	2.6	1.2	0.6	0.0	0.0	0.0	0.0	0.0	0.0	32	0
UNDERESTIMATE	-1.2	-0.3	-0.2	0.0	0.0	0.0	0.0	0.0	0.0	31	0
UNDERMINE	-2.0	-0.7	-0.1	0.0	0.0	0.0	0.0	0.0	0.0	29	2
UNDERSTAND	2.8	2.2	0.6	0.0	0.0	0.0	0.0	0.0	0.0	30	0
UNDRESS	0.4	0.7	1.0	1.4	0.0	0.0	0.0	0.0	0.0	28	0
UNNERVE	-1.6	-0.1	0.4	0.0	0.0	0.0	0.0	0.0	0.0	27	1
UPBRAID	0.3	0.7	0.5	0.0	0.0	0.0	0.0	0.0	0.0	14	18
UPLIFT	2.3	1.7	0.9	0.0	0.0	0.0	0.0	0.0	0.0	29	1
UPSET	-1.6	0.4	0.7	0.0	0.0	0.0	0.0	0.0	0.0	34	0
UPSTAGE	-1.0	1.2	0.7	0.0	-2.2*	0.0	0.0	0.0	0.0	23	7
URGE	0.4	1.2	0.9	0.0	0.0	0.0	0.0	0.0	0.0	32	0
USE	-2.8	-2.7	-0.2	0.0	1.7*	0.0	0.0	0.0	0.0	29	0
VALUE	2.5	1.8	1.2	-0.9	0.0	-0.8	0.0	0.0	0.0	33	0
VANQUISH	-1.4	1.1	1.0	0.0	0.0	0.0	0.0	0.0	0.0	21	9
VENERATE	0.3	0.3	1.3	0.0	0.0	-1.5	0.0	0.0	0.0	11	20
VEX	-1.5	-0.8	0.3	-0.9	1.7	0.0	0.0	0.0	0.0	27	5
VICTIMIZE	-2.3	0.7	0.8	0.0	-2.3*	-1.4	0.0	-0.5	0.0	28	0
VISIT	2.2	1.2	1.3	0.0	0.0	0.0	0.5	0.0	0.0	34	0
WAKEN	0.1	0.0	0.3	0.0	0.8	0.9	0.0	0.0	0.0	30	0
WARN	2.4	1.1	2.0	0.0	0.0	-1.2	0.0	0.0	-0.6	33	0
WATCH	0.3	0.0	-0.2	0.0	0.0	0.0	0.0	0.0	0.0	30	1
WELCOME	2.7	1.8	1.2	0.0	0.0	0.0	0.0	0.0	0.0	28	0
WHACK	-1.7	0.9	1.5	0.0	0.0	0.0	0.0	0.0	0.0	33	1
WHEEDLE	-1.0	-1.4	0.7	-1.1	0.0	0.0	0.0	0.0	0.0	19	12
WHIP	-1.1	0.6	1.5	-0.8	0.0	0.0	0.0	0.0	0.0	32	0
WORK	0.2	1.0	0.9	0.0	0.0	0.0	0.0	0.0	-0.8	28	1
WORSHIP	0.4	0.3	0.6	0.0	0.0	0.0	0.0	0.0	0.0	32	0
WRESTLE	-0.1	1.9	2.3	0.0	-1.1	0.0	0.0	0.0	0.0	29	0
WRONG	-2.4	0.0	0.7	0.0	0.0	0.0	0.0	0.7	0.0	30	0
ZAP	-1.0	0.1	1.3	0.0	0.0	0.0	0.0	0.0	0.0	23	9

Notes

Chapter 1. Affect control and situated action

1 Affective associations to cognitive categories generally are recognized as "attitudes" when they relate to good–bad sentiments (Osgood, Suci, and Tannenbaum, 1957; Fishbein and Ajzen, 1975). Research on attitudes and attitude change provides a rich source of insights and hypotheses concerning affective processes in general, and the literature on attitudes frequently is examined here as a way of approaching issues in general affect theory.

2 Actually, following Fishbein and Ajzen (1975), we might suppose that salient beliefs are retrieved, and then fundamentals are regenerated by affectual processing of these belief statements. Whether it is beliefs or affects that are stored in memory does not affect the discussion here. Similarly, we might suppose that fundamental feelings about identities are regenerated from "pivotal attributes" (Nadel, 1964:32) or "exemplars" (Imershein, 1976), without affecting the discussion here.

3 Examining a given actor–object combination should require no more than half a second. Accordingly, if there are two persons interacting, there always are two frames to be considered, and the processing time would be one second. With three persons, there are six interaction frames for consideration, so that processing would run three seconds. Nearing the limits of the attention span – say seven persons – there are forty-two possible interaction frames requiring about twenty-one seconds of processing time. The processing time in a large group is lengthy but not crippling, particularly because people often begin identifying events before actions have terminated.

4 DiVesta and Dick (1966) and Boshier (1969) used the semantic differential for measurements, and the figures reported here are for evaluation factor scores. Test–retest correlations for potency and activity measurements were .55 and .54, respectively, in the DiVesta and Dick study, and .56 and .61, respectively, in the Boshier study.

5 Both quoted definitions are from *The Doubleday Dictionary* (Landau, 1975).

6 Isen, Clark, and Schwartz (1974) studied the duration of transient feelings; a mood induced by a positive event manifested itself in acts ten minutes and more after the event.

7 The time scale of group dynamics has only a rough relation to physical time: we may wait seconds or years for another to complete an action, and a similar range of time may be involved as we organize our own event constructions in response.

8 They used a semantic differential for attitude measurement and identified agreement on the potency dimension as particularly crucial for continued association.

9 An important elaboration of this model introduces behavioral intentions as a variable between attitudes and behavior (Triandis, 1964; Fishbein and Ajzen, 1975). That idea contributed significantly to development of the present theory.

Chapter 2. Affective reactions

1 The Gollob (1968) article introduced this tradition of research, using the symbols S, V, and O for subject, verb, and object. The transition here to A, B, and O is to emphasize that events are the matter of concern.

179

2 Dr. Chester Cassel in a personal communication reports another replication with sixty-four sentences and 106 University of Delaware students, using a 7-point scale that yielded $A' = -.23 + .43A + .39B + .23BO$ and $R^2 = .69$.

3 An attempt to define a similar corpus in the Heise (1969a) study was unsuccessful because of difficulties in finding "weak" behaviors.

4 Johnson did find that the objects were rated as significantly more passive than subjects, contrary to what would be expected from activity-dimension formulas presented by Heise (1969a). However, Johnson reported that respondents in his study employed activity scales and potency scales similarly, the two together forming a single "animate–inanimate" dimension.

5 The complete model defining both fundamentals and transients involves a second equation:

$$T_{t+1} = F_t + d_{t+1}$$

which says that the transient at time $t + 1$ consists of a fundamental component plus a signed deflection, d, generated externally at time $t + 1$.

Chapter 3. Event construction and retroduction

1 Because people typically bring somewhat different transient feelings to event recognition, and thereby produce somewhat different affective responses, we might also average in-context ratings in order to define the typical profile of response transients.

2 The quoted words are part of the definition of "expect" in the *Doubleday Dictionary* (Landau, 1975).

3 These averages do not include the responses obtained when children were asked what they themselves would do, this condition serving as S (+). Averaging those data separately, the correlation with predictions is .76.

4 This finding links *ABO* research to research on subjective probabilities: See, for example, Wyer (1974) or Fishbein and Ajzen (1975: chap. 5).

Chapter 4. Analyzing social processes

1 The identity and act catalogs have been mapped (using the potency and activity dimensions as axes and indicating evaluation variations by special symbols), and by visually scanning the maps, one can easily find concepts having a given profile. Regrettably, it is not possible to include the identity and act maps in this monograph, because each is constructed from thirty-six pages of computer output that assembles into a chart five feet square.

2 Figures for "Child" and for "Rehabilitate" (p. 97) are computed by taking the values in columns 1, 2, or 3 in the Appendix plus one-half the increments for males in columns 4, 5, or 6. Male increments with an asterisk are significant at the .01 level and are treated distinctly. The other increments are too unreliable for analyses, and they are treated in this way to recover the average profile for males and females combined.

3 This example is worked out using an earlier parameterization of the model, reported in Heise (1977) and Heise (1978:app. B). The data were collected in a 1976 student course project, and they no longer are available for conversion to the metric used in the current parameterization.

4 The analysis of state troopers is based on data from a student paper in an undergraduate social psychology course. Students volunteering for special projects were provided with copies of the identity and act catalogs and a sheaf of semantic differential rating forms, and were instructed to obtain sentiment measurements on ten key concepts from respondents in special groups. Then they used their measurements to run computer-assisted comparative analyses comparable to the trooper–criminal illustration. The project introduced them to

attitude measurement, data analyses, and computer usage; they were stimulated to ponder the theoretical relations of affect, behaviors, and group norms; and the analytic results provided them with a framework for reflecting on their field observations.

Debbie Gilchrist obtained the trooper ratings with the help of her trooper father. The other pioneers in undergraduate use of Program INTERACT were Thomas Gerbe, who studied policemen and police science students; Marsha Hirsch, who studied feminists in a NOW chapter; Chuck Rechsteiner, who studied nationally known psychics and a group of psychic cultists; Elizabeth Walker, who studied young attorneys clerking at the North Carolina Supreme Court or attorney general's office; and Michael Priddy, who studied children of isolated black tenant farmers in eastern North Carolina.

5 If this assumption were wrong, the analytic results would have to be interpreted as reflecting the kinds of events students would expect if they had trooper sentiments about the two identities, state trooper and criminal.

6 The formulas will be rederived in a study of Ulster adolescents.

Chapter 5. Social roles

1 Quoted definitions are from *The Doubleday Dictionary* (Landau, 1975). Nadel (1964:36) emphasized the difference between identities defined in terms of states, which give rise to "recruitment roles," and identities defined in terms of behaviors, which yield "achievement roles."

2 The reference here is to the learning process by which individuals can acquire understanding of their culture. However, we might speculate that similar processes are involved in the development of culture itself, in the spirit of Nadel (1964:36). Perhaps a new recruitment role is invented when an aggregate of people are found to share states that define previously unnamed profiles of attitudes and semantic–syntactic features. Perhaps a new achievement role is created when inferring the kind of person who would perform an observed act leads to a previously unnamed meaning profile in a given institutional context.

3 These identities are not listed in the identity catalog because the data were obtained at a different time in the formula study described in Chapter 2. EPA profiles are God 3.0, 3.1, 2.0; minister 2.4, 1.6, 1.1; Christian 2.1, 1.6, 1.6; the Devil −3.0, 1.8, 2.0. Sex and conservatism increments have not been calculated.

4 Covert reidentifications – for one's own understanding only – probably are more common. Covert reidentifications leading to nonshared definitions of the situation need not disrupt a relationship: as McCall and Simmons (1966) said, "All that is needed is a sufficient lack of disagreement about one another for each to proceed in some degree with his own plans of action" (p. 127, italics removed). However, Bord (1976) demonstrated experimentally that covert identifications of others do affect others' behaviors.

5 It may be productive to view other aspects of these two processes in a unified framework also. For example, negotiations are required to label another publicly in a romantic identity, and such labeling entails new demands on the other – expectations for secondary deviance, so to speak. Agencies like the courts are chartered to assign stigma; agencies like universities are chartered to assign esteem (Meyer, 1972).

6 Triandis's work focuses explicitly on relationships, rather than on behaviors alone or actors alone. Marwell and Hage (1970) also collected and factored data on relationships, obtaining intimacy, visibility, and regulation dimensions; they had role relationships rated on such variables as frequency of occurrences and public or private occurrences. Wish, Deutsch, and Kaplan (1976) applied a multidimensional scaling analysis to adjective ratings of relationships and found four dimensions: cooperative and friendly versus competitive and hostile; equal versus unequal; intense versus superficial; socioemotional and informal versus task-oriented and formal.

7 One might suppose that Parson's pattern variables (Parsons and Shils, 1951:76–88) would relate to the *EPA* dimensions. Affectivity versus affective neutrality seems to correspond to the activity dimension, but other relationships are not so evident.

8 Some correspondence also exists between *EPA* location and the clusterings of deviant types obtained empirically by Cancian (1975:66–8) in a Mexican community: "violent" roles are at right middle; "crafty" roles are at bottom middle, toward the right; and "lazy" roles are in the bottom left corner. "Incompetent" roles do not appear in Table 5.11 because they receive middling evaluation, but they cluster at the lower left. It is not obvious what the Zinacantan "irreligious" cluster would correspond to in American society.

9 This characterization seems to fit the contrasts in terms of underlying pattern variables: universalism and neutrality versus affectivity and particularism. However, it should be noted that Parsons explicitly labeled the family as an institution dealing with latent pattern maintenance (Parsons, Bales, and Shils, 1953:265–6), putting it at the opposite end of this dimension.

10 Bales (1970:100–35) classifies acts according to their expected usage by individuals in different sectors of his three-dimensional character space. As Bales notes (p. 53), his dimensions can be related to the *EPA* dimensions, and so his specifications can be compared with the distributions shown in Table 5.12 (and the complete distributional information available in the Appendix). The correspondence is moderately good for positive acts. It is poor in the case of negative acts, because Bales associates his UN type (our upper right corner) with behaviors that are distributed all over the negative regions in Table 5.12

11 The estimate might well be off by a constant. If we suppose that zero deflection should be associated with a likelihood of 1.0, then we need to add .14 to all estimates, according to the equation used to convert deflections to likelihoods. Also, these computations were conducted with an earlier parameterization of the model (Heise, 1977*b*) and are intended to be only illustrative.

References

Abelson, Robert P. and Milton J. Rosenberg, 1958. "Symbolic Psycho-Logic: A Model of Attitudinal Cognition." *Behavioral Science* 3:1–13.

Aderman, David, Sharon S. Brehm, and Lawrence B. Katz, 1974. "Empathic Observation of an Innocent Victim: The Just World Revisited." *Journal of Personality and Social Psychology* 29:342–7.

Albert, Stuart, 1977. "Temporal Comparison Theory." *Psychological Review* 84:485–503.

Anderson, Norman H. and Arthur J. Farkas, 1973. "New Light on Order Effects in Attitude Change." *Journal of Personality and Social Psychology* 28:88–93.

Back, Kurt W., Stephen Bunker, and Catherine B. Dunnagan, 1972. "Barriers to Communication and Measurement of Semantic Space." *Sociometry* 35:347–56.

Bales, Robert Freed, 1970. *Personality and Interpersonal Behavior*. New York: Holt, Rinehart and Winston.

Barker, Roger G. and H. F. Wright, 1955. *Midwest and Its Children*. New York: Harper & Row.

Beckmann, Petr, 1972. *The Structure of Language: A New Approach*. Boulder, Colo.: Golem.

Bem, D. J., 1968. "Attitudes as Self-Descriptions: Another Look at the Attitude–Behavior Link," in A. G. Greenwald, T. C. Brock, and T. M. Ostrum (eds.), *Psychological Foundations of Attitudes*, pp. 197–225. New York: Academic.

Benjamin, Lorna Smith, 1974. "Structural Analysis of Social Behavior." *Psychological Review* 81:392–425.

Berger, Joseph, M. H. Fisek, R. Z. Norman, and M. Zelditch, Jr., 1977. *Status Characteristics and Social Interaction: An Expectation-States Approach*. New York: Elsevier.

Bickman, Leonard, 1974. "Social Roles and Uniforms: Clothes Make the Person." *Psychology Today* 7:49–51.

Biddle, Bruce J. and Edwin J. Thomas (eds.), 1966. *Role Theory: Concepts and Research*. New York: Wiley.

Blood, R. O., Jr. and D. M. Wolfe, 1960. *Husbands and Wives*. New York: Free Press.

Blum, Alan F. and Peter McHugh, 1971. "The Social Ascription of Motives." *American Sociological Review* 36:98–109.

Blumstein, Philip W., 1973. "Subjective Probability and Normative Evaluations." *Social Forces* 52:98–107.

Boorman, Scott A. and Harrison C. White, 1976. "Social Structure from Multiple Networks: II. Role Structures." *American Journal of Sociology* 81:1384–1446.

Bord, Richard J., 1976. "The Impact of Imputed Deviant Identities in Structuring Evaluations and Reactions." *Sociometry* 39:108–16.

Borgatta, Edgar F. and Betty Crowther, 1965. *A Workbook for the Study of Social Interaction Process*. Chicago: Rand McNally.

Boshier, Roger, 1969. "Factor Scores and Reliabilities of Some Semantic Differential Concepts High in *n* Achievement or *n* Affiliation Motivational Content." *Psychological Reports* 24:17–18.

Box, George E. P. and Gwilym M. Jenkins, 1970. *Times Series Analysis: Forecasting and Control*. San Francisco: Holden-Day.

183

Bruner, Edward M., 1973. "The Missing Tins of Chicken: A Symbolic Interactionist Approach to Culture Change." *Ethos* 1:219–38.

Buckley, Walter (ed.), 1968. *Modern Systems Research for the Behavioral Scientist: A Sourcebook*. Chicago: Aldine.

Burke, Richard L. and Warren G. Bennis, 1961. "Changes in Perception of Self and Others during Human Relations Training." *Human Relations* 14:165–82.

Calder, Bobby J. and Michael Ross, 1973. "Attitudes and Behavior." Pamphlet. Morristown, N.J.: General Learning Press.

Cancian, Francesca M., 1975. *What are Norms? A Study of Beliefs and Action in a Maya Community*. Cambridge: Cambridge University Press.

Capel, W. C., 1967. "Continuities and Discontinuities in Attitudes of the Same Persons Measured through Time." *Journal of Social Psychology* 73:125–6.

Cartwright, D. and Frank Harary, 1956. "Structural Balance: A Generalization of Heider's Theory." *Psychological Review* 63:277–93.

Chafe, Wallace L., 1970. *Meaning and the Structure of Language*. Chicago: University of Chicago Press.

Church, Joseph, 1961. *Language and the Discovery of Reality: A Developmental Psychology of Cognition*. New York: Random House.

Cicourel, Aaron V., 1974. *Cognitive Sociology: Language and Meaning in Social Interaction*. New York: Free Press.

Cloward, Richard and Lloyd E. Ohlin, 1960. *Delinquency and Opportunity – a Theory of Delinquent Gangs*. New York: Free Press.

Collins, Randall, 1975. *Conflict Sociology: Toward an Explanatory Science*. New York: Academic.

Cressey, Donald R., 1962. "Role Theory, Differential Association, and Compulsive Crimes," in A. M. Rose (ed.), *Human Behavior and Social Processes*, chap. 23. Boston: Houghton Mifflin.

Davitz, Joel R. (ed.), 1964. *The Communication of Emotional Meaning*. New York: McGraw-Hill.

Deutsch, Morton, 1968. "Field Theory in Social Psychology," in G. Lindzey and E. Aronson (eds.), *The Handbook of Social Psychology*, vol. 1, chap. 6. Reading, Mass.: Addison-Wesley.

DiVesta, Francis J. and Walter Dick, 1966. "The Test–Retest Reliability of Children's Ratings on the Semantic Differential." *Educational and Psychological Measurement* 26:605–16.

Donahoe, John W., 1961. "Changes in Meaning as a Function of Age." *Journal of Genetic Psychology* 99:23–8.

Emerson, Joan P., 1970. " 'Nothing Unusual Is Happening,' " in T. Shibutani (ed.), *Human Nature and Collective Behavior: Papers in Honor of Herbert Blumer*, chap. 15. New Brunswick, N.J.: Transaction Books, E. P. Dutton.

Endler, Norman S. and David Magnusson, 1976. "Toward an Interactional Psychology of Personality." *Psychological Bulletin* 83:956–74.

Fillenbaum, Samuel and A. Rapoport, 1971. *Structures in the Subjective Lexicon*. New York: Academic.

Fishbein, Martin and Icek Ajzen, 1975. *Belief, Attitude, Intention and Behavior: An Introduction to Theory and Research*. Reading, Mass.: Addison-Wesley.

Foa, Uriel G., 1958. "Behavior, Norms, and Social Rewards in a Dyad." *Behavioral Science* 3:323–34.

Frake, Charles O., 1964. "A Structural Description of Subanun 'Religious Behavior' " in W. H. Goodenough (ed.), *Explorations in Cultural Anthropology*, pp. 111–29. New York: McGraw-Hill.

Friendly, Michael L. and Sam Glucksberg, 1970. "On the Description of Subcultural Lexicons: A Multidimensional Approach." *Journal of Personality and Social Psychology* 14:55–65.

Fu, King-Sun, 1974. *Syntactic Methods in Pattern Recognition.* New York: Academic.

Garfinkel, Harold, 1964. "Studies of the Routine Grounds of Everyday Activities." *Social Problems* 11:225-50.

Gerth, Hans H. and C. Wright Mills (eds. and trans.), 1958. *From Max Weber: Essays in Sociology.* New York: Oxford University Press.

Goffman, Erving, 1959. *The Presentation of Self in Everyday Life.* New York: Doubleday.

1974. *Frame Analysis: An Essay on the Organization of Experience.* Cambridge, Mass.: Harvard University Press.

Goldberger, Arthur S., 1964. *Econometric Theory.* New York: Wiley.

Goldfried, Marvin R. and Stanley Kissel, 1963. "Age as a Variable in the Connotative Perceptions of Some Animal Symbols." *Journal of Projective Techniques and Personality Assessment* 27:171-80.

Goldstein, Ira, and Seymour Papert, 1977. "Artificial Intelligence and the Study of Knowledge." *Cognitive Science* 1:84-123.

Gollob, Harry F., 1968. "Impression Formation and Word Combination in Sentences." *Journal of Personality and Social Psychology* 10:341-53.

1974a. "Some Tests of a Social Inference Model." *Journal of Personality and Social Psychology* 29:157-72.

1974b. "The Subject-Verb-Object Approach to Social Cognition." *Psychological Review* 81:286-321.

Gollob, Harry F. and Gregory W. Fischer, 1973. "Some Relationships between Social Inference, Cognitive Balance, and Change in Impression." *Journal of Personality and Social Psychology* 26:16-22.

Gollob, Harry F. and Betty B. Rossman, 1973. "Judgments of an Actor's 'Power and Ability to Influence Others.' " *Journal of Experimental Social Psychology* 9:391-406.

Goodenough, Ward H., 1969. "Rethinking 'Status' and 'Role': Toward a General Model of the Cultural Organization of Social Relationships," in Stephen A. Tyler (ed.), *Cognitive Anthropology*, pp. 311-30. New York: Holt, Rinehart, & Winston.

Gove, P. B. (ed.), 1971. *Webster's Third New International Dictionary of the English Language, Unabridged.* Springfield, Mass.: Merriam.

Gove, Walter R. (ed.), 1975. *The Labelling of Deviance: Evaluating a Perspective.* New York: Wiley.

Greenberg, J. H., 1963. "Some Universals of Grammar with Particular Reference to the Order of Meaningful Elements," in J. Greenberg (ed.), *Universals of Language*, pp. 58-90. Cambridge, Mass.: MIT Press.

Greenstein, Theodore, 1976. "Behavior Change through Value Self-Confrontation: A Field Experiment." *Journal of Personality and Social Psychology* 34:254-62.

Gross, Neal, Ward S. Mason, and A. W. McEachern, 1958. *Explorations in Role Analysis: Studies of the School Superintendency Role.* New York: Wiley.

Hanson, Norwood R., 1958. *Patterns of Discovery: An Inquiry into the Conceptual Foundations of Science.* Cambridge: Cambridge University Press.

Harris, Marvin, 1964. *The Nature of Cultural Things.* New York: Random House.

Hartley, Ruth E., 1966. "A Developmental View of Female Sex-Role Identification," in B. Biddle and E. Thomas (eds.), *Role Theory: Concepts and Research*, pp. 354-60. New York: Wiley.

Hawkes, Roland K., 1975. "Norms, Deviance, and Social Control: A Mathematical Elaboration of Concepts." *American Journal of Sociology* 80:886-908.

Hawkins, Richard and Gary Tiedeman, 1975. *The Creation of Deviance: Interpersonal and Organizational Determinants.* Columbus, Ohio: Charles E. Merrill.

Hayes, Donald P. and Sally Sievers, 1972. "A Sociolinguistic Investigation of the 'Dimensions' of Interpersonal Behavior." *Journal of Personality and Social Psychology* 25:254-61.

Heider, Fritz, 1946. "Attitudes and Cognitive Organizations." *Journal of Psychology* 21:107-12.

1958. *The Psychology of Interpersonal Relations*. New York: Wiley.

1967. "On Social Cognition." *American Psychologist* 22:25–31.

Heise, D. R., 1965. "Semantic Differential Profiles for 1,000 Most Frequent English Words." *Psychological Monographs* 70, no. 8 (whole no. 601).

1968. "Norms and Individual Patterns in Student Deviancy." *Social Problems* 16:78–92.

1969a. "Affective Dynamics in Simple Sentences." *Journal of Personality and Social Psychology* 11:204–13.

1969b. "Some Methodological Issues in Semantic Differential Research." *Psychological Bulletin* 72:406–22.

1970. "Potency Dynamics in Simple Sentences." *Journal of Personality and Social Psychology* 16:48–54.

1975. *Causal Analysis*. New York: Wiley.

1977a. "Group Dynamics and Attitude–Behavior Relations." *Sociological Methods and Research* 3:259–88.

1977b. "Social Action as the Control of Affect." *Behavioral Science* 22:163–77.

1978. *Computer-Assisted Analysis of Social Action: Use of Program INTERACT and SURVEY.UNC75*. Institute for Research in Social Science, University of North Carolina, Chapel Hill, 27514.

Heise, D. R. and Essie P. M. Roberts, 1970. "The Development of Role Knowledge." *Genetic Psychology Monographs* 82:83–115.

Helson, Harry, 1973. "A Common Model for Affectivity and Perception: An Adaptation-Level Approach," in D. E. Berlyne and K. B. Madsen (eds.), *Pleasure, Reward, Preference: Their Nature, Determinants, and Role in Behavior*, chap. 7. New York: Academic.

Herbst, P. G., 1952. "The Measurement of Family Relationships." *Human Relations* 5:3–35.

Hilgard, Ernest R., 1965. *Hypnotic Susceptibility*. New York: Harcourt, Brace & World.

Hinde, R. A. (ed.), 1972. *Non-Verbal Communication*. Cambridge: Cambridge University Press.

Hovland, Carl I., 1959. "Reconciling Conflicting Results Derived from Experimental and Survey Studies of Attitude Change." *American Psychologist* 14:8–17.

Imershein, Allen W., 1976. "The Epistemological Bases of Social Order: Toward Ethnoparadigm Analysis," in D. Heise (ed.), *Sociological Methodology: 1977*, chap. 1. San Francisco: Jossey-Bass.

Insko, Chester A., Elaine Sanger, and William McGarvey, 1974. "Balance, Positivity, and Agreement in the Jordan Paradigm: A Defense of Balance Theory." *Journal of Experimental Social Psychology* 10:53–83.

Isen, Alice M., Margaret Clark, Mark F. Schwartz, 1974. "Duration of the Effect of Good Mood on Helping: 'Footprints on the Sands of Time.' " *Journal of Personality and Social Psychology* 34:385–93.

Izard, Carroll E., 1971. *The Face of Emotion*. New York: Appleton-Century-Crofts.

Jenkins, Gwilym M. and Donald G. Watts, 1968. *Spectral Analysis and Its Applications*. San Francisco: Holden-Day.

Johnson, Michael G., 1967. "Syntactic Position and Rated Meaning." *Journal of Verbal Learning and Verbal Behavior* 6:240–6.

Jöreskog, K. G., and D. Sörbom, 1976. *LISREL III: Estimation of Linear Structural Equation Systems by Maximum Likelihood Methods: A Fortran IV Program*. National Eduational Resources, Inc., Box 1025, Chicago, 60690.

Katz, Jerold J., 1972. *Semantic Theory*. New York: Harper & Row.

Kelly, E. Lowell, 1955. "Consistency of the Adult Personality." *American Psychologist* 10:659–81.

Kelman, Herbert C., 1974. "Attitudes Are Alive and Well and Gainfully Employed in the Sphere of Action." *American Psychologist* 29:310–24.

Kemper, Theodore, 1972. "Power, Status, and Love," in D. Heise (ed.), *Personality and Socialization*, chap. 10. Chicago: Rand McNally.

1978. *A Social Interactional Theory of Emotions*. New York: Wiley-Interscience.

Kendon, Adam, 1973. "The Role of Visible Behaviour in the Organization of Social Interaction," in M. Von Cranach and I. Vine (eds.), *Social Communication and Movement*, chap. 2. New York: Academic.

Kenrick, Douglas T., John W. Reich, and Robert B. Cialdini, 1976. "Justification and Compensation: Rosier Skies for the Devalued Victim." *Journal of Personality and Social Psychology* 34:654–7.

Kirby, D. M. and R. C. Gardner, 1972. "Ethnic Stereotypes: Norms on 208 Words Typically Used in Their Assessment." *Canadian Journal of Psychology/Review of Canadian Psychology* 26:140–54.

Kohlberg, L. and R. Kramer, 1969. "Continuities and Discontinuities in Childhood Moral Development." *Human Development* 12:93–120.

Köhler, Wolfgang, 1969. *The Task of Gestalt Psychology*. Princeton, N.J.: Princeton University Press.

Kohn, Melvin L. and Robin M. Williams, 1956. "Situational Patterning in Intergroup Relations." *American Sociological Review* 21:164–74.

Komarovsky, Mirra, 1973. "Presidential Address: Some Problems in Role Analysis." *American Sociological Review* 38:649–62.

Krech, David, R. S. Crutchfield, and E. L. Ballachey, 1962. *Individual in Society: A Textbook in Social Psychology*. New York: McGraw-Hill.

Kulik, James A., Theodore R. Sarbin, and Kenneth B. Stein, 1971. "Language, Socialization, and Delinquency." *Developmental Psychology* 4:434–9.

Kutner, Nancy G. and Donna Brogan, 1974. "An Investigation of Sex-Related Slang Vocabulary and Sex-Role Orientation among Male and Female University Students." *Journal of Marriage and the Family* 36:474–84.

Landau, Sidney I. (ed.), 1975. *The Doubleday Dictionary*. Garden City, N.Y.: Doubleday.

Lazarsfeld, Paul F., 1972. *Qualitative Analysis: Historical and Critical Essays*. Boston: Allyn and Bacon.

Leeuwenberg, E. L. J., 1971. "A Perceptual Coding Language for Visual and Auditory Patterns." *American Journal of Psychology* 84:307–49.

Lerman, Paul, 1967. "Argot, Symbolic Deviance and Subcultural Delinquency." *American Sociological Review* 32:209–24.

Lerner, Melvin J., 1971. "Observer's Evaluation of a Victim: Justice, Guilt, and Veridical Perception." *Journal of Personality and Social Psychology* 20:127–35.

Levi-Strauss, Claude, 1963. *Structural Anthropology*. Trans. by C. Jacobson and B. G. Schoepf. New York: Basic Books.

Lewin, Kurt, 1951. *Field Theory in Social Science: Selected Theoretical Papers*. Ed. by D. Cartwright. New York: Harper & Row.

Lincoln, Alan and George Levinger, 1972. "Observers' Evaluations of the Victim and the Attacker in an Aggressive Incident." *Journal of Personality and Social Psychology* 22:202–10.

Linton, Ralph, 1945. *The Cultural Background of Personality*. New York: Appleton-Century-Crofts.

Loevinger, Jane and Ruth Wessler, 1970. *Measuring Ego Development*, vol. 1. San Francisco: Jossey-Bass.

Lofland, John, 1969. *Deviance and Identity*. Englewood Cliffs, N.J.: Prentice-Hall.

1976 *Doing Social Life: The Qualitative Study of Human Interaction in Natural Settings*. New York: Wiley–Interscience.

McCall, George J. and J. L. Simmons, 1966. *Identities and Interactions*. New York: Free Press.

Maccoby, Eleanor Emmons and Carol Nagy Jacklin, 1974. *The Psychology of Sex Differences*. Stanford, Calif.: Stanford University Press.

McGrew, W. C., 1972. *An Ethological Study of Children's Behavior*. New York: Academic.

McHugh, Peter, 1968. *Defining the Situation: The Organization of Meaning in Social Interaction*. New York: Bobbs-Merrill.

Manis, Jerome G. and Bernard N. Meltzer (eds.), 1972. *Symbolic Interaction: A Reader in Social Psychology* (2nd edn). Boston: Allyn and Bacon.

Marwell, Gerald and Jerald Hage, 1970. "The Organization of Role-Relationships: A Systematic Description." *American Sociological Review* 35:884–900.

Merton, Robert K., 1957. *Social Theory and Social Structure*. New York: Free Press.

Meyer, John W., 1972. "The Effects of the Institutionalization of Colleges in Society," in K. A. Feldman (ed.), *College and Student: Selected Readings in the Social Psychology of Higher Education*, chap. 9. New York: Pergamon.

Milgram, Stanley, 1974. *Obedience to Authority: An Experimental View*. New York: Harper & Row.

Miller, George A., E. Galanter, and K. H. Pribram, 1960. *Plans and the Structure of Behavior*. New York: Holt, Rinehart, and Winston.

Miller, George A. and P. N. Johnson-Laird, 1976. *Language and Perception*. Cambridge, Mass.: Harvard University Press.

Minsky, Marvin, 1975. "A Framework for Representing Knowledge," in P. Winston (ed.), *The Psychology of Computer Vision*, pp. 211–77. New York: McGraw-Hill.

Nadel, Siegfried F., 1964. *The Theory of Social Structure*. New York: Free Press.

Newcomb, Theodore M., 1953. "An Approach to the Study of Communicative Acts." *Psychological Review* 60:393–404.

Newell, Allen and Herbert A. Simon, 1972. *Human Problem Solving*. Englewood Cliffs, N.J.: Prentice-Hall.

Newtson, Darren, G. Engquist, and J. Bois, 1977. "The Objective Basis of Behavior Units." *Journal of Personality and Social Psychology* 35:847–62.

Orcutt, James D., 1973. "Societal Reaction and the Response to Deviation in Small Groups." *Social Forces* 52:259–67.

Osgood, Charles E., 1962. "Studies of the Generality of Affective Meaning Systems." *American Psychologist* 17:10–28.

1963. "On Understanding and Creating Sentences." *American Psychologist* 18:735–51.

1970. "Interpersonal Verbs and Interpersonal Behavior," in J. L. Cowan (ed.), *Studies in Thought and Language*, chap. 6. Tucson: University of Arizona Press.

1977. "Toward an Abstract Performance Grammar." Unpublished manuscript, Institute of Communications Research, University of Illinois, Champaign.

Osgood, Charles E., W. H. May, and M. S. Miron, 1975. *Cross-Cultural Universals of Affective Meaning*. Urbana: University of Illinois Press.

Osgood, Charles E., George J. Suci, and Percy H. Tannenbaum, 1957. *The Measurement of Meaning*. Urbana: University of Illinois Press.

Osgood, Charles E. and Percy H. Tannenbaum, 1955. "The Principle of Congruity in the Prediction of Attitude Change." *Psychological Review* 62:42–55.

Osgood, Charles E. and Christine Tanz, 1976. "Will the Real Direct Object in Bitransitive Sentences Please Stand Up?" Unpublished manuscript, Institute of Communications Research, University of Illinois, Champaign.

Osterhouse, Robert A. and Timothy C. Brock, 1970. "Distraction Increases Yielding to Propaganda by Inhibiting Counterarguing." *Journal of Personality and Social Psychology* 15:344–58.

Palmer, Stephen E., 1975. "Visual Perception and World Knowledge: Notes on a Model of Sensory-Cognitive Interaction," in D. A. Norman and D. E. Rumelhart (eds.), *Explorations in Cognition*, chap. 11. San Francisco: W. H. Freeman.

Parsons, Talcott, 1951. *The Social System*. New York: Free Press.

Parsons, Talcott, R. F. Bales, and E. A. Shils, 1953. *Working Papers in the Theory of Action*. Glencoe, Ill.: Free Press.

Parsons, Talcott and Edward A. Shils (eds.), 1951. *Toward a General Theory of Action*. Cambridge, Mass.: Harvard University Press.

Piaget, Jean, 1970. "Piaget's Theory," in P. H. Mussen (ed.), *Carmichael's Manual of Child Psychology* (3rd edn), vol. 7, chap. 9. New York: Wiley.

Powers, William T., 1973. *Behavior: The Control of Perception*. Chicago: Aldine.

Price, Richard H. and Dennis L. Bouffard, 1974. "Behavioral Appropriateness and Situational Constraint as Dimensions of Social Behavior." *Journal of Personality and Social Psychology* 30:579–86.

Raush, Harold L., 1965. "Interaction Sequences." *Journal of Personality and Social Psychology* 2:487–99.

Raush, Harold L., I. Farbman, and L. G. Llewellyn, 1960. "Person, Setting, and Change in Social Interaction: II. A Normal-Control Study." *Human Relations* 13:305–32.

Reed, Stephen K., 1973. *Psychological Processes in Pattern Recognition*. New York: Academic.

Regan, Dennis T. and Judith Totten, 1975. "Empathy and Attribution: Turning Observers into Actors." *Journal of Personality and Social Psychology* 32:850–6.

Rokeach, Milton, 1971. "Long-Range Experimental Modification of Values, Attitudes, and Behavior." *American Psychologist* 26:453–9.

Rose, Arnold M. (ed.), 1962. *Human Behavior and Social Processes*. Boston: Houghton Mifflin.

Rubenstein, Herbert, 1973. "Some Problems of Meaning in Natural Languages," in I. Pool et al. (eds.), *Handbook of Communication*, chap. 2. Chicago: Rand McNally.

Sacks, Harvey, 1972. "An Initial Investigation of the Usability of Conversational Data for Doing Sociology," in D. Sudnow (ed.), *Studies in Social Interaction*, pp. 31–74. New York: Free Press.

Sarbin, Theodore R. and Vernon L. Allen, 1968. "Role Theory," in G. Lindzey and E. Aronson (eds.), *The Handbook of Social Psychology* (2nd edn), vol. 1, chap. 7. Reading, Mass.: Addison-Wesley.

Schachter, Stanley, 1951. "Deviation, Rejection, and Communication." *Journal of Abnormal and Social Psychology* 46:190–207.

Schank, Roger C., 1973. "Identification of Conceptualizations Underlying Natural Language," in R. C. Schank and K. M. Colby (eds.), *Computer Models of Thought and Language*, chap. 5. San Francisco: W. H. Freeman.

Schank, Roger C. and Robert P. Abelson, 1977. *Scripts, Plans, Goals and Understanding: An Inquiry into Human Knowledge Structures*. Hillsdale, N.J.: Lawrence Erlbaum Associates.

Schank, Roger C. and Kenneth Mark Colby, 1973. *Computer Models of Thought and Language*. San Francisco: W. H. Freeman.

Schlenker, Barry R. and P. A. Schlenker, 1975. "Reactions following Counterattitudinal Behavior Which Produces Positive Consequences." *Journal of Personality and Social Psychology* 31:962–71.

Schutz, Alfred and Thomas Luckman, 1973. *The Structures of the Life-World*. Trans. by R. M. Zaner and H. T. Engelhardt, Jr. Evanston, Ill.: Northwestern University Press.

Schwartz, Gary and D. Merten, 1967. "The Language of Adolescence: An Anthropological Approach to the Youth Culture." *American Journal of Sociology* 72:453–68.

Scott, John F., 1954. "Two Dimensions of Delinquent Behavior." *American Sociological Review* 24:240–3.

Secord, Paul F. and Carl W. Backman, 1965. "An Interpersonal Approach to Personality," in

B. A. Maher (ed.), *Progress in Experimental Personality Research*, pp. 91–125. New York: Academic.

Shaver, Kelly G., 1975. *An Introduction to Attribution Processes*. Cambridge, Mass.: Winthrop.

Skinner, B. F., 1957. *Verbal Behavior*. New York: Appleton-Century-Crofts.

Smith, Edward E., Edward J. Shoben, and Lance J. Rips, 1974. "Structure and Process in Semantic Memory: A Featural Model for Semantic Decisions." *Psychological Review* 81:214–41.

Smith, Gene F. and Donald D. Dorfman, 1975. "The Effect of Stimulus Uncertainty on the Relationship Between Frequency of Exposure and Liking." *Journal of Personality and Social Psychology* 31:150–5.

Snider, James G. and C. E. Osgood (eds.), 1969. *Semantic Differential Technique: A Sourcebook*. Chicago: Aldine.

Snyder, Mark, E. D. Tanke, and E. Berscheid, 1977. "Social Perception and Interpersonal Behavior: On the Self-Fulfilling Nature of Social Stereotypes." *Journal of Personality and Social Psychology* 35:656–6.

Spiro, Melford E., 1961. "Social Systems, Personality, and Functional Analysis," in B. Kaplan (ed.), *Studying Personality Cross-Culturally*, chap. 2. New York: Harper & Row.

Stryker, Sheldon, 1977. "Developments in 'Two Social Psychologies': Toward an Appreciation of Mutual Relevance." *Sociometry* 40:145–60.

Szalay, Lorand B. and Jack E. Brent, 1967. "The Analysis of Cultural Meanings through Free Verbal Associations." *Journal of Social Psychology* 72:161–87.

Szalay, Lorand B. and Jean A. Bryson, 1974. "Psychological Meaning: Comparative Analyses and Theoretical Implications." *Journal of Personality and Social Psychology* 30:860–70.

Thibaut, John W. and John Coules, 1952. "The Role of Communication in the Reduction of Interpersonal Hostility." *Journal of Abnormal and Social Psychology* 47:770–7.

Triandis, Harry C., 1964. "Exploratory Factor Analyses of the Behavioral Component of Social Attitudes." *Journal of Abnormal and Social Psychology* 68:420–30.

1971. *Attitude and Attitude Change*. New York: Wiley.

1977. *Interpersonal Behavior*. Monterey, Calif.: Brooks/Cole.

Triandis, Harry C. (ed.), 1972. *The Analysis of Subjective Culture*. New York: Wiley–Interscience.

Truzzi, Marcello (ed.), 1974. *Verstehen: Subjective Understanding in the Social Sciences*. Reading, Mass.: Addison-Wesley.

Turner, Ralph H., 1962. "Role-Taking: Process versus Conformity," in Arnold M. Rose (ed.), *Human Behavior and Social Processes*, chap. 2. Boston: Houghton Mifflin.

Tversky, Amos, 1977. "Features of Similarity." *Psychological Review* 84:327–52.

von Cranach, M., and I. Vine, 1973. *Social Communication and Movement: Studies of Interaction and Expression in Man and Chimpanzee*. New York: Academic.

Wallace, Anthony F. C., 1970. *Culture and Personality* (2nd edn). New York: Random House.

Weitzenhoffer, André M., 1953. *Hypnotism: An Objective Study in Suggestibility*. New York: Wiley.

1957. *General Techniques of Hypnotism*. New York: Grune & Stratton.

Werner, Oswald and Joann Fenton, 1970. "Method and Theory in Ethnoscience or Ethnoepistemology," in R. Naroll and R. Cohen (eds.), *A Handbook of Method in Cultural Anthropology*, chap. 29. Garden City, N.Y.: Natural History Press.

Wheaton, Blair, Bengt Muthén, Duane F. Alwin, Gene F. Summers, 1976. "Assessing Reliability and Stability in Panel Models," in D. Heise (ed.), *Sociological Methodology: 1977*, chap. 3. San Francisco: Jossey-Bass.

Wilks, Yorick A., 1972. *Grammar, Meaning and the Machine Analysis of Language*. London: Routledge & Kegan.

1973. "An Artificial Intelligence Approach to Machine Translation," in R. C. Schank and K. M. Colby (eds.), *Computer Models of Thought and Language*, chap. 3. San Francisco: W. H. Freeman.

1977. "What Sort of Taxonomy of Causation Do We Need for Language Understanding?" *Cognitive Science* 1:235–64.

Wilson, Glenn D. (ed.), 1973. *The Psychology of Conservatism*. New York: Academic.

Wilson, Thomas P., 1970. "Conceptions of Interaction and Forms of Sociological Explanation." *American Sociological Review* 35:697–710.

Winograd, Terry, 1972. *Understanding Natural Language*. New York: Academic.

Wish, Myron, M. Deutsch, and S. J. Kaplan, 1976. "Perceived Dimensions of Interpersonal Relations." *Journal of Personality and Social Psychology* 33:409–20.

Wrong, Dennis H., 1961. "The Oversocialized Conception of Man in Modern Sociology." *American Sociological Review* 26:183–93.

Wyer, Robert S., Jr., 1974. *Cognitive Organization and Change: An Information Processing Approach*. Potomac, Md.: Lawrence Erlbaum.

Yinger, J. M., 1960. "Contraculture and Subculture." *American Sociological Review* 25:625–35.

Index

192